D1196122

THE ULTIMATE GUIDE TO HOMEMADE ICE CREAM

THE ULTIMATE GUIDE TO HOMEMADE ICE CREAM

Jan Hedh   Klas Andersson

Translated by Monika Romare

S P

Copyright © 2012 by Jan Hedh

All rights reserved. No part of this book may be reproduced in any manner without the express
written consent of the publisher, except in the case of brief excerpts in critical reviews or articles.
All inquiries should be addressed to Skyhorse Publishing, 307 West 36th Street, 11th Floor,
New York, NY 10018.

Skyhorse Publishing books may be purchased in bulk at special discounts for sales promotion,
corporate gifts, fund-raising, or educational purposes. Special editions can also be created to
specifications. For details, contact the Special Sales Department, Skyhorse Publishing, 307 West
36th Street, 11th Floor, New York, NY 10018 or info@skyhorsepublishing.com.

Skyhorse® and Skyhorse Publishing® are registered trademarks of Skyhorse Publishing, Inc.®,
a Delaware corporation.

www.skyhorsepublishing.com

10 9 8 7 6 5 4 3 2 1

Library of Congress Cataloging-in-Publication Data is available on file.

Printed in China

ISBN 978-1-61608-604-6

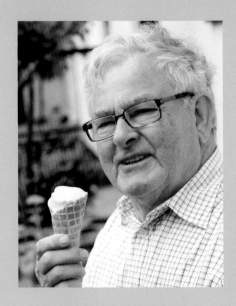
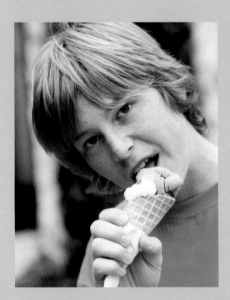

Table of Contents

PREFACE

As Swedes, we are one of the peoples that eat the most ice cream in the world. Unfortunately, most of it is factory made ice cream.

Today, very few bakeshops make their own ice cream and much of what is called homemade ice cream is based on powder products and pastes from Italy that have few things in common with ice cream made from natural produce.

I remember when Östen Brolin and I began making our own ice cream at the bakeshop, *Vete Katten*, in Stockholm. Ice cream quickly became a favorite craving in the neighborhood! The bakeshops began to make ice cream bombs just like back in the day. Ice cream in cups or in cones was served at every pastry shop. At Olof Viktors bakery in Glemminge, close to Ystad, where we are famous for making bread, jam, marmalade—and ice cream—with fresh produce, and without E numbers and stabilizers. In the summer, we make about 2,642 gallons or 10,000 liters of ice cream every week.

My first memory of homemade ice cream is from when my mother, Kerstin, stirred ice cream in the freezer with a ladle and served it freshly frozen for Sunday

dessert. Sometimes, she would simply make frozen cream and serve it with berries. During the summer she used to make Popsicle sticks out of frozen juice, something we loved as kids. Parfait was often served when we had guests, or during various holidays. Most of the time, my mother would make strawberry or pineapple parfait. Sometimes, when someone in the family had a birthday, mother would order frozen pudding or *Meringue Suisse* from Brauns Bakeshop at Gustav Adolfs torg in Malmö. Back then it was considered the nicest bakeshop in the entire city. Their window display was always filled with ice cream bombs and frozen puddings that had been decorated with spun sugar and other goodies, depending on the holidays.

Desserts and ice creams were always part of the bakeshop and most of the cake shops used to make their own ice cream parfaits and frozen puddings. I have always worked at places where we make our own ice cream. At my first job, we always received many orders for frozen pudding with spun sugar every Friday and Saturday. Bomb molds were lined with different ice creams and filled with various types of filling, such as parfait and fruit mousse. As an apprentice, I sometimes helped delivering the ice cream on my bike. Then, the ice cream would be stored in a metal container inside a very heavy bucket. 2.2 pounds of ice was mixed with 10.6 oz of salt to lower the freezing point so that the ice cream would hold up for hours. Eventually, artificial ice was introduced to us and made the delivery process a lot easier.

Meringue Suisse used to be a very common dessert back in the day. The tall creations were delivered in large boxes. They contained circles of classic French meringue and chocolate cream and vanilla cream. Other popular desserts included lemon or orange fromage, savarin, and charlotte russe. At weddings, croquembouches out of almond paste solved in egg whites were desired. The ice cream was placed on top of the crown and it was embedded in spun sugar. The entire creation was usually decorated with roses and leaves in pulled caramel. For baptisms, decorations often consisted of cradles made with hippenmasse or chocolate, with a baby covered in a marzipan blanket, or a stork out of caramel. For the children's birthday party, the cake would be adorned with a marzipan train for a boy or a marzipan bear when it was for a girl. We sold loads of ice cream for graduation ceremonies, and for anniversaries, or birthdays. Not to mention the demand for ice cream for New Year's Eve parties and Christmas.

The storefront windows at pastry shops were often adorned with *croquembouches* made with almond paste and egg whites, and a beautiful cornucopia filled with tea biscuits and chocolate pralines. Both of these baked goods were often served with ice cream desserts, especially at weddings, baptisms, festivals, and anniversaries. Last year I received an order for 13 *croquembouches*, all for the same wedding. It is fun when you receive a big order like that, but it also requires a lot of work.

This book is dedicated to my mother, father and grandmother who taught me to love good food and appreciate the importance of high quality ingredients.

I still recall my father's conversations with butchers and fishmongers in Malmö's three market halls, which had floors covered in sawdust. I was a young boy, and stood there all ears and listened. I used to go shopping with dad every Saturday, while mom was at work. We spent a lot of time and effort on our cooking every weekend. Walks with my grandmother often ended up at the meat shops in Tomelilla, and to the market square, where they sold fresh vegetables, fruits, and berries every day. Every Saturday for breakfast, I would get sugar biscuits filled with vanilla custard or Berliner pastries with apple marmalade filling from Ekerlund's local bakery. These are the memories that have stuck with me!

July 2008 | *Jan Hedh, pastry chef and master baker*

A special thank you to expert herb grower Magne Haugen, for his generosity with his knowledge about herbs and edible flowers and the use of his herb garden in Klevane. Go to his website to learn all about edible herbs and flowers!

A Brief History of Ice Cream

Gastronomic encyclopedias disagree on who invented the ice cream. Some of them credit the Chinese, others the Romans, and sometimes the Indians. However, most of them agree that it was the Chinese who invented the ice cream many thousands years ago, although there are no similarities between the archaic ice cream and the one we eat today. The story goes that Marco Polo tried Chinese ice cream during his trip to China in 1292 (despite the ongoing debate whether he visited China or not).

Ice cream in the shape of flavored snow or ice has a long history. Even during antiquity people pondered over how to improve water so that it would remain cold and taste better. Some of the methods included mixing water with wine, fruit juice, and honey, and various ways to chill it.

Emperor Nero is said to have used slaves to run with ice in relay races from the Apennines to Rome every day. Rumor has it that during the siege of Petra, Alexander the Great ordered 30 pits to be dug in the ground and filled with ice and snow. They were then covered with a thick layer of oak leaves to maintain the ice for a longer time. The ice was used to chill drinks and to cool feverish warriors.

Sorbet, which is made from fruit puree, fruit juice, or wine, is the type of ice cream that was served up to the mid 1700s. The term comes from the Arabic word, *sherbet*. Many people claim that sorbet originates from Asia. The Romans are said to have dug basements, much like our food storages on the northern slopes of the Averner Mountain. And Seneca considered the Romans were wasteful and profligate because they only wanted drinks that had been chilled. Hippocrates didn't even want to taste these drinks.

According to literature, when Catherine de Medici married the French successor to the throne, Henry II, she brought her confectioner, Bernardo Buontalenti, with her to France so that he could serve her different ice creams every day. In 1822, Antonin Carème wrote that the chefs in the 1700s had to learn how to cook Italian cuisine, which Catherine de Medici had introduced to the French court. That's when ice cream was served for the first time in France, so in literature it is agreed that in Europe ice cream originated from Italy. In Florence, it is said that the first ice cream was born in 1565, when Buontalenti created a concoction of frozen desserts, containing *zabaglione* and fruit. Many people still credit him for inventing ice cream. The only issue to that claim is that it wasn't until 14 years later that people discovered that you could lower the freezing point with salt. Buontalenti was considered an ice cream wizard and his various ice cream recipes became precious state secrets.

Italian ice cream makers spread the art of preparing ice cream to the capital of culinary art, Paris. In the mid 1670s a man from Palermo, Francesco Procopio (later changed to Procopé), opened up an ice cream café at Rue des Fossés Saint-Germain, next to the old Comédie Française. The place is rumored to have served hundreds of ice creams flavored with fine wines, delicious fruits, and rare spices, featuring other exotic flavors such as white coffee ice cream, or ice cream infused with roses, violets, and lavender. This also became one of the first ice cream cafés in Paris to serve coffee. Intellectuals, such as Rousseau, Voltaire, and Diderot are said to have met up and tried all their specialties. In 1675, there were about 250 ice cream boutiques in Paris, and in 1750, Procopio's successor, Buisson, began selling ice cream all year round in his shop. Another famous ice cream place in Paris was Le Caveau, which was known for its almond ice cream that was flavored with kirsch. Eventually, an ice cream confectioner from Naples by the name Raphael introduced the new Italian ice cream method in France. He too, was considered a wizard in his field and was met with great respect by the French confectioners.

In 1770 the first ice cream shop opened up in New York by an Italian immigrant named Giovanni Bosio. During the first half of the 1800s, ice cream parlors and confectioners shops that produced ice cream in all shapes and forms became common throughout Europe.

The first time that ice cream is mentioned in literature in Sweden is in Cajsa Warg's cookbook. The lady didn't particularly like it. "Although ice cream is very unhealthy cuisine, it may nevertheless not be omitted as many people like it." In Stockholm, ice cream consumption was very popular at cafés, bake shops, and restaurants.

The great August Escoffier, sometimes referred to as the King of chefs, was a lot more positive towards ice cream and wrote: "When ice cream is well made and elegantly served, it is the most fulfilling delicacy. No other area in culinary art offers the same creative freedom for the mind to create endless and delicious combinations."

Ice cream was still exclusive during the mid 1920s and it was ordered from the bake shops for festive occasions. It was delivered in ice buckets, which contained a cylinder and two structures that could hold two ice cream bombs. In finer homes, the maids would turn the ice cream in a cold mixture of ice and salt until it became smooth and firm. Vanilla used to be the most common ice cream flavor, and it remains the most popular flavor to this day.

When ice cream on sticks was invented (so called Popsicles), little kiosks began selling ice cream cones all over the country. America has the largest ice cream consumption in the world, but just like in Sweden, it is mostly industrially produced ice cream. The ice cream industry often makes ice cream that is flavored with nature-identical flavors and stabilizers made from locust bean gum, stabilizers, emulsifiers, and E numbers. Yellow lemon ice cream? How can it be yellow when lemon juice is white? Or green pear ice cream, how is that possible? Yellow banana ice cream when bananas are white inside? Well, there are a lot of tricks in the ice cream industry. But enough about that, in this book we will teach you how to make ice cream the way it should be done!

Ice cream is a dish that uses the delicious features of milk and cream. By freezing the ice cream it becomes firm and creamy and it is converted in the mouth from a fixed to a fluid consistency. However, it was not an easy task to learn how to freeze the cream so that it would attain a good consistency.

Pure cream will turn rock hard when it freezes. Sugar softens the ice cream but it also lowers the freezing point. Sweetened cream freezes during the freezing point for water. Back in the day, what used to make it possible to freeze the ice cream was a cold blend of ice and salt, which lowers the freezing point and makes the ice cold enough to freeze the sweetened cream (300 g (1½ cups) of salt was needed for 2.2 lbs of ice). This process was known in the Arab world back in the 1300s, and perhaps this is where this knowledge came from when it arrived in Italy. In 1292, Marco Polo is said to have brought the knowledge of how to make ice cream with a cold blend of potassium nitrate and water, a method that the Chinese were using to cool various fruit drinks. In 1530, a Sicilian from Catania further developed Marco Polo's recipe and used natural ice and potassium nitrate to freeze the ice cream mix. He named his invention "gelato."

Ice creams appeared in Italian cookbooks already during the early 1700s. The English term "ice cream" appeared in writing for the first time in 1672. The very first recipes for frozen water and cream came about in France and Naples around 1680-90. The first French ice cream recipe (*neige de fleurs d'orange*, snow of orange flowers) was published in the book, *Nouveau Confiturier*, in 1682. Year 1798 was a milestone in the history of ice cream. That's when *Paris L'Art de Faire Les Glaces (The Art of Making Ice Cream)* was published. The author of the book, Monseigneur Emy, described an ice cream machine for the first time in history that was constructed with a handle that could rotate the inner container. The rotation made the freezing process a lot quicker, but it would also produce an ice cream that was smooth and soft in texture.

In 1700s a constant mixing of the ice cream mass resulted in a much finer and smoother consistency without any ice crystals in the ice cream. In 1843, Nancy Johnson from Philadelphia patented an ice cream machine that performed continuous stirring. The next step in the development of ice cream was achieved with the invention of the refrigerator and the freezer.

The Structure and Consistency of Ice Cream

Ice cream mass is composed of three basic elements: ice crystals from pure water, concentrated cream crystals that are formed from the ice cream mass, and the air cells that are formed through the churning process during freezing.

The concentrated cream is what is left when the ice crystals are formed. Thanks to the dissolved sugar, about a fifth of the water in the ice cream blend, the cream remains unfrozen even at temperatures around - 0.4°F. The result is a thick mass containing equal parts unfrozen water, milk fat, milk proteins, and sugar. This liquid mass covers the millions of ice crystals and holds them together, but not too rigidly.

During the freezing process, air cells form in the ice cream blend. They soften the structure of the blend and make the ice cream lighter and more airy so that it becomes easier to scoop up when it is time to serve it, and so that it is easier to eat. The air cells also increase the volume of the ice cream during the freezing process. The technical jargon for the process during which the ice cream volume can increase up to 100% is called overrun. The final result is an even mix of ice cream mass and air. The lesser the volume, the harder the consistency of the ice cream will turn out.

In the 1800s, Sweden was the world's leading manufacturer of ice cream machines, most of them produced by Husqvarna. The export of ice cream makers to the USA was extensive.

It is quite an art to be able to create an ice cream blend that freezes structured, and that has a balanced mix of ice crystals, cream, and air. All these components are important to produce ice cream that is smooth, soft, and slightly chewy in texture. The less water you add to the mixture, the easier it is to achieve tiny ice crystals and a smooth and soft consistency. Too much sugar and milk produces a heavy and rich ice cream, and if you add too much cream, butter will form during the freezing process. Most good recipes produce ice cream that contains about 60 percent water and 15 percent sugar, and at least 10 percent of milk substance with a maximum fat content of 20 percent.

High quality ice cream contains a lot of egg yolks and cream and is not as airy as cheap ice cream.

Different Types of Ice Cream

American ice cream is mostly made from cream and milk, sugar, and some other ingredients, but it usually does not contain any eggs.

French ice cream contains egg yolks, as many as 12 yolks per every 34 ounces of ice cream. The egg protein creates a good emulsion that makes ice crystals in the finished ice cream relatively small, which contributes to a smooth texture, even if the milk fat content is low and the water content is high. Most French ice cream recipes are based on a *crème anglaise* made out of milk, and sometimes out of milk and cream. A blend containing egg yolks needs to be cooked first so that the protein dissolves and causes the mixture to emulsify at a temperature between 179.6°F and 185°F, but also to kill any bacteria that may form in the raw egg yolks. This blend has a vanilla sauce-like consistency and a classic egg flavor that is characteristic for this type of ice cream. Yolk emulsifying lecithins are required to produce sauces such as mayonnaise, hollandaise, *béarnaise*, and a good *crème anglaise*.

Italian ice cream, gelato, has a high fat content, contains egg yolks, and freezes with a pretty low increase in volume, which gives it a rich and smooth texture. Italian vanilla ice cream always contains lemon peel and vanilla pods. Sometimes the Italians produce a leaner ice cream with a *crème anglaise* based on milk only, instead of milk and cream. If the entire egg is used, the ice cream will turn out colder, because the egg whites contain more water. Ice cream that contains only the whites tends to feel a lot colder than it actually is. Egg whites begin to solidify at 141.8°F, but ovalbumin, which is the dominant protein in whites, coagulates at 183.2°F. Glucose, sugar, gelatin, or ice cream stabilizers are added to ice cream with a low fat content (below 10 percent), to get as tiny ice crystals as possible.

Indian ice cream, *kulfi*, is said to originate from the 1600s. It is made without the churning process by boiling the milk so that the milk sugar caramelizes to a consistency similar to condensed milk. *Kulfi* has a strong milk flavor with hints of butterscotch, and it is absolutely delectable.

What Is Good Ice Cream?

What qualities are you looking for in good ice cream? Most people are raised on industrial ice cream full of stabilizers and E numbers and skim milk powder, and inflated with air to increase the volume up to 100 percent. If you are one of those people, you have no idea how delicious handcrafted ice cream with natural ingredients tastes!

Ice cream tastes different in every country. The French are accustomed to creamy, smooth ice cream with strong fruit flavor, or ice cream that has been flavored with real vanilla pods. The Italians like their ice cream more milky with a lesser fat content, and a colder ice consistency, while Americans tend to gravitate towards sweeter, creamier, and softer ice cream.

It is paramount to serve ice cream and sorbet at the right temperature. Ice cream should be enjoyed at a temperature between 5°F and 17.6°F. The ideal temperature is 8.6°F, at least that's what my headmaster at the COBA School in Switzerland used to say. Sorbets should be eaten at a lower temperature because they melt more quickly, and *spoom* and *granite* should be consumed right out of the freezer.

Appearance

The color of the ice cream should agree with its content. Yellow banana ice cream or lemon ice cream are therefore artificially colored, because the fruit is white inside. Any additives, such as lightly candied fruit or caramelized almonds should be thoroughly mixed into the ice cream. The ice cream surface shouldn't have any ice crystals or be dry.

Consistency

You can see the "body" of the ice cream with the naked eye. When you are scooping up ice cream with an ice cream scoop or with a spoon dipped in hot water, you can tell how the ice cream shapes up in the vessel. If it is scooped up too easily, the texture is too loose and will melt too quickly. The texture should be soft and melt on the tongue, unlike some industry ice creams, whose consistency is like rubber and as a result, tends to be crumbly and waxy. A well-balanced ice cream will form a shell on the surface when served, so that it doesn't turn runny.

Texture

The right texture is smooth, soft, and melts on the tongue. If the ice cream melts in the mouth but has a rough texture, it was probably frozen too slowly. If you can taste the ice crystals, either the recipe was incorrect or the ice cream is partially thawed. If it has a gritty texture on the tongue, the blend was heated too much and the egg yolk is partially coagulated.

Taste

It should be easy to identify the intended flavor, but it shouldn't be so strong that you are unable to eat one or more spoons of it. Sweetness is often a controversial and highly individual matter, and it is usually the one that is mentioned first. Because sugar tends to be one of the cheapest ingredients used in ice cream production, it is commonly overused. Too much sugar kills the fresh acidity, especially in fruit sorbet or fruit ice cream, and the result is way too sweet. It is important to add fresh lemon juice when making fruit sorbet or fruit ice cream, so that it doesn't turn too sweet. The natural flavors shouldn't get buried under added sugar, but they should leave a pleasant memory on the tongue.

Melting Point

When ice cream melts in the mouth, it should turn into a creamy liquid, and not remain in the mouth, get separated, or have a crumbly texture.

The Chemistry of Ice Cream and Sorbet

All ice cream and sorbet is a mix of water (pure water, or the water content in milk), air, and flavoring, and any addition from the following ingredients:
Sugar, glucose, honey, and naturally occuring sugar in fruits and berries.
Fat in the form of milk, cream, and butter. Skim milk powder without fat
(lactose, protein, and minerals).
Eggs, egg yolks, or egg whites.
Stabilizers, such as gelatin, which are without E numbers.
Other types of stabilizers and emulsifiers that are commonly used by industrial manufacturers (instead of eggs).

When fruit purées and juices freeze, they form a medium hard mass that is refreshing in the mouth. This type of ice cream making was refined in Italy in the 1700s, and it gave us the term *sorbet* from *sorbetto*, which comes from the Arabic term *sherbet*.

The taste and aroma comes from the fruits and berries, but often wine, spices, herbs, flowers, coffee, and other ingredients are added for additional flavor. Sugar or sugar syrup is often added, as well as fresh lemon juice and lime juice.

When making sorbet, it is very important to make sure that the sugar level is about 25-35 percent. That's about the same sugar percentage as a mature melon has. The acidity should be about 0.5 percent in the form of fresh lemon juice. The dry matter, the fruit content, should be about 33-45 percent. The purée or the juice is often diluted with water, in certain cases to reduce the acidity from the lemon and lime, and in other cases to reduce the flavor intensity. Melon and cucumbers often need to be diluted with water because otherwise their flavor can be overwhelming.

Italians tend to add milk to their lemon sorbet and lemon ice cream to round off the flavor. In my opinion, classic Italian lemon ice cream (sorbet) is among the best ice creams. Another good ice cream is mandarin ice cream. Unfortunately, it is very difficult to find mandarins in Sweden, because the Swedes think that they contain too many seeds. In Switzerland, it used to be a Christmas Eve tradition to serve hollowed mandarins filled with mandarin ice cream. I remember how we used to rub the skin of the mandarins with sugar cubes to enhance the ice cream flavor. This takes a really long time, and it is unusual today, but there is no other method that produces a better citrus ice cream.

We used to mix about 50 percent vanilla ice cream with sorbet blend when making strawberry, black currant, or passion fruit ice cream. This trick produces a very nice fruit ice cream with a velvety structure, despite that it might not be as refreshing as when mixed only with water or milk. Sometimes, the Italians add sweet condensed milk to give light ice creams a richer flavor. When it comes to sorbet and fruit ice cream, the texture can vary from rock hard to velvety, this all depends on sugar levels, manufacturing process, and serving temperature. During the freezing process, the water transforms into millions of little ice crystals surrounded by the other ingredients in the blend. It is mainly copious amounts of water that forms a sugar syrup with the dissolved sugar and the sugar in the fruit, combined with the pulp. The more sugar syrup and fruit pulp, the more malleable the ice crystals will be, which produces a soft sorbet or ice cream. You will be able to taste this right away on the tongue. Most fruit ice creams are made with 25-35% sugar. Very sweet fruits don't require as much added sugar to achieve the right sugar content. Fruits and berries that contain a lot of pectin also don't require as much sugar. The ice cream producer often uses an aerometer, a device that measures sugar, which was invented by the French scientist, Antoine Baumé (1782-1804). Baumé is a measurement that measures the density of liquid. The Brix scale is used to measure the sugar level in a solution at a given temperature, and it is measured with a refractometer. Clean water is 0 Brix, a 10 percent sugar solution is 10 Brix; 20° Brix = 11.1° Baumé. Most fruit ice creams and sorbet without alcohol should be on a scale between 17 and 18° Baumé, or 30-31° Brix.

For ice cream, 18° Baumé is common and it means that the ice cream has a sugar content of 34 percent and requires a minimum temperature of 1.4°F to freeze, otherwise syneresis occurs, which means that separation of the water occurs in the ice cream or sorbet. The refractometer is inserted into the mixture in a big measuring cup, and the degrees can be read on the scale. If needed, you add sugar syrup until you achieve the right degree. If the sugar content is too high, you can dilute the blend with water, fruit purée, or fruit juice.

A refractometer

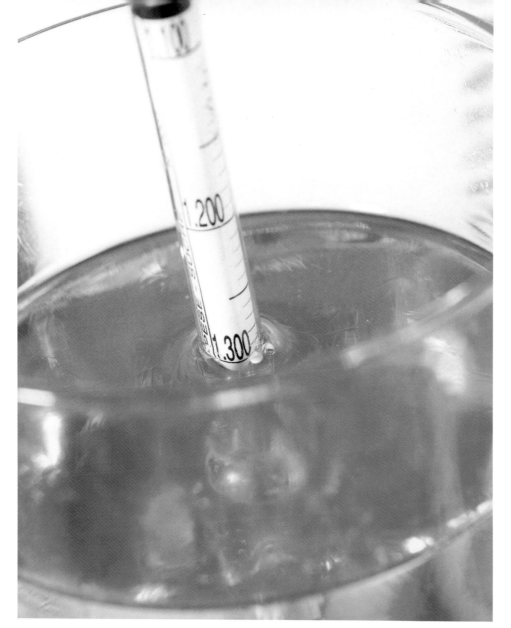

Tip!

Remember that the sorbet mixture should be at a temperature of about 68°F when you are measuring it with the hydrometer and the refractometer, in order to get the correct degrees.

Example: The sugar content is measured with a hydrometer and has dropped to 17° Baumé, which means that sorbet mixture has a density of 1.17 or that the sugar syrup weighs 1170 g (41.3 oz).

Most ice cream manufacturers add up to ⅓ of glucose syrup, invert sugar, to give the ice cream or sorbet a smoother texture and prevent it from crystallizing while it settles. It provides a good consistency and does not add as much sugar. Sugar and glucose syrup, honey, glucose, or invert sugar makes the ice shape into small crystals during freezing, which also improves the consistency of sorbet and ice cream and prevents the formation of larger crystals, which makes ice cream grainy.

Ice cream or sorbet served directly from the freezer is usually pretty hard, but if you allow it to sit in room temperature for a bit it becomes much softer and smoother in texture. Therefore freshly frozen ice cream and sorbet always tastes the best.

Making Ice Cream

If you use a pacojet (see the photo on the opposite page), you can reduce the sugar content of your ice cream by 50 percent due to the rapid freezing process. This professional machine is still expensive, but remember that computers too used to be expensive not long ago.

Hygiene During Ice Cream Production

Remember to wash your hands thoroughly with liquid soap and a nail brush, and rinse them in clean running water and dry them with paper, not with a towel.

Always wash your ice cream machine with detergent, rinse well, and allow it to dry before you freeze ice cream. Wash and rinse all tools and bowls before you begin the process. Never use plastic bowls; metal is much easier to keep clean.

Always cover the frozen ice cream with a lid or plastic wrap so that it does not assimilate flavors from other products in the freezer.

There are three classic moments in ice cream production: the preparing and cooling of the ice cream mass, the freezing, and the solidifying process.

Preparing and Cooling the Ice Cream Mass

The first step is to choose your ingredients and combine them. The base ingredients are milk, cream, and sugar. A mixture of 17 percent of milk fat (equal parts whipping cream and milk) and 6.4 oz (180 g) of sugar per 34 oz (1 liter) of fluid is nice and smooth in texture and freezes quickly in an ice cream machine, even the home model.

If you want a smooth cream with lower fat content, there are several ways to achieve this: you can make a crème anglaise with egg yolks, replace some of the cream with condensed milk, add milk powder, and replace some sugar with glucose, glucose syrup, invert sugar, or honey, which is nature's own invert sugar.

During commercial production, the entire ice cream mass needs to be heated so that all the ingredients dissolve and the flavors are released. It must be pasteurized by being heated to 181.4-185°F for 2 minutes. Cooking enhances the ice cream texture and its agility by breaking down proteins, which helps to reduce the ice crystals in size. Mixtures containing egg and egg yolk are always heated to 181.4-185°F, until they begin to thicken and form an emulsion.

Then the ice cream mass should be cooled down as quickly as possible to 39.2°F to prevent bacteria from forming through slow cooling. After that, the ice cream blend should be left to swell for at least 4 hours but preferably for 12 hours, according to ice cream experts (in my opinion, however, 24 hours is ideal). During this process, the milk proteins swell and form a good emulsion, which gives ice cream a smoother, softer and silkier texture. It also increases in volume when it swells, because the ice crystals become smaller once the ice cream is frozen.

You should store the ice cream blend in the fridge at a temperature of 39.2°F during the swelling process.

Freezing

During this process you will be able to tell if the result of your work is good or a failure. By controlling the overrun, the percentage increase in volume, you can tell how the ice cream will develop during the freezing process.

What is overrun then? When the ice cream hardens during freezing and air enters it, the volume of the ice cream increases. This creates the proper ice cream texture. The ideal overrun is 25-50 percent for handcrafted ice cream. But this is also a personal choice and will vary with each manufacturer's own personal taste.

Then the ice cream is frozen in an electric ice cream machine with chilled walls as quickly as possible. The ice cream blend is churned and chilled by the machine and during the process the ice cream is scraped down from the walls by the machine so that the ice cream gets a smooth and even texture, and so that it can absorb air and

increase in volume until it becomes flexible, light, and slightly chewy. A slow freezing process gives the ice cream a rough structure with big ice crystals and mushy consistency. The faster an ice cream mass freezes, the better the consistency. Rapid freezing during stirring ensures that production of small ice crystals is spreading quickly, because it divides the available water molecules that surround the ice crystals, which prevents them from growing. Rapid freezing also prevents the crystals from lining up next to each other and forming chains. Instead, the many small crystals give a wonderfully smooth, melting, and slightly chewy texture.

Hardening

When the ice cream is firm and feels ready, only half of the water in the ice cream has frozen into ice crystals. Now the ice cream needs to be frozen as soon as possible, and then another 40 percent of the water will freeze. If freezing occurs slowly, some of the ice crystals will absorb more water than others and worsen the texture of the ice cream. The freezing process can be speeded up by dividing the ice cream into smaller containers.

Ingredients and Methods During Ice Cream Production

Sugar

Sweet is the first taste that humans are able to perceive; breast milk is sweet. Humans have always appreciated sweet flavors and experienced them as a positive, good, and pleasant.

The sugar cane was the first plant used to produce sugar on a large scale. The process of squeezing juice out of the sugar cane was discovered in India about 300 BC. Eventually, humans discovered how to produce sugar in solid form by concentrating it through boiling so that it crystallized.

Sugar is necessary for all types of ice cream production to provide the proper sweetness. Sugar provides volume and acts as a flavor enhancer. Sugar also gives the ice cream body and viscosity and contributes to making it soft and smooth in texture. Because sugar provides body and texture in ice cream, it counts as a solid in well-balanced ice cream or sorbet. It also affects the freezing point, when the sugar dissolves in the milk, cream, and eggs. This means that the freezing point must be reduced, which is done by creating a lower temperature to cause the water to form ice. When the ice cream begins to freeze, tiny frozen crystals of almost pure water begin to form. Therefore, the remaining sugar syrup becomes even more concentrated, and the freezing point is lowered further. The lower the temperature, the more ice crystals are formed and the more concentrated the sugar solution. However, it can reach a point where the sugar concentration becomes too high, as there always has to be some water moving freely in the ice cream.

Sugar makes the ice cream retain its moisture, last longer, and retain its texture. It enhances flavor and texture and increases the rising capacity during stirring in the ice cream machine.

The more sugar ice cream contains, the colder the temperature needs to be during the freezing process. If you add too much sugar to the ice cream, it will not freeze. If you don't add enough sugar, the ice cream becomes too hard. Sugar also plays an important role in the production of caramel ice cream, as it is the caramelization and the Maillard reaction that produces the brown color.

Various Sugars and Sweeteners

Sucrose, or regular granulated sugar, is also known as K5. It is a disaccharide composed of a glucose and a fruit molecule, joined by a glucose binding. It gives a sweet taste without any off-flavors and it is the most common sugar used in ice cream production. Other varieties can provide interesting combinations and flavors that regular sugar doesn't provide with its neutral flavor.

Cassonade is a raw sugar with a strong aroma. It comes from the Old French colony of Mauritius.

Demerara sugar was originally the name of brown sugar from the town of Demerara Guiana in South America. Today it comes mostly from Mauritius.

Brown sugar is produced by adding cane molasses or dark syrup during the sugar boiling process.

Powdered sugar is very finely ground sugar (sucrose) produced by grinding and sieving the sugar. Powdered sugar often contains anti-caking agents such as starch or maltodextrin.

Glycerine, which is a liquid sugar that comes from fermented products such as wine, has now started being used in ice cream production. Because 1 g (0.035 oz) of glycerine lowers the freezing point as much as 4 g (0.14 oz) of ordinary sugar, it is especially useful when making less sweet appetizer ice cream.

Honey is the oldest sweetener in the world. Cave paintings from the time of Cro-Magnon show that honey was collected 10,000 years BC. The sugar content is 78-84 percent. Honey is a liquid solution of invert sugar, where the fructose content is higher than the sucrose level.

Invert sugar, trimoline, is a mixture of equal parts glucose and fructose. Invert sugar prevents the sugar (sucrose) from crystallizing and makes the ice cream smoother. Trimoline should only be used in problematic ice cream like chocolate ice cream, which tends to get too hard, hazelnut ice cream, praline ice cream, and gianduja ice cream.

Molasses made from cane sugar is delicious in ice cream, but not molasses from beet sugar, which used to be used as animal feed. Molasses is a by-product of sugar manufacturing. It is used in the production of brown sugar and licorice and is a raw material in rum production.

Muscovado is a brown sugar with a little more color and flavor than the Demerara sugar.

Raw sugar is an intermediate product in sugar cane processing, and it contains 96-98 percent of sugar, while the rest is molasses residue.

Sorbitol is a sugar alcohol in liquid form in a 70-percent solution or in powder form. It keeps the ice cream soft and supple. Measure about 10 percent of the sugar additive.

Glucose syrup is a clear, viscous liquid sugar. The addition of glucose syrup prevents sucrose crystallization, and it increases hygroscopic capacity and viscosity, and reduces sweetness. It makes ice cream and sorbet smooth and soft and increases its shelf life.

Usually, between 200 g (1 cup) and 350 g (1¾ cup) of sugar is used per 1 liter (4¼ cup) of milk, or 1 liter (4¼ cup) of a milk and cream blend. Since sugar does not freeze during the hardening process, the following chart should be taken into consideration to achieve a fine texture when serving the ice cream. This is the right temperature when portioning the ice cream:

250 g (1¼ cup) of sugar per 1 liter (34 oz)	53.6°F storage temperature
300 g (1½ cup) of sugar per 1 liter (34 oz)	57.2°F storage temperature
350 g (1¾ cup) of sugar per 1 liter (34 oz)	59°F storage temperature

Water

Pure water freezes to solid ice, but when it is combined with other ingredients in ice cream, the freezing process changes in many ways. When the temperature is about 17°F, about 67 percent of the water has formed ice crystals, but this varies slightly depending on the recipe. These ice crystals should be as small as possible to produce an ice cream that is smooth and melts. Rapid freezing ensures the growth of minimal crystals throughout the entire ice cream blend and it keeps them in motion so that they don't attach to each other.

If an ice-cream is frozen without stirring or only with the occasional stir by using a spoon, it will contain large ice crystals, as opposed to an ice cream frozen during continuous stirring.

Air

The process of incorporating air into the ice cream during freezing has great influence on texture, because stirring also separates the ice crystals and fat molecules and causes them to produce foam. In industrial ice cream the volume is often doubled by injecting air with a compressor during freezing. Handcrafted ice cream increases about 25 percent with regular ice cream machines. Fancier ice cream machines can increase the yield (increase in volume) to about 50 percent. The technical term for this process is overrun.

Milk-Based Ice Creams

Milk-based ice creams contain ice crystals, fat molecules, and air cells, all distributed in the water of the milk, which contains sugar, milk protein, and minerals. The ingredients get stabilized in a foam during freezing.

Milk, cream, yogurt, quark cheese, and various kinds of cheese, such as ricotta and mascarpone, and in some cases unsalted butter, are the most common milk products used in ice cream production. Milk and cream from cows is most common, but there is also ice cream made from goat's milk, which I recently ate in Sicily.

The Art of Handling Cream and Milk

Both cream and milk should always be stored in a refrigerator at a temperature as low as 39.2°F, but they should not freeze. Good taste and durability is achieved by storing them in well-sealed packaging as milk and cream easily absorb flavors from other ingredients.

Fat

Fat is the most expensive ingredient in ice cream, and air is the cheapest. Therefore, commercial ice cream is low in fat and filled with plenty of air. In small-scale ice cream production, the fat comes mostly from milk and cream and in some cases from butter, and the fat molecules inhibit the growth of larger ice crystals. The amount of fat in ice cream determines how rich the flavor and how smooth the texture will turn out.

Stabilizers

Gelatin improves texture and prevents the ice cream from becoming runny when temperature differences occur during transportation or other situations when the temperature is likely to shift. Gel strength is measured in bloom. Preferably use gold gelatin, which has 200 bloom, while silver gelatin has 180 bloom. Gelatin doesn't have an E number, but it contains animal elements, which vegetarians should be aware of.

Other stabilizers used in ice cream and sorbet production are:

E 401 Sodium Alginate
E 403 Ammonium Alginate
E 406, Agar Agar
E 407 Carrageenan
E 440 Pectin

Emulsifiers

The most important emulsifier in ice cream is egg. Egg yolk contains 50 percent water, 10 percent lecithin, 30 percent fat, and 10 percent other substances, and it affects the ice cream consistency. Add eggs to make ice cream appear smoother and fattier than it is. By binding the ice cream mass with eggs, the ice crystals will turn out small in the frozen ice cream and this will prevent the texture from becoming icy.

Eggs

It is easy to see if an egg is fresh or stale. A fresh egg sinks in water, has a high yellow and the white folds tightly around the yolk when the egg is turned up. It has a small air bubble.

Eggs contain pure protein and are often used as the standard for measuring protein in other foods. Protein is composed of amino acids, and the composition of amino acids in eggs is so great in quantity and quality, that it contains almost 100 percent of the amino acids that are necessary for body and muscle maintenance.

Sizes

After candling the eggs, they are sorted by size into four classes: XL (very large), more than 2.5 oz, L (large), 2.2–2.5 oz, M (medium), 1.8–2.2 oz, s (small), 1.5–1.8 oz. In a regular egg, the egg yolk weighs about 0.7 oz and the egg white approximately 1 oz.

Eggs last in the refrigerator for a long time. The membranes inside the egg protect both the yolk and the white. Most vitamins can be found in eggs, except for vitamin C. Professionals always buy eggs with pasteurized yolks.

Eggs are important fresh produce when it comes to making high quality ice cream. It is known that the albumins in eggs have a binding effect. The egg white usually consists of 75 percent water. When you boil or fry eggs, you can see how their binding capacity increases through heating. In order for the ice cream mass to thicken, a process known as coagulation is required, which occurs when the ice cream mass is heated to a so-called rose test between 179.6 and 185°F. During this process pasteurization occurs that kills any bacteria. Ice cream manufacturers do the same process in an ice cream maker.

I add about 8.5 oz egg yolks (about a dozen) per 34 oz of milk or, milk and cream mix, or any other liquid that would bind the same way. You can use more or less egg yolks, 10 yolks is fine (7 oz), but 6-8 yolks provide weak binding in the finished ice cream.

Pasteurization

The purpose of pasteurization is to minimize the risk of microbiological bacteria from developing, as they are always present in raw materials. Pasteurization does not kill all the bacteria, but it slows down their development and prolongs the shelf life a few days.

There are two different pasteurization methods: HTST (high temperature, short time) and LTLT (low temperature, long time). HTST is the most commonly used in ice cream production.

The mixture is heated to a minimum temperature of 185°F for 2-3 minutes and then it is cooled down as soon as possible to 39.2°F.

Confectioners, ice cream manufacturers, and chefs mostly cook the ice cream blend in a professional ice cream maker with automatic pasteurization, and a swell tank on the side. It is the same process but with automatic stirring.

Rose Test and Ladle Test at 179.6-185°F

The better the binding of the ice cream mass, the better the ice cream will be. These tests were among the first things I learned as an apprentice pastry chef. For the rose test, you need to blow on the backside of a spoon that has been dipped in the ice cream mass. When a rose shape appears in the ice cream batter when you blow on it, it is because the sugar has dissolved and bound with the egg yolk, milk, and cream. During the ladle test, you dip a ladle in the batter and drag the finger through the mass on the backside of the ladle. You know the batter is good when you drag the finger through the batter and it separates without flowing back together.

Is a Thermometer Useful?

Yes, you can use a thermometer to assist you, but it requires a little bit of training before you will be able to tell when the cream begins to thicken as you stir it. If the ice cream mass becomes too hot, it may coagulate completely and curdle. Use a regular household thermometer. It is important to remove the pot from the stove to prevent the ice cream mass from coagulating on the bottom. Keep stirring for a little while once you remove the pot from the heat, because it will still be hotter close to the bottom.

Is There Anything That Can Be Done if the Ice Cream Mass Curdles?

Yes, if the cutting process hasn't reached too far, you can pour the ice cream mass in a blender and mix until it is smooth. A hand blender won't be useful, because it isn't strong enough. When you're done mixing, sieve the ice cream mass through a chinois or a very fine sieve, or twist it through a straining-cloth.

Storage and Serving

Ice cream gets better the colder it is stored; −0.4°F or an even lower temperature is required for the ice cream to retain its texture, flavor, and smoothness. The ideal temperature is −22°F. The lower the storage temperature, the better the result will be during thawing. Repeatedly thawing and freezing the ice cream will worsen its quality. Then the little ice crystals melt completely and they reshape into bigger ice crystals, worsening the texture of the ice cream.

Ice cream is negatively affected in two ways during storage. First off, fat absorbs odors and flavors in the freezer. Second, the ice cream can get ruined and dried out by the air in the freezer. You can prevent these issues by pressing plastic over the ice cream to get rid of any air bubbles, and then cover with a tightly fitting lid.

Ideally, you should thaw the ice cream slowly in the fridge until it reaches 8.6°F. Then the ice cream will taste delicious and have a smooth and soft texture. It will contain more flowing water, which contributes to a softer consistency.

Vanilla

Vanilla is the most popular ice cream flavor in the world, closely followed by chocolate, and strawberry ice cream. The legend says that the people of the kingdom of Totonacopan had a fertility goddess by the name Xanath, who descended to the people on Earth and fell in love with a mortal man—which was an impossible union. Xanath transformed herself into a vanilla plant to be able to remain on Earth with the people. The people of Totonacopan began growing vanilla plants and produce vanilla from the pods about a thousand years ago. The plant was their secret until the mid 1800s.

The first European to taste vanilla was Columbus. It happened on the 14th of September, 1502, in Nicaragua. He was on his fourth trip when he tasted vanilla along with a chocolate drink. The Spaniards also came across the vanilla plant during their encounter with the Aztecs in Mexico, and they brought vanilla pods to Europe in 1510. In the 1520s, Hernán Cortés sent vanilla plants to Spain from Mexico, but they wouldn't grow in Spain.

Europeans used vanilla in chocolate production during the first hundred years. The French started using vanilla in perfume making in the 1600s. Vanilla became a popular aphrodisiac in Europe in the 1700s, after a German doctor published a pamphlet in 1762 about how he had healed 342 impotent men with vanilla. Vanilla is a climbing orchid plant that originates from Central America. After the green seed pods are harvested, they undergo a lengthy and complicated procedure before

they are distributed for sale. Vanilla aroma consists of approximately 170 different substances. The substance vanillin is important, but not the determining factor for flavor and aroma. During fermentation a transformation occurs to vanillin. The entire process takes about 6 months and is important to maintain quality. According to legend, it was the Indians in Mexico who discovered how to ferment vanilla pods. Mexico has excellent vanilla beans, which can be difficult to come by in Europe.

Bourbon Vanilla (Vanilla planifolia) and Tahitian vanilla (Vanilla tahitiensis) have about 7.5–12 inches and 6–7 cm long pods and they grow in Réunion and Madagascar and Tahiti. Tahitian vanilla is my absolute favorite vanilla, because of its rounder tones and sweetness.

High quality vanilla beans should be long and moist with a strong aroma and only a slight bitterness. They are best when they have white, needle-like crystals on the pods. The little black seeds inside are pretty tasteless, so the pod quality is crucial for the final result. Divide the vanilla bean in the middle and scrape out the seeds with a small sharp knife before they are added to the ice cream mass, often together with the pod itself.

WINE PAIRINGS FOR ICE CREAM, SORBETS, AND PARFAITS

Ice cream and parfait with berries or citrus flavors are always well paired with sweet and sparkling muscat wine. Ice cream and parfait with its creamy, rich texture of cream and eggs go well with the mousse in the wine. Spices also combine well with the sweet muscat wine.

Vanilla ice cream goes well with sweet sherry, which has a rich fig/raisin characteristic with the scent of chocolate. Ice creams and parfaits that are spiced with cardamom, cinnamon, and saffron require a wine with more flavor, such as Marsala Florio, or Marsala Floriovo Aromatizzato.

Sweet Madeira or the very sweetest Tokay wine goes well with caramel ice cream. Commandaria from Cyprus is also suitable, it has a rich sweetness, body, and a burned characteristic, just like the ice cream.

With chocolate ice cream and chocolate parfait, which are both flavorful, sweet and rich with a light bitter taste, I recommend Madeira with its burnt character and rich sweetness. However this is very potent combination. You can also serve Port wine as it also has a burnt character and rich flavor. If you want to serve something more elegant, I would go with a sweet, heavy muscat wine that has a higher alcohol content.

Fruit ice creams made with summer berries go well with sweet and light wines and sweet champagne. Ice cream with strawberries, wild strawberries, raspberries, and blackberries is well paired with noble sweet wines from Bordeaux and noble sweet wines from Austria and Germany. Sweet wines from Vouvray and Coteaux du Layon in the Loire Valley are also suitable. Even sweet muscat wines, both sparkling and still, will do. muscat grape flavors marry well with the berries.

Currants, cranberries, and blueberries, with their tangy flavors can be difficult to pair with wine. Blueberries and black currants fit well with a young fruity red Port wine, while sweet muscat wine, either sparkling or still, balances the cranberries and currants. The cherry beer, Kriek, can be served with cranberry and currant ice cream. Cloudberries are best combined with Tokayer.

Fruit and berry sorbet should have a raw characteristic. Sorbet is a refreshing dessert or side dish that is well paired with a heavy dinner, such as a black currant sorbet after a wild game dinner. In the summer, when we crave lighter food, raspberry sorbet and melon sorbet, garnished with some fresh berries, provide the perfect finish to a good dinner. Personally, I prefer sorbet without any wine combination. However, if you'd like to pair it with something, I recommend Asti Spumante wines from Italy, they have a nice sweetness and mild acidity. Demi-Sec champagne is also a good choice.

Apple sorbet and apple ice cream go well with the Hungarian wine Tokayer. Specifically a Tokayer with 3-5 Puttonyos or 60-90 grams of residual sugar. The fine acid and the slightly burnt character provides an excellent combination, as does the sweet ripe Loire wines, such as Moulin Touchais, which is sweet, yet refreshing. You can also serve red Port with apple desserts.

Exotic fruits, such as pineapple, kiwi, papaya, starfruit, and citrus fruits are not great with wine. The high acidity and the enzymes tend to interfere with the taste experience. Sweet muscat wine usually manages them quite well.

Peaches, apricots, and honeydew melon are sweet with a mild acidity, and suit sweet or noble sweet wines with a high fruit acidity, such as Sauternes, German, and Austrian sweet wines, and sweet Loire wines.

Italy is the epicenter of ice cream culture. The Italians love ice cream of all shapes and forms. In Italy you can find high quality, handcrafted ice cream on nearly every street corner. These wonderful photographs were taken on a beautiful fall afternoon in Rome in 2007.

1. *Pacojet* 3. *Springform pan* 5. *Sugar thermometer* 7. *Chinois* 9. *Ice cream baller* 11. *Refractometer* 13. *Circle pan*

2. *Blender* 4. *Ice cream machine* 6. *Hydrometer* 8. *Balloon wire whisk* 10. *Handheld stick blender* 12. *Digital scale*

ICE CREAMS

About quantities, fat content, etc.

It is very important that the proportions of the ingredients are exact when making ice cream, or any other dessert. Therefore, traditional measurements are preferred over volume measuring tools. Today, most enthusiastic home chefs also have a digital scale, so the amateur chef shouldn't encounter any problems when using a cookbook like this one. Just in case, I have created a little cheat sheet that could be helpul. It also indicates the recommended fat content for the dairy products, which sometimes varies in different countries.

1 egg yolk = approximately 0.7 oz
1 egg white = approximately 1 oz
1 gelatin leaf = approximately 0.07 oz (use gold gelatin, their leaves always weigh exactly 0.07 oz)

3.5 oz granulated sugar = 3.7 fl. oz
3.5 oz brown sugar = 4.6 fl. oz
3.5 oz confectioner's sugar = 5.6 fl. oz
3.5 oz syrup/honey = 2.4 fl. oz
3.5 oz almonds/nuts = 5.2 fl. oz
3.5 oz raisins = 4.9 – 6.8 fl. oz

Milk fat content = 3%
Whipping cream fat content = 40%

Basic Ice Cream Recipe (Ice Cream Base), approx. 18% milk fat

During my long career at various work places and trade schools, I've been involved in making many different types of ice creams, but this recipe is my absolute favorite. This classic ice cream is also an excellent basic recipe that can be mixed with many different flavors. If you want a lighter ice cream, you can add less cream, but the ice cream won't turn out as creamy. Also be careful not to add too much fat, then the fat tends to crystallize and give the ice cream a grainy texture. If you don't want to use gelatin leafs, you can exclude them, but the consistency is always better if you add them. In this recipe we use the crème anglaise method. In America, this type of ice cream is called double cream ice cream, the lighter variations are referred to as cream ice cream.

(4g) 2 gelatin leaves
1-2 vanilla pods, divided and scraped
500 g (2 cups) milk
500 g (2 cups) whipping cream
50g (2½ tbsp) light honey or glucose syrup
240 g (1 cup) egg yolks
250 g (1¼ cups) granulated sugar

Day 1
1. Soak the gelatin leaves in cold water for at least 10 minutes.

2. Place the vanilla pod and the seeds in a big pan and add milk, cream, honey or glucose syrup.
3. Beat the yolks and sugar fluffy. Bring the cream mixture to a boil. Add the warm cream blend into the frothy yolk mix, and whisk thoroughly. Pour everything back into the pan.
4. Heat to 185°F while you continuously stir the ice cream blend with a ladle. You will be able to tell when you reach the right temperature, because the mixture will start to thicken. Use a thermometer, or do a rose test (p. 25).
5. Lift the gelatin leaves out of the water and add to the ice cream blend. Stir until they have dissolved.
6 Sieve through a chinois or a fine sieve, into a stainless steel bowl. Cool the ice cream blend as quickly as possible in an ice cold water bath, stirring occasionally to speed up the process.
7. Cover with plastic wrap and allow the ice cream to swell for 4-12 hours, or preferably 24 hours, in a refrigerator at 39.2°F.

Day 2
1. Mix the ice cream blend with an immersion hand blender before you freeze it to get a smoother texture.
2. Pour the ice cream mass into the ice cream machine so that you fill up to half of the container, and freeze during continuous stirring so that the ice cream gets smooth and firm. Time will vary depending on the ice cream machine that you are using. If you don't have one of those machines, you can put the ice cream blend in the freezer and occasionally stir it with a ladle until the ice cream is firm. Serve right away.

Remember…
If you freeze an ice cream for too long, the texture may become strange and buttery, because the butter fat tends to crystallize.

Italian Vanilla Ice Cream

It is typically Italian to cut the vanilla flavor with a slight tinge of lemon, a nice and refreshing addition to an old classic. If you add the cream right before you are about to freeze the ice cream, it will lighten up the flavor a bit. If you want to lighten it even further, you can exclude the cream completely and remove half of the gelatin leaves and 1.8 oz of the sugar. You can also replace the cream with greek yogurt if you want a refreshing vanilla yogurt ice cream.

Day 1
4 gelatin leaves (8 g)
1-2 vanilla pods, divided and scraped
1000 g (4 cups) milk
50 g (2½ tbsp) light Swedish honey or glucose syrup
240 g (1 cup) egg yolks
300 g (1½ cups) sugar
Lemon peel from half a lemon

Prepare the same way as in the previous basic ice cream recipe, but add the lemon peel.

Day 2
Add 200 g (⅘ cup) of cream to the ice cream blend and whisk with an immersion hand blender. Freeze in an ice cream machine.

Modern Italian Vanilla Ice Cream

This recipe doesn't require as many eggs. Instead, skim milk powder is used to add body to the ice cream and bind the cream.

5 gelatin leaves (10 g)
1000 g (4 cups) milk
68 g (⅗ cup) skim milk powder
100 g (⅓ cup) glucose or corn syrup
160 g (¾ cup) unsalted butter, melted and lukewarm
2 vanilla pods, divided and scraped
120 g (½ cup) egg yolks
235 g (1⅛ cups) sugar

1. Soak the gelatin leaves in cold water for at least 10 minutes.
2. Slowly heat the milk and skim milk powder to 77°F, add the glucose syrup.
3. At 95°F, add the melted butter. At 98.6°F, add the vanilla. At 104°F, add yolks. At 113°F, add sugar. Heat everything to 185°F,
4. Mix everything in an electric blender. Quickly cool down to 39.2°F. Allow the blend to swell in the fridge for at least 4 hours, but preferably 12 hours.
5. Freeze the ice cream in an ice cream machine.

Vanilla Ice Cream without Eggs

2 gelatin leaves (4 g)
1 vanilla pod, divided and scraped
700g (2⁹⁄₁₀ cups) milk
300 g (1¼ cups) whipping cream
250 g (1¼ cups) sugar
50 g (2½ tbsp) light honey, or glucose syrup

1. Soak the gelatin leaves in water for at least 10 minutes.
2. Add the vanilla pod and the seeds together with the milk, cream, sugar, and honey or glucose syrup. Bring everything to a boil, and add the gelatin leaves and mix until they have dissolved.
3. Strain the ice cream blend through a chinois or a fine sieve. Cool down as quickly as possible to 39.2°F.
4. Freeze the ice cream blend in an ice cream machine.

LUXURIOUS SOFT ICE CREAM

Soft ice cream can be flavored in many different ways. There are very expensive machines especially made for soft ice cream, but you can also use a regular ice cream machine. Just interrupt the freezing process when the ice cream has a nice and soft consistency.

5 gelatin leaves (10 g)
150 g (1¼ cups) skim milk powder
250 g (1¼ cups) sugar
1500 g (6⅓ cups) milk
500 g (2 cups) whipping cream
50 g (2½ tbsp) glucose
2 vanilla pods, divided and scraped

1. Soak the gelatin leaves in cold water for at least 10 minutes.
2. Mix the skim milk powder with sugar, add the milk, cream, glucose, and vanilla.
3. Heat to 179.6°F. Lift the gelatin leaves out of the soak and let the water that is left on the leaves join them into the mix. Stir until they have dissolved.
4. Take out the vanilla pods. Mix the ice cream blend thoroughly and strain it through a chinois or a fine meshed sieve. Rapidly cool mix to 39.2°F.
5. Freeze the ice cream blend in an ice cream machine.

Vanilla Ice Cream with Other Types of Sugar

You can exchange regular sugar for molasses or cassonade sugar for a delicious variation. It will give a rich flavor that is excellent with red wine poached prunes with spices, or with pears poached in red wine.

CARAMEL ICE CREAM WITH FLEUR DE SEL GUÉRANDE

Absolutely delectable with vanilla poached pears! Salt from Guérande comes from a process that has remained unchanged for over thousand years. The beach fields around Guérande are nature reserves nowadays. Several of them have been used since the 1800s. It is a unique white salt with fine crystals that are excellent to add to ice cream. Caramelization is a thermal decomposition of the sugar that occurs when a sugar solution is heated to 212°F and above. The degree of caramelization increases with the rising temperature and particularly occurs at low pH values. The sugar molecules disintegrate at first, and then the disintegrated particles react with each other and with the water and the sugar that hasn't been broken down. Together they build a varied, brown colored and slightly sweet molecule. Caramel ice cream and sauce are based on caramelization.

2 gelatin leaves (4 g)
500 g (2 cups) milk
500 g (2 cups) whipping cream
1 vanilla pod (unopened)
240 g (1 cup) egg yolks
50 g + 200 g (¼ cup + 1 cup) sugar
80 g (⅓ cup) water
50 g (2½ tbsp) glucose syrup
5 g (1 tsp) fleur de sel Guérande

1. Soak the gelatin leaves in water for at least 10 minutes.
2. Boil the milk, cream, the whole vanilla bean, and set the pot aside.
3. Whisk egg yolks with 50 g (¼ cup) of sugar until you get a foamy blend and set aside.
4. Boil the remaining sugar and water until you have a dark brown caramel sauce (it has a good color at 356°F). Immediately pour it into the warm milk/cream blend (be cautious as a lot of bubbles will occur). Put the pot back on the stove and bring to a boil again and make sure that all the sugar is dissolved. Immediately pour it over the foamy yolk blend and mix well.
5. Pour everything back into the pot and heat to 185°F, when it begins to thicken, or do a rose test or a ladle test (p. 25). Lift the gelatin leaves out of the water and add them to the ice cream blend. Stir until they dissolve. Add salt.
6. Remove the vanilla pod from the batter, rinse it and allow it to dry so you can reuse it.
7. Strain the ice cream mass through a strain it through a chinois or a fine meshed sieve into a stainless steel bowl. Rapidly cool mix to 39.2°F, whisk occasionally so that it cools down quicker.
8. Continue as you would with the vanilla ice cream.

CARAMEL BRITTLE ICE CREAM

1 batch of caramel ice cream with fleur de sel (above)
200 g (1½ cups) crushed almond praliné (p. 229)

Mix the almond praliné into the frozen ice cream.

NOUGAT ICE CREAM

1 batch of the vanilla ice cream base (p. 32)
150 g (1 cup) crushed almond praliné (p. 229)

Freeze the ice cream batter in an ice cream machine and mix in the crushed almond praliné.

Alcohol in Ice Cream

Grand Marnier, Punch, Cointreau, whiskey, cognac, calvados, and rum all provide a good flavor addition in ice cream. It may be tempting to just pour alcohol into the ice cream batter until you think it tastes great, but because alcohol affects the freezing point, this can pose a problem. Adding too much may prevent the ice cream from freezing.

The following is a calculation based on 34 oz of vanilla ice cream base or parfait:

Spirits with 40% alcohol: 15 ml (1 tbsp) alcohol reduces the freezing point by 1.8°F, the same amount added to sorbet will reduce the freezing point by 1.08°F.

Fortified wine, like sherry, port, and Madeira, with an alcohol level around 20%: ice cream and parfait about 1.08°F, water ice about 0.54°F.

Wine, about 10% alcohol: ice cream and parfait 0.54°F, sorbets 0.36°F.

You can reduce the amount of sugar by 100 g (½ cup) if you add the same quantity of alcohol per 34 oz of ice cream or parfait.

The sugar level should be about 12° baumé in liquor sorbet, and 14° baumé in sorbet that contains wine.

Pistachio Ice Cream

1 batch of the vanilla ice cream base (p. 32)
200 g (4/5 cup) pistachio paste (p. 229)
1 drop of orange blossom water
1 drop of oil of bitter almonds
2 cl (1½ tbsp) kirschwasser (cherry brandy), Maraschino liqueur, or rum.

Add all the ingredients to the ice cream batter. Strain through a fine sieve or chinois. Cool rapidly to 39.2°F and allow the batter to sit until the next day. Freeze the batter in an ice cream machine. When the ice cream is frozen, you can add 100 g (¾ cup) caramelized pistachios (p. 228).

Praliné Ice Cream

1 batch vanilla ice cream base (p. 32) with 250 g (1 cup) added milk
250 g (1 4/5 cups) mixed almond and hazelnut praliné (p. 229)

Mix thoroughly with a stick blender until the ice cream blend is homogenous. Cool rapidly to 39.2°F. Let it stand in the fridge overnight. Freeze in an ice cream machine.

Gianduja Ice Cream

1 batch vanilla ice cream base (p. 32) with 250 g (1 cup) added milk
250 g (1 cup) gianduja (p. 229)

Mix the ginaduja into the batter until the ice cream is homogenous. Cool rapidly to 39.2°F. Let it stand in the fridge overnight. Freeze in an ice cream machine.

Mascarpone or Ricotta Ice Cream

Make a batch of the vanilla ice cream base (p. 32), but use 650 g (2¾ cups) milk and 350 g (1⅖ cups) mascarpone or ricotta ice cream instead of cream. Cool rapidly to 39.2°F. Let it stand in the fridge overnight. Freeze in an ice cream machine.

Honey Ice Cream

Make a batch of vanilla ice cream base (p. 32), but replace 150 g (¾ cup) of the sugar with honey. Cool rapidly to 39.2°F. Let it stand in the fridge overnight. Freeze in an ice cream machine.

Rum Raisin Ice Cream

Make a batch of the vanilla ice cream base (p. 32) but with 75 g (⅖ cup) less sugar. Marinate 150 g (1 cup) raisins in 100 g (⅖ cup) dark rum overnight. Freeze the batter and mix in the marinated raisins once the ice cream is frozen.

Prune Ice Cream with Armagnac

Make a batch of the vanilla ice cream base (p. 32) with 225 g (1 1/10 cups) muscovado sugar, 0.4 inch true cinnamon, half a lemon peel, and peel from half an orange. Strain through a chinois or a fine mesh and cool rapidly to 39.2°F. Marinate 200 g (1½ cup) finely chopped prunes in 100g (⅖ cup) Armagnac overnight. Freeze the ice cream the next day and add the prunes into the frozen ice cream.

Almond Ice Cream

Begin by making 2 cups of almond milk:

6 bitter almonds
250 g (1 cup) water
100 g (½ cup) sugar
170 g (1⅘ cups) almond flour
optional: 1 cl (2 tsp) kirschwasser (cherry brandy)
(200 g) vanilla ice cream base (p. 32)

1. Bring ⅖ cup of water to a boil and blanch the bitter almonds about 1 minute. Rinse them cold in a sieve. Remove the shells. Crush the almonds in a mortar.
2. Boil 250 g (1 cup) water with the sugar, and remove the pan from the heat. Add the almond flour and the bitter almonds, and kirschwasser (cherry brandy) if you decide to use it.
3. Mix the milk in a blender until all the almond oil has dissolved. Drain it through a chinois or a fine mesh. Cool rapidly to 39.2°F. Let it stand in the fridge overnight.
4. Freeze in an ice cream machine with the vanilla ice cream base.

Dulche De Leche Ice Cream

This Argentinean specialty can be found all over the world today. The hermitic boiling

method caramelizes the condensed milk lightly.

1 can sweetened condensed milk (14 oz)
2 gelatin leaves (4 g)
50 g (¼ cup) sugar
375 g (1½ cups) milk
250 g (1 cup) heavy cream

1. Place the unopened can of condensed milk in a pan with boiling water for 3 hours (place a newspaper on the bottom of the pot to isolate the can from direct heat). Allow it to cool off entirely by rinsing it with cold water.
2. Soak the gelatin leaves in cold water for at least 10 minutes.
3. Place the sugar in a pot and melt it while you stir it continuously until it turns into golden brown caramel. Add milk and cream and bring everything to a boil.
4. Remove the gelatin leaves from the water and add them to the blend. Mix until they dissolve.
5. Add the boiled milk from the can and mix the mass vigorously with a handheld stick whisk until you have an emulsion. Strain it through a chinois or a fine sieve. Cool rapidly to 39.2°F.
6. Freeze in an ice cream machine.

QUARK ICE CREAM

Place the quark in a mesh towel overnight to drain it from liquid. This way you'll achieve a nice texture.

600 g (2⅖ cups) quark cheese (drained weight 17.6 oz)
2 gelatin leaves (4 g)
300 g (1¼ cups) water
110 g (½ cup) sugar
50 g (2½ tbsp) honey
1 lemon, the zest
15 g (1 tbsp) lemon juice

1. Soak the gelatin leaves in cold water for at least 10 minutes.
2. Bring water, sugar, and honey to a boil. Add the cleaned lemon zest, and the drained gelatin leaves and stir until they have dissolved.
3. Once the blend has cooled to 95°F, strain it over the drained quark and the lemon juice and mix until smooth with a whisk. Cool rapidly to 39.2°F.
4. Freeze the ice cream in an ice cream machine.

RISOTTO ICE CREAM

2 gelatin leaves (4 g)
150 g (⅘ cup) Arborio rice
1125 g (4⅗ cups) milk
1 Tahitian vanilla pod, split and scraped
95 g (⅖ cup) heavy cream
40 g (2 tbsp) orange blossom honey
190 g (1 cup) sugar
4 g (¾ tsp) fleur de sel
95 g (⅓ cup) plain yogurt

1. Soak the gelatin leaves in cold water for at least 10 minutes.
2. Preheat the oven to 300°F. Boil the rice in the milk with the vanilla pod and seeds until you have a loose porridge. Cover with a lid and put the pan in the oven for 20-30 minutes. Stir occasionally to prevent the rice from getting stale.
3. Lift the gelatin leaves and add them to the warm porridge, stir until dissolved. Remove the vanilla pods. Add cream, honey, sugar, salt, and yogurt and stir until all the sugar has dissolved.
4. Cool rapidly to 39.2°F.
5. Freeze in an ice cream machine.

Herb Ice Creams

You can add any edible herbs or flowers to your ice cream: bay leaf, lemon verbena, thyme (orange and lemon), basil (Thai, cinnamon, orange, lemon, chocolate), different types of mint, dill, or fennel seeds, French tarragon, rosemary, pineapple sage, etc. Coriander, almost tastes like almond. You use the stems and the flowers in angelica ice cream or sorbet; it adds a gin like character to the ice cream.

1 batch of the vanilla ice cream base (p. 32)

Blanch 40 g (⅘ cup) herbs in boiling water and cool them in ice water to retain their color and to kill any bacteria. Allow them to soak in the warm ice cream batter for about 15 minutes. Mix the herbs with the cold ice cream mass and strain through a fine sieve. Cool rapidly to 39.2°F. Freeze in an ice cream machine. You can also make an infusion by soaking the herbs in the batter for 15 minutes before you remove them through straining. Both these processes work well, but will vary taste and appearance.

ELDERFLOWER ICE CREAM OR MEADOWSWEET ICE CREAM

1 batch vanilla ice cream base (p. 32)

Add 40 g (⅘ cup) elderflower or meadowsweet to the batter and allow it to soak for 10 minutes. Mix and strain through a chinois or a fine meshed sieve. Cool rapidly to 39.2°F. Freeze in an ice cream machine.

Ice Cream with Spices

The intensity of spices is a nice addition to ice cream. You can try different spices to create exciting flavors. I even count tea and coffee as spices.

Caraway Ice Cream

Make a batch of vanilla ice cream base (p. 32). Add 100 g (¾ cup) caraway seeds and let them sit in the batter for 5 minutes before you mix and strain through a sieve or a chinois. Cool rapidly to 39.2°F, and let the batter sit in the fridge overnight. Freeze in an ice cream machine.

Cinnamon Ice Cream

Make a batch of vanilla ice cream base (p. 32), but replace the sugar with cassonade sugar, and replace the vanilla pod with 1.4 oz true cinnamon (not cassia), and 4 cl (2¾) dark rum. Mix the ice cream batter with the cinnamon thoroughly before you strain it through a chinois or a fine meshed sieve. Cool rapidly to 39.2°F. Store in the fridge overnight. Freeze in an ice cream machine.

Cardamom Ice Cream

Make a batch of vanilla ice cream base (p. 32), but replace the vanilla pod with 60 g (⅖ cup) peeled, whole, green cardamom seeds. Mix with a stick whisk and strain through a chinois or sieve. Cool rapidly to 39.2°F, and let the batter sit in the fridge overnight. Freeze in an ice cream machine.

Tea Ice Cream

Make a batch of vanilla ice cream base (p. 32), but add 30 g (¼ cup) tea, preferably classic Earl Grey, green tea, or red tea. Add 2 cl (1½ tbsp) dark rum. Mix vigorously with a stick hand blender, and strain through a chinois or a fine meshed sieve. Cool rapidly to 39.2°F. Store in the fridge overnight. Freeze in an ice cream machine.

Saffron Ice Cream

Make a batch of vanilla ice cream base (p. 32), and add 6 g (1 tsp) saffron, or according to your own preference. Cool rapidly to 39.2°F. Store in the fridge overnight. Freeze in an ice cream machine.

Licorice Ice Cream

Make a batch of vanilla ice cream base (p. 32), and add about 2 tbsp (40 g) poudre de reglisse (a licorice concentrate that can be found at spice stores or at Werner's Gourmet Service in Skara), and 4 g (¾ tsp) fleur de sel. Continue as you would with the vanilla ice cream.

Mocha Ice Cream with Nougat

Make a batch of vanilla ice cream base (p. 32), and add 10 g (2 tbsp) dark roast Nescafé. Cool rapidly to 39.2°F. Store in the fridge overnight. Freeze in an ice cream machine. Mix 200 g (1½ cup) almond praliné (p. 229) into the frozen ice cream.

Mint Chocolate Ice Cream

Make a batch of vanilla ice cream base (p. 32), but exchange the granulated sugar for 300 g (1½ cup) light demerara sugar. Allow 40 g (⅘ cup) of peppermint to sit in the batter for 10 min. Add 200 g (1 cup) dark chocolate (preferably Valrhona Grand Cru Pur Caribé 66%) and mix until the batter is smooth. Strain through a chinois or a fine mesh sieve. Cool rapidly to 39.2°F. Store in the fridge overnight. Freeze in an ice cream machine.

Basic Chocolate Ice Cream Recipe

Dark Chocolate Ice Cream

1 batch of the vanilla ice cream base (p. 32)
200-250 g (1 cup – 1¼ cup) dark chocolate, preferably Valrhona Grand Pur Caribé, Grand Cru Manjari, or Grand Cru Guanaja

1. Chop the chocolate finely and mix it into the warm and strained batter with a stick hand blender, until it dissolves. Cool rapidly to 39.2°F. Store in the fridge overnight.
2. Freeze the batter in the ice cream machine.

Milk Chocolate Ice Cream

1 batch vanilla ice cream base (p. 32) + 100g (⅖ cup) additional milk
350 g (1¾ cup) milk chocolate, preferably

Valrhona Jivara Lactée with 40% cacao

Follow the same instructions as for dark chocolate ice cream.

White Chocolate Ice Cream

1 batch of vanilla ice cream base (p. 32) + 150 g (⅗ cup) additional milk
350 g (1¾ cup) milk chocolate, preferably Valrhona Ivoire, or Lindt
50 g (⅕ cup) Cointreau or light rum

Follow the same instructions as for dark chocolate ice cream.

Variations on Chocolate Ice Cream

All the recipes above can be used as basic recipes, and can be varied.

Chocolate Ice Cream with Rosemary

1 batch of the dark chocolate ice cream

Soak 20 g (⅓ cup) of fresh rosemary in the warm batter for 15 minutes. Cool rapidly to 39.2°F. Store in the fridge overnight. Freeze in an ice cream machine.

Chocolate Macadamia Ice Cream

1 batch of the dark chocolate ice cream

Add 125 g (⅘ cup) caramelized macadamias (p. 228) once the ice cream is frozen.

Chocolate Brownie Ice Cream

1 batch dark chocolate ice cream

Mix in 125 g (1 cup) of brownie bits once the ice cream is frozen.

NOSTRA PRODUZIONE
GELATERIA A. CECERE

CHOCOLATE ICE CREAM WITH LEMON VERBENA

1 batch of the dark chocolate ice cream

Soak 20 g (⅓ cup) fresh lemon verbena in the warm batter. Follow the directions for the chocolate ice cream with rosemary.

CHOCOLATE ICE CREAM WITH CANDIED ORANGE PEEL

I batch dark chocolate ice cream (p. 37)

Mix 150 g (1⅕ cup) of finely chopped candied orange peel (p. 228) into the frozen ice cream.

CHOCOLATE ICE CREAM WITHOUT EGGS

Many people prefer chocolate ice cream without egg yolks, because it isn't as rich. It is a personal taste matter. This eggless variation doesn't need as much time to swell, as ice cream with yolks.

2 gelatin leaves (4 g)
750 g (3 cups) milk
70g (⅓ cup) granulated sugar
30 g (¼ cup) skim milk powder
50 g (2½ tbsp) honey
230 g (1⅕ cup) dark chocolate, preferably Valrhona Grand Cru Pur Caribé

1. Soak the gelatin in cold water for at least 10 minutes.
2. Bring milk, sugar, skim milk powder, and honey to a boil. Remove the pan from the heat. Remove the gelatin leaves from the water and add to the milk blend and mix until they dissolve.
3. Add the finely chopped chocolate and mix with a stick hand blender until you have a homogenous batter. Cool rapidly to 39.2°F.
4. Freeze in an ice cream machine.

COCONUT CHOCOLATE ICE CREAM

Day 1
Make a basic vanilla ice cream batter (p. 32), but replace the milk with frozen unsweetened coconut milk.

Day 2
Ripple:
100g (⅖ cup) heavy cream
25 g (3½ tsp) honey
1 cup (200 g) dark chocolate, preferably Valrhona Grand Cru Araguani 72%

Boil the cream and honey and pour the boiling hot mix over the chopped chocolate. Mix with a stick blender until you have a smooth emulsion. Allow the batter to cool to 95–104°F. Fill a disposable pastry bag with the batter and cut a little hole at the bottom of the bag. Freeze the ice cream, and squeeze the batter on and use a ladle to carelessly mix it into the ice cream.

CHOCOLATE CHIP ICE CREAM

Make a batter for the basic vanilla ice cream (p. 32), but replace the granulated sugar with 1 ½ cup (300 g) light demerara sugar, and add 200 g (1 cup) of dark chocolate, preferably Valrhona Grand Cru Guanaja 70. 5%. Mix until the chocolate dissolves into the batter. Cool rapidly to 39.2°F. Store in the fridge overnight. Freeze in an ice cream machine the following day, and chop 150 g (¾ cup) of the same chocolate and mix into the frozen ice cream.

STRACCIATELLA

I batch basic vanilla ice cream (p. 32)
1 cup 200g (1 cup) dark chocolate, preferably Valrhona Grand Cru Araguani 72%

Melt the chocolate to 122–131°F. Freeze the ice cream batter in an ice cream machine. Fill a paper cone with the melted chocolate, and cut a little hole at the bottom and squeeze out the chocolate (thinly) over the ice cream while you stir.

ICE CREAM WITH EGG WHITES

Ice creams that are bound with egg whites instead of yolks get a different texture and has a colder feel to it on the tongue. Egg whites begin to coagulate at 141.8°F, but the albumins in the egg whites bind at 183.2°F.

WHITE COCONUT ICE CREAM WITH LEMON GRASS

Coconut milk varies widely in quality and taste. I prefer the Philippine kind.

2 gelatin leaves (4 g)
4 lemon grass stalks
500 g 2 cups milk
500 g (2 cups) unsweetened frozen coconut milk.
50 g (2½ tbsp) honey
200g (⅘ cup) egg whites
200 g (1 cup) sugar
The juice from 2 limes

1. Soak the gelatin in cold water for at least 10 minutes.
2. Crush the lemon grass with a kitchen hammer and put into a pot. Add milk, coconut milk and honey, and bring everything to a boil. Remove the pan from the heat and let it stand for 30 minutes.
3. Beat egg whites and sugar, until stiff peaks form, in a very clean stainless steel bowl.
4. Remove the lemon grass stalks and pour the milk over the egg whites and mix well. Heat to 183.2°F, while you continuously stir the batter. Or do a rose test or a ladle test (p. 25).
5. Lift the gelatin leaves and stir them into the ice cream batter, until they dissolve. Mix vigorously with a hand stick blender. Strain through a chinois or a fine sieve, and cool rapidly to 39.2°F. Store the batter in the fridge overnight.
6. Add the fresh juice from the limes and mix with a hand stick blender.
7. Freeze in an ice cream machine.

WHITE MOCCA ICE CREAM

2 gelatin leaves (4 g)
100 g (½ cup) whole espresso beans (French Roast)
500 g (2 cups) heavy cream
500 g (2 cups) milk
50g (2½ tbsp) glucose
80g (⅖ cup) sugar
100g (⅖ cup) white coffee liqueur, i.e. Marie Brizard or Bols

1. Soak the gelatin leaves in cold water for at least 10 minutes.
2. Put the coffee beans in a cloth bag, and crush them with a rolling pin or a kitchen hammer.
3. Boil cream, milk, and glucose. Remove the pan from the heat and add the cloth bag with the coffee beans and allow it to sit in the milk blend for 30 minutes.
4. In an absolutely clean metal bowl, beat the egg whites and sugar until stiff peaks form.
5. Remove the cloth bag with the crushed coffee beans and carefully squeeze it so that the remaining milk comes out, but without making the ice cream brown. Pour the coffee milk over the egg whites and mix well. Pour everything back into the pot and heat during continuous stirring to 183.2°F, or do a rose test or a ladle test (p. 25).
6. Lift the gelatin leaves out the water and add them to the ice cream batter, stir until they dissolve. Mix the batter vigorously with a hand stick blender. Strain through a chinois or sieve. Cool rapidly to 39.2°F. Let it stand in the fridge overnight.
7. Mix the liqueur into the batter with a stick blender and freeze in an ice cream machine.

Berry Ice Cream

If you want to add berries or fruit to ice cream, they should be lightly candied, or they will freeze to ice.

Add 250 g (2 cups) candied and drained berries (p. 228) to the frozen ice cream.

Strawberry Ice Cream

Kids absolutely love this ice cream. It is also the very first ice cream I made when I was a 15-year-old intern. Sometimes I make it only with cream instead of the vanilla ice cream base.

350 g (1¾ cups) vanilla ice cream base (p. 32)
600g (3½ cup) strawberry purée with 10% sugar

1. Make the vanilla ice cream base at least 4 hours prior, but preferably the day before.
2. Use a hand stick blender to mix the strawberry purée into the ice cream batter. Store it cold until it is time to freeze it.
3. Freeze in an ice cream machine, until the ice cream is firm and supple. If you want to make it extra delicious, add 8.8 oz candied strawberries to the frozen ice cream. See the basic recipe for the candied strawberries on page 228.

Strawberry Ice Cream, Quick and Delicious

1 gelatin leaf (2 g)
500g (4 cups) rinsed and cleaned strawberries
15 g (1 tbsp) freshly squeezed lemon juice
250 g (2 cups) powdered sugar
350 g (1½ cup) heavy cream

1. Soak the gelatin leaf in cold water for at least 10 minutes.
2. Mix strawberries, lemon juice, and sugar to a purée. Mix in the cream.
3. Lift the gelatin out of the water and add it to 2 dl (⅘ cup) of the ice cream batter and heat it to 122°F, until the gelatin has dissolved.
4. Mix into the ice cream blend and freeze in an ice cream machine.

Raspberry Ice Cream

This recipe can be used as a base for ice cream with other berries, such as blackberries, cloudberries, lingonberries, blue berries, cranberries, and wild strawberries.

500g (2⅖ cups) basic vanilla ice cream (p. 32)
600g (5 cups) raspberries
100 g (½ cup) sugar

1. Mix the berries with the sugar until the sugar has dissolved. Strain through a sieve.
2. Mix into the cold ice cream base and freeze in an ice cream machine.

If you want to make this delectable treat even tastier, you can add 250g (2 cups) of half candied berries into the ice cream once it is frozen. See the basic recipe for half-candied berries on page 228.

If you want to combine the berry ice cream with herbs, boil the herbs in the ice cream base, this will really enhance the flavor. Raspberry ice cream goes really well with lemon verbena or rosemary.

Blueberry Cheesecake Ice Cream

2 gelatin leaves (4 g)
120 g (½ cup) egg yolks
125 g (⅗ cup) sugar
300 g (1¼ cup) milk
100g (⅖ cup) heavy cream

200g (⅘ cup) cream cheese
1 vanilla pod, split and scraped
zest from one cleaned lemon
3 g (½ tsp) fleur de sel
50 g (2½ tbsp) light honey
200g (1⅗ cups) half candied blueberries (p. 228)

1. Soak the gelatin in cold water for at least 10 minutes.
2. Beat the egg whites and sugar fluffy.
3. Pour milk, cream, cream cheese, vanilla, lemon zest, salt, and honey into a pot and bring to a boil while stirring.
4. Pour the milk blend over the egg batter, mix thoroughly and heat everything while continuously stirring. The cream will begin to thicken at 185°F, or do a rose test or a ladle test (p. 25).
5. Remove the gelatin leaves from the water and add them to the batter. Mix until they dissolve. Strain through a sieve or a chinois, and cool as quickly as possible to 39.2°F. Store in the fridge overnight.
6. Freeze in an ice cream maker. Mix the berries into the ice cream once you have drained them.

Ice Cream with Nuts

Walnut Ice Cream

Make a batch of the basic vanilla ice cream (p. 32), but replace the granulated sugar with muscovado sugar. The next day, freeze the batter in an ice cream machine and add 8.8 oz caramelized walnuts (p. 228) into the frozen ice cream.

Hazelnut Ice Cream Just Like the One in Piemonte

I make hazelnut ice cream without cream, because the nuts have such a high fat content. The ice cream tends to get a grainy texture when too much fat is added.

2 gelatin leaves (4 g)
1000 g (4 cups) milk
1 vanilla pod, split and scraped out
300 g (1½ cups) cassonade sugar
50 g (2½ tbsp) honey
240 g (1 cup) egg yolks

Make the same way you would make the classic vanilla ice cream (p. 32). Mix 150g (⅗ cup) hazelnut cream (p. 229) into the batter with a stick blender. Rapidly cool to 39.2°F. Store in the fridge overnight. The following day, make 150 g (1 cup) caramelized hazelnuts (p. 228). Freeze in an ice cream machine and add the crushed caramelized nuts into the frozen ice cream.

Nougat Ice Cream Montelimar

Make a batch of the vanilla ice cream base (p. 32). Freeze in an ice cream machine and add 250g (1¼ cups) chopped white nougat (French nougat) to the frozen ice cream.

Espresso Ice Cream with Caramelized Pecans

Make a batch of the vanilla ice cream base (p. 32), but replace the sugar with cassonade sugar, and 100g (⅖ cup) crushed espresso beans and allow them to soak in the batter for 5 minutes, and add 8 g (1½ tbsp) Nescafé instant coffee. Sift through a chinois or sieve. Cool as quickly as possible to 39.2°F. Store in the fridge overnight.

The following day, make 250 g (1⅘ cups) caramelized pecans (p. 228). Freeze the batter in an ice cream machine, and mix the nuts into the frozen ice cream.

Chestnut Ice Cream with Rum

Candied chestnuts is a sought after delicacy in Italy and France. The various bakeshops compete with each other to see who can make the best *marrons glacées*. If you happen to be in Paris, you must visit Stohrer or Pierre Marcolini, and bring some home! Unfortunately, they are rare here, but you can find them in Italian and French delicatessen boutiques.

1 batch vanilla ice cream base (p. 32)
150g (2½ cups) lightly whipped cream
200g (1½ cups) chopped candied chestnuts, that have been marinating in 50g (⅕ cups) of dark rum for a few day

Freeze the ice cream batter mixed with the cream and the liquor in the ice cream machine. Mix the candied chestnuts into the frozen ice cream.

Torrone Ice Cream

Day I

1 batch of the vanilla ice cream base (p.32)

Day 2

150 g (2½ cups) lightly whipped cream
150 g (1⅕ cup) finely chopped candied fruit, marinated in
10 g (⅕ cup) Maraschino Liqueur
150 g (1 cup) crushed almond praliné (p. 229)

Use an ice cream maker to freeze the vanilla ice cream mixed with the lightly whipped cream. Mix fruit and praliné into the frozen ice cream.

My Indian Kulfi

This is a lovely creamy ice cream with a light caramel characteristic.

2 gelatin leaves (4 g)
4000 g (16 ⅔ cups) milk
1 Tahitian vanilla pod, split and scraped.
250 g (1¼ cups) sugar
25 g (5 tsp) freshly squeezed lemon juice
125 g (½ cup) water
200 g (⅘ cup) whipping cream
50 g (2½ tbsp) honey
4 g (¾ tsp) fleur de sel

1. Soak the gelatin in cold water for 10 minutes.
2. Boil the milk and vanilla seeds in a pot with a thick bottom, until only about 8 dl (3 ⅖ cups) remain.
3. Heat sugar, lemon juice, and water to 356°F, until you have dark brown caramel. Pour the caramel into the milk and let it simmer until all the sugar has dissolved.
4. Lift out the gelatin leaves and drain them before you add them to the batter. Stir until they dissolve. Add cream, honey, and fleur de sel and mix the batter smooth in a blender. Strain through a chinois or a fine sieve, and allow the batter to cool off. Rapidly chill the ice cream mass to 39.2°F.
5. Freeze in an ice cream maker.

Yogurt Ice Cream

YOGURT ICE CREAM WITH BLUEBERRIES

You can alter this recipe by using raspberries, strawberries, or blackberries instead.

2 gelatin leaves (4 g)
375 g plain Greek yogurt
125 g (½ cup) heavy cream
25 g (3½ tsp) light honey
125 g (1 cup) powdered sugar
2 g fleur de sel
200 g (1⅗ cup) half-candied blue
    berries (228)

1. Soak the gelatin leaves in cold water for 10 minutes.
2. Mix the other ingredients, except for the berries, in a blender until all the sugar has dissolved.
3. Transfer 1 dl (⅖ cup) of the blend to a pot and bring to a boil. Lift the gelatin leaves out of the water and add to the pot, stir until dissolved. Mix everything with a stick blender.
4. Freeze the batter in an ice cream machine.

FROZEN YOGURT WITH FRUIT

2 gelatin leaves (4 g)
500 g (2¾ cup) fruit purée with 10% sugar
500 g (2 cups) plain Greek yogurt
250 g (2 cups) powdered sugar
about 50 g (⅕ cup) freshly squeezed lemon
    juice, depending on fruits are being used

1. Soak the gelatin in cold water for at least 10 minutes.
2. Mix the other ingredients with a stick blender.
3. Lift the gelatin leaves out of the water and add to 2 dl (⅘ cup) of the ice cream batter. Heat to 113–122°F, until the gelatin has dissolved. Mix everything with a stick blender.
4. Freeze the batter in an ice cream machine.

YOGURT ICE CREAM WITH VANILLA

2 gelatin leaves (4 g)
1 lemon
250 g (1¼ cup) sugar
250 g (1 cup) water
2 vanilla pods, split and scraped
500 g (2 cups) plain Greek yogurt
250 g (1 cup) whipping cream

1. Soak the gelatin in cold water for at least 10 minutes.
2. Clean and peel the lemon with a potato peeler.
3. Bring sugar, water, lemon peel, and vanilla to a boil, and allow it to sit for 10 minutes.
4. Lift the gelatin out of the water and add to the sugar solution. Stir until they have dissolved. Strain the sugar solution through a chinois or a sieve. Add yogurt and cream and mix until smooth with a stick blender.
5. Freeze in the ice cream machine.

BASIL YOGURT ICE CREAM

1 gelatin leaf (2 g)
120 g (½ cup) egg yolks
25 g (2 tbsp) sugar
500 g (2 cups) plain Greek yogurt
100 g (⅓ cup) honey
1 lemon, the peel
1 oz basil leaf, preferably Genoese

1. Soak the gelatin in cold water for at least 10 minutes.
2. Whisk the egg yolks and the sugar until fluffy.
3. Bring yogurt, honey, and the lemon peel to a boil. Pour the yogurt blend over the yolks and mix thoroughly. Heat to 185°F while stirring continuously, or do a rose test or a ladle test (p. 25).
4. Remove the gelatin from the water and add to the batter.
5. Mix vigorously with a stick blender and strain the batter through a chinois or a sieve. Cool rapidly to 39.2°F. Store in the fridge overnight.
6. The following day, blanch the basil leaf for 10 seconds in boiling hot water and cool them off in ice water.

7. Mix ⅔ cup of the ice cream batter with the basil leaf until you have a purée. Mix it into the batter.
8. Freeze the batter in an ice cream machine.

Flower Ice Cream

Flowers make an excellent flavor addition to ice cream. The rose ice cream is a classic. Hansa Park is a good rose to use, according to herb guru, Magne Haugen, at the herb garden in Klevane. The hollyhock has a very rich aroma. Four organically grown wild roses are enough to flavor the basic vanilla ice cream batter, but don't add vanilla, instead replace it with the rose petals and allow the flavors to marinate. You can add a drop of rose water to enhance the flavor.

When it comes to lavender ice cream, you can use either dried or fresh flowers. However, be cautious with the dosage. About 0.7 oz dried lavender is enough for the entire batch.

In Switzerland, we used to serve an exclusive violet ice cream with violet Queen Charlotte, which is only around a few weeks in early spring. 5.3 oz violet petals, and 1.8 oz dried violet root got to marinate in the ice cream batter before it was removed, and we added fresh lemon juice. We added candied violets into the ice cream once it was frozen.

All edible flowers that are organically grown can be used to flavor ice cream: lilac, hibiscus, violet Queen Charlotte, lavender, and scented pelargonium with lemon and orange. Fennel flowers or fennel hyssop, mallow, honeysuckle, mint flowers of all varieties, Cicely flower, basil flowers, and primrose flower. Cowslip, rosemary, and sage flowers, thyme flower, borage, calendula, chamomile, garland chrysanthemum, chicory, cloves, fuchsia, sunflower, daylily, garden orchid, myrtle, catnip, schiso, perilla, mint leaf, summer phlox, primrose, dandelion, red clover, Indian cress, valerian, sweet violet, wild pansy…the possibilities are limitless.

Three flower sorbets:
Wild Pansy Sorbet (closest to camera)
Indian Cress Sorbet
Mint Sorbet

Sorbets

When making sorbet or fruit ice cream, the thickening process occurs a little bit differently than when making cream ice cream with egg yolks during heating. Instead, you need to add sugar syrup with glucose (corn syrup or honey), or just sugar.

Adding glucose or honey prevents the sugars from crystallizing in the sorbet.

Simple Sugar Syrup for Sorbet and Fruit Ice Cream

This sugar syrup is 30° Baumé, or 60° Brix, when made only on water and sugar. With glucose added to this sugar solution, the sugar content changes to 32° Baumé, and 64° Brix,

1350 g (6¾ cups) sugar
1000 (4⅕ cup) water
250 g (¾ cup) glucose (glucose syrup)

1. Pour the water into a clean pot and add the sugar, stir thoroughly. Bring the sugar solution to a boil while you continuously keep brushing the inside walls of the pot with a brush that has been dipped in water (to prevent the sugars from crystallizing in the finished sugar syrup).
2. Add glucose and bring to a boil again, skim off the sugar syrup.
3. Pour into a plastic pail with a lid, or into a glass jar.
4. Store in the fridge once it has cooled off.

Appropriate storage temperatures:

16° Baumé: about 51.8°F
17° Baumé: about 53.6°F
18° Baumé: about 57.2°F

When I began my career as a pastry chef, commis pâtissier, we always used to serve sorbet in tall glasses, topped with some sort of liquor or wine. Most of the time we added Italian meringue or beaten warm meringue to make the sorbet extra airy, which I recommend when you want to serve the sorbet as an entremets. The meringue (egg white foam) has an important stabilizing function in sorbet.

Because of the increased viscosity, the production of larger ice crystal is diminished. During the beginnings of the French cuisine in 1970s, the meringue was removed. Instead they made what used to be called fruit ice cream or water ice cream, and it was served in the shape of beautiful eggs with fruit coulis and fresh berries.

Back in the day, we used to add a lot of wine to the sorbets, red wine with berries, and white wine with light colored berries or fruit juices. I rarely do this today, as I believe it ruins the fruit flavor. However, Côtes du Rhône red wine tastes great in a black currant sorbet, or in a rich raspberry sorbet.

You can spike your strawberry sorbet with champagne. Orange sorbet goes well with Campari.

In America, it is very common to add milk in the sorbet, but I rarely do this, with the exception for lemon and lime sorbet, and sometimes the green apple sorbet. The milk tends to balance out the acid in these flavors and give the sorbet a nice and smooth texture.

You can make your own herb and spice infusions in boiling water, and add them to flavor your sorbets. It will give your sorbet an exotic flavor combination, especially in your entremets sorbets. Raspberry sorbet will not get any tastier with rosemary, tarragon, or lemon verbena, but it will definitely acquire a fascinating flavor that will become an interesting topic of conversation at the dinner table. Other interesting combinations includes lemon sorbet with rosemary, strawberry sorbet with French tarragon, orange sorbet with orange thyme, passion fruit sorbet with lemon verbena, apple sorbet with meadowsweet, jasmine tea sorbet with lemon basil. Sage fruit and pineapple sage also add an exotic kick to your sorbet.

If You Measure the Sugar Content Like a Professional

Sorbets should have a sugar content of 25-35 percent, and 0.5 percent acidity. You can sweeten it with sugar syrup or with powdered sugar if you want them more concentrated. Personally, I always use a sugar scale, a Baumé hydrometer, to control the sugar levels.

Pour the sugar solution into a tall glass and insert the Baumé hydrometer. The solution for fruit ice cream/sorbet should be about 17–18° Baumé, or 30–31 Brix if you are using a refractometer. The solution should be at about 68°F, in order for the meter to display correctly. If the mixture is higher than 18° Baumé, or 33 Brix, it is necessary to add more fruit juice, purée, or water, otherwise the sorbet won't freeze correctly. If it is less than 17° Baumé, or 31 Brix, you need to add more sugar syrup or powdered sugar.

If you make a sorbet the old fashioned way, with meringue, it should be 16° Baumé, or 28–29 Brix, because there is already sugar in the meringue. Count 1 egg white (30 g) and 60 g (⅓ cup) sugar per every 34 oz of sorbet (see Italian meringue, p. 230).

Wine sorbets should have a lower sugar content, depending on if you are using fortified wine or cooking wine, it will be about 14° Baumé.

I'll share an old trick with you on how to measure the sugar content by dropping a fresh egg into the blend. If the egg breaks the surface so that it is about as big as a quarter when it floats to the surface, it is about 17–18° Baumé.

Old Fashioned Sorbet

If you want to make an old fashioned sorbet, lessen the simple sugar syrup recipe with 50 g (2½ tbsp), and make a warm meringue blend by beating 1 egg white (30 g) with 60 g (⅓ cup) sugar and 5 g (1 tsp) freshly squeezed lemon juice. Use a spatula to mix it into the frozen sorbet. Squeeze the sorbet from a plastic pastry bag (with a big plain tube) into frozen champagne glasses.

If you want to make fruit ice cream the French way, you will need to make a sorbet base and add 50 percent vanilla ice cream base (p. 32). Mix vigorously with a stick blender and freeze. Most fruits and berries contain about 10 percent sugar, so keep that in mind. It is often necessary to add lemon juice so that the sorbet doesn't become too sweet. When I learned to make sorbet (when it used to be called water ice cream), the following classic mixing procedure was used: 1 part fruit purée or fruit juice was mixed with 1 part sugar syrup. Then, water

Recommended Alcohol to Serve over Sorbet

Pour the liquor over the sorbet when you serve it, and serve it with a tall spoon.

· *Lemon sorbet with vodka or Cherry Heering*
· *Lime sorbet with gin, tequila, or Pisco*
· *Orange sorbet with Cointreau, or Campari*
· *Grapefruit sorbet with gin*
· *Cherry sorbet with Maraschino liqueur, or kirschwasser (cherry brandy)*
· *Pineapple sorbet with kirschwasser (cherry brandy)*
· *Peach sorbet with Framboise eau de vie*
· *Pear sorbet with eau de vie Poire Williams*
· *Chocolate sorbet with Grand Marnier or cognac*
· *Ginger sorbet with Drambuie*
· *Raspberry sorbet with Framboise eau de vie*
· *Strawberry sorbet with kirschwasser (cherry brandy) or Maraschino liqueur*
· *Coconut sorbet with dark rum*
· *Banana sorbet with dark rum*

3 different herb sorbets:
Lemon Verbena (at the bottom)
Pineapple Sage (right)
Vanilla basil (left)

was added, in addition to fresh lemon juice to achieve the correct sugar level at 16–18° Baumé, depending on the temperature the freezer kept at portioning, so that the ice cream wouldn't get too hard. Then, meringue was also added to make the sorbet light and airy. Today pastry chefs buy first class frozen fruit purées with 10 percent sugar, by brands like Boiron, Sicolly, and Ravifruit, which all come from France.

Rhubarb Sorbet

(18° Baumé or 32 Brix degrees)

2 gelatin leaves (4 g)
about 800 g (6 cups) fresh pink rhubarb (450 g, approx. 1⅘ cup purée)
50 g (¼ cup) sugar
350 g (1 cup) simple sugar syrup (pg 44)
50 g (⅕ cup) water
freshly squeezed lemon juice according to your own preference

1. Soak the gelatin leaves in cold water for at least 10 minutes.
2. Rinse, peal and clean the rhubarb and cut it into small cubes. Boil them soft in 1000 g (4⅕ cups) water. Drain them in a sieve.
3. Mix the rhubarb into a mass and strain it through a fine-meshed sieve.
4. Measure 450 g (1 ⅘ cup) purée, add sugar and mix until it dissolves. Add sugar syrup and water and add lemon juice until you are satisfied with the taste. Mix thoroughly with a stick blender.
5. Lift the gelatin leaves out of the water and add them to a pot with ⅖ cup of the sorbet batter. Heat to 104–122°F, until the gelatin has dissolved. Pour back to the rest of the batter and mix.
6. Freeze the sorbet in an ice cream maker.

If you want to make fruit ice cream, take 450 g (2¼ cup) of the vanilla ice cream base (p. 32) and mix with the sorbet blend to get a nice and smooth rhubarb ice cream. You can add lightly candied rhubarb to the ice cream once it is frozen; see frozen fruit for ice cream on page 228.

Blackberry Sorbet

(17° Baumé or 30.5 Brix)

2 gelatin leaves (4 g)
about 600 g (5 cups) blackberries (450 g, approx. 1⅘ cups purée)
50 g (¼ cup) sugar
400 g (1⅕ cups) simple sugar syrup (p. 44)
100 g (⅖ cup) water
freshly squeezed lemon juice according to your own preference

1. Soak the gelatin leaves in cold water for at least 10 minutes.
2. Mix the blackberries in a blender until you have a purée, and strain it through a fine-meshed sieve.
3. Measure 450 g (1⅘ cups) purée, add sugar and mix until it has dissolves. Mix it with the sugar syrup and water and add lemon juice.
4. Lift the gelatin leaves out of the water and add them to a pot with 1 dl (⅖ cup) of the sorbet batter. Heat to 104–122°F, until the gelatin has dissolved.
5. Pour the blend back to the rest of the batter and mix vigorously.
6. Freeze the sorbet in an ice cream maker.
7. If you want to make blackberry ice cream instead, take 500 g (2½ cups) of the vanilla ice cream base (p. 32) and mix with the sorbet blend. If you want to add lightly candied blackberries to the ice cream once it is frozen, see frozen fruit for ice cream on page 228.

Kiwi Sorbet

(18° Baumé or 32.5 Brix)

About 700 g (3⅘ cups) kiwi (450 g, approx. 1 ⅘ cups purée)
50 g (¼ cup) sugar
700 g (2 cups) simple sugar syrup (p. 44)
150 g (⅗ cup) water
freshly squeezed lemon juice according to preference

1. Peel the fruit, but don't run it in the blender to get a purée, because then it tends to get bitter. Instead, strain it through a fine-meshed sieve.
2. Measure 450 g (approx. 1⅘ cups) purée, add sugar and mix until it has dissolved.
3. Mix the sugar syrup and water and add lemon juice.
4. Freeze the sorbet in an ice cream maker.

Black Currant Sorbet

(17.5° Baumé or 31.5 Brix)

2 gelatin leaves (4 g)
about 750 g (6 cups) black currants (450 g, approx. 1 ⅘ cups purée)
50 g (¼ cup) sugar
450 g (1⅓ cups) simple sugar syrup (p. 44)
150 g (⅗ cup) water
freshly squeezed lemon juice according to preference

1. Soak the gelatin leaves in cold water for at least 10 minutes.
2. Mix the currants in a blender until you have a purée. Strain it through a fine-meshed sieve.
3. Measure 450 g (approx. 1⅘ cups) purée, add sugar and mix until it has dissolved.
4. Mix vigorously with the sugar syrup and water and add lemon juice.
5. Lift the gelatin leaves out of the water and add them to a pot with ⅔ cup of the sorbet batter. Heat to 104–122°F, until the gelatin has dissolved. Pour back to the rest of the batter and mix.
6. Freeze the sorbet in an ice cream machine.

If you want to make black currant ice cream instead, mix 550 g (2¾ cups) of the vanilla ice cream base into the sorbet.

Red or White Currant Sorbet

(18° Baumé or 32 Brix)

2 gelatin leaves (4 g)
about 750 g (6 cups) red or white currants (450 g, approx. 1⅘ cup purée)
50 g (¼ cup) sugar
350 g (1 cup) simple sugar syrup (p. 44)
50 g (⅕ cup) water
freshly squeezed lemon juice according to preference

Follow the same instructions as for black currant sorbet.

Gooseberry Sorbet

(18° Baumé or 32 Brix)

2 gelatin leaves (4 g)
about 750 g (6 cups) green, unripe gooseberries (450 g, approx. 1 ⅘ cups purée)
50 g (¼ cup) sugar
350 g (1 cup) simple sugar syrup (p. 44)
50 g (⅕ cup) water
freshly squeezed lemon juice according to preference

1. Soak the gelatin leaves in cold water for at least 10 minutes.
2. Mix the gooseberries into a fine purée. Strain it through a sieve.
3. Measure 450 g (1⅘ cups) purée, add sugar and mix until it has dissolved.
4. Mix sugar syrup and water into the blend with a stick blender, and add lemon juice.
5. Lift the gelatin leaves out of the water and add them to a pot with ⅔ cup of the sorbet batter. Heat to 104–122°F, until the gelatin has dissolved. Pour back to the rest of the batter and mix with a stick blender. Taste and see if you need to add more lemon juice.
6. Freeze the sorbet in an ice cream machine.

Banana Sorbet

(17° Baumé or 30.5 Brix)
2 gelatin leaves (4 g)
about 800 g (4 cups) ripe bananas, preferably small and sweet (450 g, approx. 1⅘ cup purée)
50 g (¼ cup) sugar
400 g (1⅕ cups) simple sugar syrup (p. 44)
150 g (⅗ cup) water
freshly squeezed lemon juice according to preference

1. Soak the gelatin leaves in cold water for at least 10 minutes.
2. Peel the bananas and mix them into a purée. Measure 450 g (approx. 1⅘ cup) purée and mix with sugar until it has dissolved.
3. Mix sugar syrup and water into the purée, and add lemon juice.
4. Lift the gelatin leaves out of the water and add them to a pot with ⅔ cup of the sorbet batter. Heat to 104–122°F, until the gelatin has dissolved. Pour back to the rest of the batter and mix. Add more lemon juice if needed.
5. Freeze the sorbet in an ice cream machine right away; otherwise the bananas may turn brown.

If you want to make banana ice cream instead, mix 550 g (2¾ cups) of the vanilla ice cream base into the sorbet. Mix with a stick blender, and add 2 cl (1½ tbsp) dark rum. Freeze the ice cream in an ice cream maker right away, so that it doesn't turn brown.

Avocado Sorbet

(18° Baumé or 32 Brix)

Use the same recipe as for the banana ice cream (p. 47), but replace the banana pulp with avocado pulp from ripe avocados, and use fresh lime juice instead of lemon juice. If you want to make the avocado ice cream, replace the rum with tequila.

Green Apple Sorbet

(17° Baumé or 30.5 Brix)

2 gelatin leaves (4 g)
about 1000 g (8 cups) green apples, i.e. Granny Smith, or Golden Delicious (450 g, approx. 1 ⅘ cups purée)
50 g (¼ cup) sugar
350 g (1 cup) simple sugar syrup (p. 44)
50 g (⅕ cup) water
freshly squeezed lemon juice according to preference

1. Soak the gelatin leaves in cold water for at least 10 minutes.
2. Rinse the apples and remove the core. Cut each apple into 4 pieces (leave the peel on) and mix them for a long time in a blender until you have a fine purée. Rapidly strain through a fine-meshed sieve, so that the purée doesn't turn brown.
3. Measure 450 g (approx. 1⅘ cups) purée and mix it with the sugar until it dissolves.
4. Mix with sugar syrup and water and add lemon juice.
5. Lift the gelatin leaves out of the water and mix them with ⅔ cup of the sorbet batter. Add to the rest of the batter and mix well.
6. Freeze the sorbet in an ice cream machine right away; otherwise the apples may turn brown.

If you want to make apple ice cream instead, mix 450 g (2¼ cups) of the vanilla ice cream base (p. 32) into the sorbet. Mix and freeze in an ice cream machine right away, so that the ice cream doesn't turn brown. You can also add lightly candied apple pieces to the ice cream; see candied fruit for ice cream on page 228.

Pineapple Sorbet

(17° Baumé or 30.5 Brix)

Pineapple contains bromelain, a substance that breaks down gelatin. Therefore, pineapple sorbet is made without gelatin.

About 800 g (6½ cups) fresh, ripe pineapple, i.e. Del Monte extra sweet (450 g, approx. 1 ⅘ cups purée)

50 g (¼ cup) sugar
500 g (1½ cups) simple sugar syrup
100 g (⅖ cup) water
freshly squeezed lemon juice according to preference

1. Peel the pineapple and mix in a blender until you have a purée. Measure 450 g (approx. 1⅘ cups) purée and mix it with 50 g (¼ cup) sugar until it has dissolved.
2. Mix with the sugar syrup and water with a stick blender. Add the lemon juice.
3. Freeze the sorbet in an ice cream machine.

If you want to make pineapple ice cream instead, mix 550 g (2 ¾ cups) of the vanilla ice cream base (p. 32) into the sorbet with a stick blender. You can also add lightly candied pineapple pieces to the ice cream; see lightly candied pineapple on page 228.

Pineapple Sorbet without Sugar Syrup

You can enhance the flavor by adding kirschwasser (cherry brandy) to the batter.

500 g (2 cups) pineapple purée with 10% sugar
150 g (1⅕ cups) powdered sugar
25 g (3½ tsp) glucose
optional: freshly squeezed lemon juice
2 cl (1½ tbsp) kirschwasser (cherry brandy)

1. Mix purée, sugar, and glucose until the sugar and glucose has dissolved.
2. If you wish, add lemon juice with kirschwasser (cherry brandy), which tastes excellent with pineapple.
3. Freeze sorbet in an ice cream machine.

Piña Colada Sorbet

About 600 g (4½ cups) fresh pineapple (325 g, approx. 1 ⅓ cups purée)
175 g (¾ cup) frozen coconut milk
150 g (1⅕ cups) powdered sugar
50 g (⅕ cup) dark rum
100 g (⅗ cup) whipping cream
freshly squeezed lemon juice

1. Peel the pineapple and cut into pieces and mix into a fine purée.
2. Measure 325 g (1⅓ cups) purée into a blender and mix with coconut milk, powdered sugar, rum, and whipping cream, until all the sugar has dissolved. Add lemon juice.
3. Freeze the sorbet in an ice cream machine.

APRICOT SORBET
(17° Baumé or 30.5 Brix)

You can spike this sorbet with a little bit of kirschwasser (cherry brandy), to make it even tastier.

2 gelatin leaves (4 g)
about 800 g (6 ½ cups) apricots, really ripe
    (450 g. approx. 1 ⁴⁄₅ cups purée)
50 g (¼ cup) sugar
350 g (1 cup) simple sugar syrup
50 g (⅕ cup) water
optional: a drop of bitter almond oil
2 cl (1 ½ tbsp) kirschwasser (cherry brandy)
freshly squeezed lemon juice

1. Soak the gelatin in cold water for at least 10 minutes.
2. Blanch the apricots in 2 liter (8 ½ cups) boiling water, and transfer them to ice cold water. Then pull the peel off with a knife.
3. Mix the apricots vigorously in a blender until you have a fine purée.
4. Measure 450 g (1 ⁴⁄₅ cups) purée into a bowl, and mix with sugar until it has dissolved.
5. Mix the sugar syrup and water, add a drop of bitter almond oil and the kirschwasser (cherry brandy) to enhance the flavor. Carefully add the lemon juice according to your personal preference.
6. Lift the gelatin leaves out of the water and add them to a pot with ⅔ cup of the sorbet batter. Heat to 104–122°F, until the gelatin has dissolved. Pour back to the rest of the batter and mix.
7. Freeze the sorbet in an ice cream machine.

You can add 450 g (approx. 1 ⁴⁄₅ cups) of the vanilla ice cream base (p. 32) to the sorbet if you want to make apricot ice cream instead. Mix with a stick blender. Optional, is to add candied apricot pieces into the frozen ice cream, see page 228 for lightly candied fruits.

MANGO SORBET
(18° Baumé or 32 Brix)

2 gelatin leaves (4 g)
about 800 g (6 ½ cups) ripe mango, preferably
    Thai (450 g, approx. 1 ⁴⁄₅ cups purée)
50 g (¼ cup) sugar
450 g (1 ½ cups) simple sugar syrup (p. 44)
50 g (⅕ cup) water
freshly squeezed lemon juice

1. Soak the gelatin in cold water for at least 10 minutes.
2. Peel the mango and remove the pulp from the seed with a knife. Mix in a blender until you have a fine purée.
3. Measure 450 g (approx. 1 ⁴⁄₅ cups) purée and mix it with 50 g (¼ cup) sugar until it has dissolved. Mix vigorously with the sugar syrup and water, by using a stick blender.
4. Lift the gelatin leaves out of the water and add them to a pot with ⅔ cup of the sorbet batter. Heat to 104–122°F, until the gelatin has dissolved. Pour back to the rest of the batter and mix with a stick blender. Carefully add lemon juice.
5. Freeze the sorbet in an ice cream machine.

You can add 500 g (2 ½ cups) of the vanilla ice cream base (p. 32) to the sorbet if you want to make apricot ice cream instead. Mix with a stick blender. Optional, is to add candied mango pieces into the frozen ice cream, see page 228 for lightly candied fruits.

Papaya Sorbet

(18° Baumé or 32 Brix)

Use the same recipe as for the mango sorbet.

Melon Sorbet

(17° Baumé or 30.5 Brix)

2 gelatin leaves (4 g)
about 800 g (6½ cups) ripe melon, preferably
*   cantaloupe or galia (450 g, approx. 1⅘*
*   cups purée)*
50 g (¼ cup) sugar
300 g (9⁄10 cup) simple sugar syrup (p. 44)
50 g (⅕ cup) water
freshly squeezed lemon juice according to
*   preference*

1. Soak the gelatin in cold water for at least 10 minutes.
2. Cut the melon in half, remove the seeds and peel. Mix in the blender into a purée.
3. Mix 450 g, approx. (1⅘ cups) purée with sugar until it has dissolved.
4. Mix sugar syrup, water, and melon purée with a stick blender.
5. Lift the gelatin leaves out of the water and add them to a pot with 1 dl (⅖ cup) of the sorbet batter. Heat to 104–122°F, until the gelatin has dissolved. Pour back to the rest of the batter and mix with a stick blender. Carefully add lemon juice.
6. Freeze the sorbet in an ice cream machine.

Mirabelle Plum Sorbet

(18° Baumé or 32 Brix)

These wonderful and aroma rich plums produce a scrumptious sorbet. You can also use Reine-Claudes or prune plums.

2 gelatin leaves (4 g)
about 800 g (6½ cups) really ripe plums
*   (450 g, approx. 1⅘ cups purée)*
50 g (¼ cup) sugar
400 g (1⅕ cups) simple sugar syrup (p. 44)
50 g (⅕ cup) water
freshly squeezed lemon juice according to
*   preference*

1. Soak the gelatin in cold water for at least 10 minutes.
2. Blanch the plums in 67.6 oz boiling hot water for about 1 minute. Transfer the plums to a bowl with ice water and remove the peel and the seeds with a knife. Mix into a fine purée.
3. Mix 450 g (approx. 1⅘ cups) purée with sugar until it has dissolved.
4. Mix sugar syrup, water, and purée vigorously with a stick blender. Carefully add lemon juice.
5. Lift the gelatin leaves out of the water and add them to a pot with 1 dl (⅖ cup) of the sorbet batter. Heat to 104–122°F, until the gelatin has dissolved. Pour back to the rest of the batter and mix with a stick blender.
6. Freeze the sorbet in an ice cream machine.

You can make a fruit ice cream by adding 500 g (2½ cups) of the vanilla ice cream base (p.32), and mix it with the sorbet batter before you freeze it in the ice cream machine.

Raspberry Sorbet

(17° Baumé or 30.5 Brix)

Sometimes I replace half of the raspberry purée with black currant purée. This delicious combination is called Sorbet Cardinal. You can also combine half a batch of raspberry sorbet with half a batch of gooseberry sorbet, or red currant sorbet, for a refreshing flavor.

2 gelatin leaves (4 g)
about 600 g (5 cups) fresh or frozen raspber-
*   ries (450 g, approx. 1⅘ cups purée)*
50 g (¼ cup) sugar
450 g (1½ cups) simple sugar syrup (p. 44)
150 g (⅗ cup) water
freshly squeezed lemon juice

1. Soak the gelatin in cold water for at least 10 minutes.
2. Mix the raspberries into a purée and strain through a sieve.
3. Mix 450 g (approx. 1⅘ cups) purée with sugar until it has dissolved. Mix with sugar syrup and water and mix vigorously with a stick blender.
4. Lift the gelatin leaves out of the water and add them to a pot with ⅖ cup of the sorbet batter. Heat to 104–122°F, until the gelatin has dissolved. Pour back to the rest of the batter and mix with a stick blender. Add lemon juice.
5. Freeze the sorbet in an ice cream machine.

If you want to make raspberry ice cream instead, you can add 550 g (2¾ cups) of the vanilla ice cream base (p. 32) to the sorbet and mix with a stick blender. Optional, is to add candied raspberries into the frozen ice cream, see page 228 for candied berries.

Raspberry sorbet with Sugar Only

Use the same recipe as for the strawberry sorbet with sugar only (p.52), but replace the strawberries with raspberries.

Strawberry Sorbet

(17° Baumé or 30.5 Brix)

You can mix half a batch of strawberry purée with half a batch of rhubarb purée for a delectable combination, or you can also add elderflower juice. A little bit of kirschwasser (cherry brandy) or Maraschino liqueur will enhance the flavors in the strawberry sorbet.

2 gelatin leaves (4 g)
about 550 g (4 cups) ripe, rinsed, and hulled
*   strawberries (450 g, approx. 1⅘ cups*
*   purée)*
50 g (¼ cup) sugar
400 g (1⅕ cups) simple sugar syrup (p. 44)
75 g (⅓ cup) water
freshly squeezed lemon juice

1. Soak the gelatin in cold water for at least 10 minutes.
2. Mix the strawberries into a purée.
3. Mix 450 g (approx. 1⅘ cups) purée with sugar until it has dissolved. Mix vigorously with sugar syrup and water with a stick blender. Carefully add lemon juice.
4. Lift the gelatin leaves out of the water and add them to a pot with 1 dl (⅖ cup) of the sorbet batter. Heat to 104–122°F, until the gelatin has dissolved. Pour back to the rest of the batter and mix with a stick blender.
5. Freeze the sorbet in an ice cream machine.

If you want to make strawberry ice cream instead, add 500 g (2½ cup) of the vanilla ice cream base (p. 32) to the sorbet and mix with a stick blender. Optional, is to add candied strawberries into the frozen ice cream, see page 228 for candied berries.

STRAWBERRY SORBET WITH SUGAR ONLY

2 gelatin leaves (4 g)
1000g (8 cups) ripe strawberries
250 g (2 cups) powdered sugar
freshly squeezed lemon juice

1. Soak the gelatin in cold water for at least 10 minutes.
2. Mix the strawberries with sugar in a blender, until all the sugar has dissolved.
3. Lift the gelatin leaves out of the water and add them to a pot with 1 dl (⅖ cup) of the sorbet batter. Heat to 104–122°F, until the gelatin has dissolved. Pour back to the rest of the batter and mix with a stick blender. Add lemon juice.
4. Freeze the sorbet in an ice cream machine.

STRAWBERRY DAIQUIRI SORBET

Mix 150 g (2½ cups) lightly whipped cream and ⅖ cup dark rum into the strawberry sorbet once it is frozen.

WILD STRAWBERRY SORBET

(17° Baumé, or 30.5 Brix)

Use the same recipe as for the strawberry sorbet with sugar only. It will turn out absolutely delicious! Woodland strawberries work really well, the garden grown kind doesn't have the same rich flavor as the ones that grow in the wild.

CHERRY SORBET

(18° Baumé or 32 Brix)

A specialty dessert from the famous Pâtisserie Wittamer at Place du Grand Sablon in Brussels is the delicious ice cream bomb with almond ice cream and cherry sorbet. It is a heavenly combination. This recipe calls for tart cherries, such as amarelles.

2 gelatin leaves (4 g)
about 900 g (cherries (450 g, approx. 1⅘ cups purée)
50 g (¼ cup) sugar
375 g (simple sugar syrup (p. 44)
50 g (⅕ cup) water
freshly squeezed lemon juice
1 drop bitter almond oil

optional: 2 cl (1½ tbsp) kirschwasser (cherry brandy)

1. Soak the gelatin in cold water for at least 10 minutes.
2. Rinse the cherries and remove the pits. Mix them into a fine purée.
3. Mix 450 g (approx. 1⅘ cups) purée with the sugar until it has dissolved.
4. Mix purée vigorously with sugar syrup and water, add lemon juice and bitter almond oil to enhance the flavor. Add kirschwasser (cherry brandy) if you want to intensify the flavors even more.
5. Lift the gelatin leaves out of the water and add them to a pot with 1 dl (⅖ cup) of the sorbet batter. Heat to 104–122°F, until the gelatin has dissolved. Pour back to the rest of the batter and mix.
6. Freeze the sorbet in an ice cream machine.

If you want to make cherry ice cream instead, add 500 g (2½ cups) of the vanilla ice cream base (p. 32) and mix vigorously with a stick blender. You can add cherries that have been marinated in alcohol, *griottes*, once the ice cream is frozen.

Peach Sorbet

(17° Baumé or 30.5 Brix)

White donut peaches work the best, but you can also use red vigneronne peaches. Whatever peaches you decide to use, make sure that they are ripe, or it won't be worth your time. Follow the same instructions as for the apricot sorbet (p. 50), but use ripe peaches instead.

Pear Sorbet

(17° Baumé or 30.5 Brix)

Nothing beats the aroma of really ripe and soft Williams pears. Allow them to ripen until you can smell the pear aroma, before using them. Otherwise, the pear sorbet will turn out flavorless.

2 gelatin leaves (4 g)
about 900 g (7½ cups) ripe Williams pears (450 g, approx. 1 ⅘ cups purée)
50 g (¼ cup) sugar
300 g (9⁄10 cup) simple sugar syrup (p. 44)
50 g (⅕ cup) water
freshly squeezed lemon juice
optional: 2 – 4 cl (1½ tbsp – 3 tbsp) Poire Williams Eau De Vie

1. Soak the gelatin in cold water for at least 10 minutes.
2. Peel the pears and remove the core and mix them into a smooth purée.
3. Mix 450 g (approx. 1⅘ cups) purée with 50 g (¼ cup) sugar until the sugar has dissolved.
4. Mix with the sugar syrup and add the lemon juice, and the pear brandy if you decide to use it.
5. Lift the gelatin leaves out of the water and add them to a pot with ⅖ cup of the sorbet batter. Heat to 104–122°F until the gelatin has dissolved. Pour back to the rest of the batter and mix with a stick blender.
6. Freeze the sorbet in an ice cream machine.

Passion Fruit Sorbet

(18° Baumé or 32 Brix)

Garnish with a few passion fruit seeds in the sorbet batter for a beautiful dessert.

3 gelatin leaves (6 g)
1500 g (12½ cups) passion fruit (450 g, approx. 1 ⅘ cups juice)
50 g (¼ cup) sugar
650 g (2 cups) simple sugar syrup (p. 44)
100 g (⅖ cup) freshly squeezed orange or lemon juice

1. Soak the gelatin leaves in cold water for at least 10 minutes.
2. Cut the fruits in half and use a spoon to scoop out the pulp. Strain through a fine-meshed sieve (don't put the pulp through a blender, because it will taste bitter).
3. Mix 450 g (approx. 1⅘ cups) passion fruit juice with sugar until it dissolves. Add the sugar syrup and orange juice and mix with a stick blender.
4. Lift the gelatin leaves out of the water and add them to a pot with ⅖ cup of the sorbet batter. Heat to 104–122°F, until the gelatin has dissolved. Pour back to the rest of the batter and mix.
5. Freeze the sorbet in an ice cream machine.

If you want to make passion fruit ice cream, add 625 g (3 cups) of the vanilla ice cream base (p. 32) to the sorbet batter, and mix with a stick blender. Freeze the ice cream in an ice cream machine.

Sea-Buckthorn Sorbet

(18° Baumé or 32 Brix)

Follow the instructions in the passion fruit sorbet recipe, but you only need about 1000 g (approx. 8 cups) sea-buckthorn to produce 500 g (2 cups) juice.

Blueberry Sorbet

(17.5° Baumé or 31.5 Brix)

2 gelatin leaves (4 g)
about 700 g (5½ cups) fresh or frozen blueberries (450 g, approx. 1⅘ cups purée)
50 g (¼ cup) sugar
300 g (9⁄10 cup) simple sugar syrup (p. 44)
50 g (⅕ cup) water
freshly squeezed lemon juice

1. Soak the gelatin in cold water for at least 10 minutes.
2. Mix the blueberries into a purée and strain through a sieve. Mix the purée with sugar syrup and water with a stick blender. Add lemon juice.
3. Lift the gelatin leaves out of the water and add them to a pot with ⅖ cup of the sorbet batter. Heat to 104–122°F, until the gelatin has dissolved. Pour back to the rest of the batter and mix thoroughly.
4. Freeze the sorbet in an ice cream machine.

If you want to make blueberry ice cream instead, add 425 g (2 ⅕ cups) of the vanilla ice cream base (p. 32) to the sorbet batter and mix with a stick blender. Optional, is to add candied blueberries into the frozen ice cream, see page 228 for candied berries.

ELDERFLOWER OR MEADOWSWEET SORBET

(17° Baumé or 30.5 Brix)

The Juice

50 g (⅕ cup) Elderflower, or Meadowsweet
1 lemon
250 g (1¼ cups) sugar
250 g (1 cup) water

1. Rinse the flowers and allow them to dry off.
2. Wash and finely slice the lemon. Layer the slices and flowers in a metal bowl.
3. Bring the water and sugar to a boil and pour the boiling hot water over the flowers. Cover with plastic wrap and store in the fridge for 5 days.
4. Pour the juice into a strainer and press the flowers.

The Sorbet

2 gelatin leaves (4 g)
Elderflower, or meadowsweet juice
350 g (1½ cups) water
150 g (⅗ cup) freshly squeezed lemon juice

1. Soak the gelatin leaves in cold water for at least 10 minutes.
2. Mix the juice with lemon juice and water with a stick blender. Pour ⅔ cup of the blend into a pot.
3. Lift the gelatin leaves out of the water and add them to the pot. Heat to 104–122°F, and stir until the gelatin has dissolved. Pour into the sorbet batter and mix thoroughly with a stick blender.
4. Freeze the sorbet in an ice cream machine.

LINGONBERRY, OR CRANBERRY SORBET

(17° Baumé or 30.5 Brix)

Follow the same steps as when making blueberry sorbet. These berries have a higher acidity.

FIG SORBET

Follow the instructions in the blueberry sorbet recipe, but replace the berries with ripe figs.

Beet Sorbet

(17° Baumé or 30.5 Brix)

Beets are naturally sweet and have a gorgeous color, which makes them a perfect addition in sorbet.

2 gelatin leaves (4 g)
500 g (2 cups) fresh raw beet juice (extracted with a centrifugal juicer)
(about 1000 g (7⅓ cups) fresh beets)
125 g (⅗ cup) sugar
25 g (5 tsp) freshly squeezed lemon juice
50 g (2½ tbsp) honey
fleur de sel, freshly ground white pepper, and a little bit of ground cloves

1. Soak the gelatin leaves in cold water for at least 10 minutes.
2. Extract the beet juice and bring 2 liters (⅘ cup) of it to a boil with sugar, lemon juice, honey, and the spices.
3. Lift the gelatin leaves out of the water and add them to the pot and stir until the gelatin has dissolved. Mix with the rest of the beet juice.
4. Thoroughly mix the blend, and taste to see if you need to add more spices.

Strain through a chinois or fine-meshed sieve.
5. Freeze the sorbet in an ice cream machine.
6. Sprinkle some fleur de sel over the ice cream.

Pumpkin Sorbet

(17° Baumé or 30.5 Brix)

Use butternut pumpkin (butternut squash) to make this delicious sorbet.

2 gelatin leaves (4 g)
about 1000 g (approx. 4 cups) butternut squash (450 g, approx. 1⅘ cups purée)
50 g (¼ cup) sugar
300 g (9⁄10 cup) simple sugar syrup
50 g (⅕ cup) freshly squeezed orange juice
freshly squeezed lemon juice

1. Soak the gelatin leaves in cold water for at least 10 minutes.
2. Peel the squash and remove the seeds, cut into pieces and cook them in 2 liters (8 ½ cups) of water until they

are soft. Place them in a colander to strain off liquid.
3. Mix the butternut squash until you have a smooth purée. Mix 450 g (1⅘ cups) purée with sugar until it dissolves. Add the sugar syrup and the orange juice.
4. Lift the gelatin leaves out of the water and add them to 450 g (⅖ cup) of the sorbet batter. Heat to 104–122°F, until the gelatin has dissolved.
   Pour into the remaining sorbet batter and mix thoroughly. Add lemon juice.
5. Freeze the sorbet in an ice cream machine.

Quince Sorbet

Follow the directions in the pumpkin sorbet recipe, but replace the butternut squash with 1000 g (approx. 4 cups) large quince, or rose quince.

Lime Sorbet

(18° Baumé or 32 Brix)

2 gelatin leaves (4 g)
250 g (1¼ cups) sugar

250 g (1 cup) water
zest from a lime fruit
250 g (1 cup) lime juice (from about 10 limes)
250 g (1 cup) milk

1. Soak the gelatin leaves in cold water for at least 10 minutes.
2. Make sugar syrup by boiling the sugar and water. Remove the pot from the stove.
3. Lift the gelatin leaves out of the water and add them to the sugar syrup. Stir until they dissolve. Add the lime zest and allow the solution to get cold.
4. Add the lime juice and stir. Strain through a chinois or a fine-meshed sieve. Add the milk.
5. Freeze the sorbet in an ice cream machine.

LEMON SORBET

Follow the directions in the lime sorbet recipe. This sorbet is my personal favorite!

GRAPEFRUIT SORBET

Follow the directions in the lime sorbet recipe, but don't add any zest.

ORANGE SORBET

(17.5° Baumé or 31.5 Brix)

If you grate sugar cubes on the orange peel, it will add a better flavor than if you grate the peel on a grater. It takes a bit of work, but the flavor difference is vast and well worth it. Try adding a splash of Cointreau when you serve this sorbet as an entremets, or as a dessert. Delicious to serve with a nice almond pastry or cake.

2 gelatin leaves (4 g)
about 5 oranges
220 g (1⅛ cups) sugar cubes
100 g (⅖ cup) water
650 g (2⅗ cups) freshly squeezed orange juice
1 lemon, the juice

1. Soak the gelatin leaves in cold water for at least 10 minutes.
2. Wash the oranges with a brush. Rub the sugar cubes against the orange peel until they absorb the juice.
3. Place the sugar cubes in a pot with 100 g (⅖ cup) water. Bring to a boil. Remove the pot from the heat.
4. Remove the gelatin from the water and mix into the sugar solution. Stir until the gelatin dissolves.
5. Mix the orange juice with the sugar solution. Carefully add the lemon juice.
6. Freeze the sorbet in an ice cream maker.

MANDARIN SORBET

Follow the instructions in the orange sorbet recipe.

Raspberry and Pepper Sorbet

(17° Baumé or 30.5 Brix)

I got this recipe from the famous Parisian pastry chef, Pierre Hermé, when he visited Sweden a few years ago.

2 gelatin leaves (4 g)
250 g (approx. 2 cups) red peppers (150 g, approx. ⅗ cup blanched pulp)
360 g (2½ cups) raspberry purée with 10% sugar
90 g (½ cup) sugar
20 g (1½ tbsp) raspberry vinegar
2 drops green Tabasco

1. Soak the gelatin leaves in cold water for at least 10 minutes.
2. Cut the peppers in half and remove the seeds. Boil it three times for 2 minutes. Use fresh water each time, to remove any bitter flavor. Remove the peel from the blanched peppers.
3. Mix everything in a blender until the sugar has dissolved, about 5 minutes.

4. Remove the gelatin leaves from the water and transfer them to a pot. Heat to 113–122°F, pour the dissolved gelatin into the batter and mix it until smooth with a stick blender.
5. Freeze the sorbet in an ice cream maker.

Carrot and Orange Sorbet

(17.5° Baumé or 31.5 Brix)

2 gelatin leaves (4 g)
125 g (⅗ cup) sugar
75 g (⅓ cup) water
60 g (⅕ cup) orange blossom honey
250 g (1 cup) fresh carrot juice
250 g (1 cup) fresh orange juice

1. Soak the gelatin leaves in cold water for at least 10 minutes.
2. Put sugar, water, and honey in a pot, and bring to a boil.
3. Remove from the heat, add the gelatin leaves (after you have drained them), and stir until they dissolve. Cool the sugar solution to 95°F. Add carrot juice and orange juice and freeze the sorbet in an ice cream machine.

Sorbet with Valrhona Gran Couva Chocolate

(18° Baumé or 32 Brix)

You get a different texture if you replace the water with milk.

4 gelatin leaves (8 g)
1000 g (4⅕ cups) water
250g (1¼ cups) sugar
400 g (2 cups) dark chocolate, Valrhona Couva

1. Soak the gelatin leaves in cold water for at least 10 minutes.
2. In a pot, bring water and sugar to a boil. Remove from heat and allow it to cool off a bit.
3. Add the gelatin leaves (after you have drained them), and stir until they dissolve.
4. Add the finely chopped chocolate, and mix the batter smooth with a stick blender.
5. Freeze the sorbet in an ice cream machine, once the batter has cooled off.

White Chocolate Sorbet

(18° Baumé or 32 Brix)

2 gelatin leaves (4 g)
400 g (1¾ cups) water
2 vanilla pods, split and scraped
125 g (⅗ cup) sugar
50 g (2½ tbsp) orange blossom honey
1 orange
350 g (1¾ cups) white chocolate, Valrhona Ivoire
600 g (2½ cups) milk
50 g (⅕ cup) Cointreau

1. Soak the gelatin leaves in cold water for at least 10 minutes.
2. Put vanilla pods and seeds in a pot, and add water, sugar, and honey. Rinse and peel the orange with a potato peeler. Bring the sugar solution with the peel to a boil, and allow it to stand and marinate for 10 minutes.
3. Add the drained gelatin leaves and stir until they dissolve.
4. Boil the milk and put it aside. Add the finely chopped chocolate and mix until well blended with a stick blender.
5. Strain the sugar solution and mix well. Add the liqueur and mix it in. Cool in an ice cold water bath as quickly as possible.
6. Freeze the sorbet in an ice cream machine.

Tapioca Sorbet with Tonka Beans

(18° Baumé or 32 Brix)

3 gelatin leaves (6 g)
1 tonka bean, or 2 split and scraped vanilla pods
400 g (1¾ cups) water
1 lemon, the peel
200 g (1 cup) sugar
4 tsp tapioca grains
600 g (2½ cups) milk
50 g (2½ tbsp) honey

1. Soak the gelatin leaves in cold water for at least 10 minutes.
2. Grate the tonka bean with a grater. Boil the water with the tonka bean, lemon peel, and half of the sugar. Add the tapioca grains and simmer until they are completely transparent. Add

the milk, and the remaining sugar, honey, and bring to a boil. Remove from the heat.

3. Remove the gelatin leaves from the water and add them to sorbet batter. Stir until they dissolve.
4. Cool the batter in an ice cold water bath as quickly as possible.
5. Freeze the sorbet in an ice cream machine.

Vanilla Sorbet

(18° Baumé or 32 Brix)

3 gelatin leaves (6 g)
2 Tahitian vanilla beans, split and
    scraped
600 g (2½ cups) milk
400 g (1¾ cups) water
200 g (1 cup) sugar
50 g (2½ tbsp) honey

1. Soak the gelatin leaves in cold water for at least 10 minutes.
2. Put vanilla, milk, water, sugar, and honey in a pot, and bring to a boil. Remove from heat.
3. Remove the gelatin leaves from the water, and add them to the batter. Stir until they dissolve. Mix with a stick blender, and allow the batter to sit for 10 minutes.
4. Strain and cool in an ice cold water bath as quickly as possible.
5. Freeze the sorbet in an ice cream machine.

Tea Sorbet with Rum Raisins

(18° Baumé or 32 Brix)

2 gelatin leaves (4 g)
75 g (⅗ cup) raisins

25 g (1¾ tbsp) dark rum
200 g (1 cup) sugar
600 g (2½ cups) water
400 g (1¾ cups) milk
50 g (2½ tbsp) honey
5 g (2 tsp) tea

1. Soak the gelatin leaves in cold water for at least 10 minutes.
2. Soak the raisins in the rum for a few hours.
3. Bring sugar, water, milk, honey, and lemon juice to a boil. Add the gelatin leaves (after you drain them from the water), and stir until they have dissolved.
4. Stir the tea into the batter and allow it to steep for 5 minutes. Strain the solution and cool it in an ice cold water bath.
5. Freeze the sorbet in an ice cream machine and stir the marinated raisins into the sorbet.

Champagne Sorbet

(14° Baumé or 25 Brix)

When you want to indulge in luxury, pulling the pink champagne sorbet out of the freezer is just right!

2 gelatin leaves (4 g)
1 bottle of good champagne, preferably Veuve Clicquot
400 g (1⅕ cups) simple sugar syrup (p. 44)
1 lemon, the juice
1 orange, the juice
4 cl (3 tbsp) cognac
60 g (¼ cup) egg whites

1. Soak the gelatin leaves in cold water for at least 10 minutes.
2. Pour the champagne into a bowl and add the sugar syrup, lemon juice, orange juice and cognac. Mix well with a stick blender.
3. Remove the gelatin leaves from the water, and add them to 1 dl (⅖ cup) of the batter. Heat at 104–122°F until the gelatin has dissolved. Add to the remaining batter and mix with a stick blender.
4. Freeze the sorbet in an ice cream machine. When it is half frozen, add the lightly beaten egg whites and mix until you have a fairly firm, fluffy, and airy sorbet.

Cider Sorbet

Follow the instructions in the champagne sorbet recipe, but replace the champagne with cider from Normandy. When you serve this sorbet, it will be extra tasty if you pour some Young Calvados over it, in a tall glass. Don't use an old Calvados, it will ruin the flavor.

Beaujolais Sorbet

Make the same way as above, but use a young, fresh, red wine. Add a dollop of French crème de cassis when you serve it.

Dessert Wine Sorbet

(12° Baumé or 22 Brix)

Port Wine Sorbet tastes delicious with fresh cantaloupe. Use the recipe above, but replace the champagne with 37 cl (1⅗ cups) red port wine and 37 cl (1⅗ cups) water (otherwise the sorbet won't freeze, because of the high alcohol content), and eliminate the cognac.

Vodka Sorbet

(12° Baumé or 22 Brix)

2 gelatin leaves (4 g)
100 g (½ cup) sugar
25 g (3½ tsp) glucose
600 g (2½ cups) water
15 g (1 tbsp) egg whites
10 g (2½ tsp) sugar
5 g (1 tsp) freshly squeezed lemon juice
1 orange
1 lemon
15 g (1 tbsp) vodka, or any other strong liquor

1. Soak the gelatin leaves in cold water for at least 10 minutes.
2. Create a sugar syrup by boiling the sugar, glucose, and water. Set aside.
3. Heat the egg whites, sugar, and lemon juice in a metal bowl in a water bath on the stove while you stir the batter continuously, until you reach 131–140°F. Remove from the stove and use a whisk to beat the meringue until cold. (Make sure that the water bath doesn't reach a temperature above 194°F, because then the egg whites may coagulate).
4. Wash and peel the orange with a potato peeler, and add the peel to the sugar solution. Do the same thing with the lemon.
5. Remove the gelatin leaves from the water and mix them into the sugar solution. Stir until they have dissolved. Place in an ice cold water bath to chill the solution.
6. Add the vodka and freeze the sorbet in an ice cream machine. Add the meringue when the sorbet is half frozen.

Tomato Sorbet

(18° Baumé or 32 Brix)

You can spice this sorbet up a bit with salt, black pepper, Worcestershire sauce, and a few drops of Tabasco. Also pour a little bit of vodka over the sorbet when you serve it. The tomato sorbet makes a great appetizer.

2 gelatin leaves (4 g)
1500 g (8½ cups) ripe plum tomatoes (1000 g, approx. 4 cups purée)
50 g (⅕ cup) freshly squeezed lemon juice
250 g (1¼ cups) sugar
50 g (2½ tbsp) orange blossom honey

1. Soak the gelatin in cold water for at least 10 minutes.
2. Blanch the tomatoes in boiling hot water. Rinse them in cold water and remove the peels with a little knife. Cut them in half and remove the core.
3. Mix the tomatoes with the lemon juice, sugar, and honey until all the sugar has dissolved.
4. Remove the gelatin leaves from the water and add them to ⅘ cup of the sorbet batter. Heat to 113–122°F, and add to the batter and mix with a stick blender.
5. Freeze the sorbet in an ice cream machine.

Spooms

Spoom is a type of sorbet with lower sugar content. It is mixed with a warm whisked cold meringue when it is newly frozen. Spoom is delicious, and just like with sorbet and ice cream, the flavor possibilities are endless.

Strawberry Spoom

Warm Whisked Meringue:

100 g (⅖ cup) egg whites
125 g (⅗ cup) sugar
5 g (1 tsp) freshly squeezed lemon juice
1 ½ gelatin leaves (0.1 oz)
500 g (2¾ cups) strawberry purée with 10% sugar
50 g (¼ cup) sugar
50 g (⅕ cup) freshly squeezed lemon juice

1. Beat egg whites, sugar, and lemon juice in a stainless steel bowl. Place it in a simmering water bath on the stove, while you continue to beat the egg batter until it reaches 131-149°F. Make sure that the water doesn't boil, and that it doesn't reach above 194°F, because then the egg whites will coagulate. Beat the meringue until it has cooled off completely.
2. Soak the gelatin leaves in cold water for at least 10 minutes.
3. Mix the strawberry purée with sugar and lemon juice until all the sugar has dissolved.
4. Remove the gelatin leaves from the water and add them to 1 dl (⅖ cup) of the strawberry batter. Heat at 113–122°F until the gelatin has dissolved. Mix with the remaining strawberry batter until smooth.
5. Freeze in an ice cream machine until it is fairly firm, and immediately fold the ice cream into the cold meringue

batter with a ladle, until you have a light
and airy spoom. Store in the freezer.

6. Pipe the spoom into frozen glasses with
a large plain tube. Serve right away.

ORANGE SPOOM WITH ORANGE THYME

Warm Beaten Meringue:

100 g (½ cup) sugar
100 g (⅖ cup) egg whites
5 g (1 tsp) fresh lemon juice
1 ½ gelatin leaves (3 g)
10 g + 25 g (2 tsp + 5 tsp) fresh lemon juice
500 g (2 cups) fresh orange juice
1 orange
10 g (2 tsp) orange thyme
20 g (1¾ tbsp) sugar cubes
25 g (3½ tsp) orange blossom honey
75 g (⅓ cup) crème fraiche

1. Beat egg whites, sugar, and lemon juice
in a stainless steel bowl. Place it in a
simmering water bath on the stove, while
you continue to beat the egg batter until
it reaches 131-140°F.

2. Beat the meringue until it is completely
cold.

3. Soak the gelatin leaves in cold water for
at least 10 minutes.

4. Caramelize the sugar with the lemon
juice in a pot until you have a light
brown caramel. Add 7 oz of the orange
juice, and the thyme. Boil until only 0.9
oz remains.

5. Strain through a chinois or a fine-
meshed sieve directly into the remaining
orange juice.

6. Clean the orange and grate the sugar
cubes on the peel, until all the peel is
absorbed.

7. Mix all the ingredients in a blender until
you have a smooth batter.

8. Remove the gelatin leaves from the water
and add them to 1 dl (⅖ cup) of the
batter. Heat at 113–122°F until the
gelatin has dissolved. Mix with the
remaining batter until smooth.

9. Freeze in an ice cream machine, until the
ice cream is fairly firm. Immediately, fold
it into the cold meringue with a ladle,
until you have a light and airy spoom.
Store in the freezer. Pipe the spoom into
frozen glasses with a large plain tube.

Punch

Ice cream punch is an old tradition in gastronomy, and is a type of sorbet, that is usually served in tall glasses with appropriate alcohol that is added with a spoon. You can vary the punch with different types of alcohol and wine, and you can serve it as an entremets, or as refreshment.

PUNCH À LA ROMAINE
(14° Baumé or 25 Brix)

2 gelatin leaves (4 g)
2 oranges
1 lemon
150 g (⅖ cup) simple sugar syrup (p. 44)
500 g (2 cups) dry champagne
180 g (3 cups) Italian meringue (p. 230)
100 g (⅖ cup) rum

1. Soak the gelatin in cold water for at least 10 minutes.
2. Wash and grate the peel of half an orange and half a lemon.
3. Boil the sugar syrup, and add the citrus zest, and the gelatin leaves (after you lift them out of the water soak). Stir until the gelatin has dissolved. Allow the blend to cool off to 68°F.
4. Add the juice from the oranges and the lemon. Add the champagne and strain.
5. Make an Italian meringue with 60 g (¼ cup) egg whites, 5 g (1 tsp) fresh lemon juice, and 120 g (½ cup) sugar (p. 230).
6. Freeze the sorbet in an ice cream maker, and fold them into the cold meringue. Serve in frozen champagne glasses, and add a little bit on top. Serve with long spoons.

PUNCH WITH APPLE CIDER AND CALVADOS

Use the same recipe as for Punch à la Romaine, but replace the champagne with apple cider from Normandy, and replace the rum with Calvados.

PUNCH À LA KIR ROYALE

Use the same recipe as for Punch à la Romaine, but replace the champagne with a young red Bourgogne or Beaujolais, and replace the rum with the black currant liqueur, Crème de Cassis.

Marquise

This type of sorbet is always mixed with lightly whipped cream at the end. Serve in glasses as a light dessert, or as an entremets, depending on the flavor you select. Can be varied, just like the sorbet.

BLACK CURRANT MARQUISE WITH LEMON VERBENA AND RUM

If you can't get a hold of lemon verbena, you can use lemon balm instead.

1 gelatin leaf (2 g)
40 g lemon verbena
600 g (5 cups) ripe black currants
100 g (⅘ cup) powdered sugar
25 g (3½ tsp) glucose
2 cl (1½ tbsp) dark rum
150 g (⅗ cup) whipping cream

1. Soak the gelatin in cold water for at least 10 minutes.
2. Blanch the lemon verbena for a few seconds in boiling hot water and immediately transfer to ice cold water.
3. Mix the currants with lemon verbena, powdered sugar, and glucose to a smooth purée. Strain through a fine-meshed sieve.
4. Add rum and mix with a stick blender. Set aside. Lift the gelatin out of the water and add them to ⅓ cup of the purée. Heat at 104-122°F until the gelatin has dissolved. Add to the remaining batter and mix.
5. Freeze in an ice cream machine.
6. Beat the cream to a loose foam in a chilled metal bowl. Add it in the ice cream machine, and freeze marquis until it has a medium firm consistency.
7. Use a star tube to pipe into frozen champagne glasses.

GRANITE

The granite can be varied with many different flavors. It can even be made with green tea aquavit, chocolate, Bloody Mary, orange, Campari, etc. Try black currant granite with Côte du Rhône, and crème de cassis, or vodka granite with Russian caviar, if you want to make it extra fancy, try cucumber granite with a fluffy salmon mousse. Or why not try tomato granite with tuna tartar, melon granite with Serrano ham? The sugar content in granite should be about 12° Baumé, the same sugar levels as all the granite recipes here.

Pour the granite onto a tray with edges, and put it in the freezer. Stir occasionally to get a grainy ice cream. Serve in frozen glasses as a side dish with desserts, as an appetizer, or as an entremets.

CHAMPAGNE, OR WINE GRANITE

2 gelatin leaves (4 g)
200 g (1 cup) sugar
100 g (⅖ cup) water
10 g (2 tsp) freshly squeezed lemon juice
750 g (3 cups) white, or pink champagne

1. Soak the gelatin leaves in cold water for at least 10 minutes.
2. Create a sugar syrup by boiling the sugar and the water.
3. Remove the gelatin from the water and add to the sugar solution. Stir until it dissolves, and allow it to cool off.
4. Mix lemon juice, champagne into the solution, and pour into a deep tray, and store in the freezer.

Wine Granite: Use the same recipe, but replace the champagne with wines with 10 percent alcohol content.

CALVADOS AND CIDER GRANITE

2 gelatin leaves (4 g)
150 g (¾ cup) sugar
90 g (⅖ cup) water
10 g (2 tsp) fresh lemon juice
700 g (2⁹⁄₁₀ cups) apple cider from Normandy

Make the same way you would make the champagne granite.

VODKA AND ORANGE GRANITE

2 gelatin leaves (4 g)
200 g (1 cup) sugar
600 g (2½ cups) water
200 g (⅘ cup) fresh orange juice
100 g (⅖ cup) vodka

Make the same way as the champagne granite.

LIME AND TEQUILA GRANITE

2 gelatin leaves (4 g)
200 g (1 cup) sugar
700 g (2⁹⁄₁₀ cups) water
100 g (⅖ cup) fresh lime juice
100 g (⅖ cup) tequila

Make the same way as the champagne granite.

MELON GRANITE

2 gelatin leaves (4 g)
160 g (⅘ cup) sugar
350 g (1 ½ cups) water
650 g (2⅗ cups) cantaloupe purée with 10% sugar

Make the same way as the champagne granite.

CUCUMBER GRANITE

2 gelatin leaves (4 g)
180 g (⁹⁄₁₀ cup) sugar
350 g (1½ cups) water
50 g (⅕ cup) fresh lemon juice
650 g (2⅗ cups) cucumber purée with 10% sugar

Make the same way as the champagne granite.

GRAPEFRUIT GRANITE

2 gelatin leaves (4 g)
650 g (2 ¾ cups) water
160 g (⅘ cup) sugar
350 g (1 ½ cups) fresh red grapefruit juice

Make the same way as the champagne granite.

LEMON GRANITE

Use the same recipe as for the grapefruit granite, but replace the grapefruit juice with lemon juice.

PASSION FRUIT GRANITE

Make the same way as the grapefruit granite, but replace the red grapefruit juice with strained passion fruit juice.

STRAWBERRY, OR RASPBERRY GRANITE

2 gelatin leaves (4 g)
120 g (⅗ cup) sugar
250 g (1¼ cups) water
about 25 g (5 tsp) fresh lemon juice
500 g (2 cups) strawberry or raspberry purée
* 10% sugar*

Make the same way as the champagne granite (p. 63). You can also use blueberries, blackberries, cloudberries.

BLACK CURRANT GRANITE

Use the recipe for strawberry granite, but replace the strawberry purée with 400 g (1⅔ cup) black currant purée, and add 100 g (⅖ cup) more water, because the black currant flavor is very potent.

MANGO GRANITE

Use the recipe for strawberry granite, but replace the strawberry purée with mango purée that you make out of 800 g (3 cups) fresh, ripe mango.

HERB, OR FLOWER GRANITE

Choose any of the herbs or flowers that you would add to your sorbet or ice cream (p. 43).

2 gelatin leaves (4 g)
50 g (1 cup) fresh peppermint or any other herb
160 g (⅘ cup) sugar
800 g (3⅖ cups) water

1. Soak the gelatin in cold water for at least 10 minutes.
2. Blanch the herbs or flowers in boiling water to kill any bacteria. Immediately chill them in ice cold water.
3. Cook sugar syrup with sugar and water. Remove the gelatin leaves from the water and add them to the sugar solution. Stir until the gelatin has dissolved.
4. Allow the solution to cool off. Mix 3 dl (1 ⅓ cup) of the simple syrup with the herbs or flowers until you have a fine purée. Strain through a chinois or a sieve, into the remaining sugar solution. Mix with a stick blender.
5. Pour into a tray with high edges, and place in the freezer. Stir occasionally to get a grainy ice cream.

CHOCOLATE GRANITE

2 gelatin leaves (4 g)
150 g (¾ cup) sugar
800 g (3 ⅖ cups) water
180 g (9⁄10 cup) dark chocolate, preferably Valrhona Grand Cru Manjari 64.5%

1. Soak the gelatin in cold water for at least 10 minutes.
2. Bring sugar and water to a boil. Set aside.
3. Add the chopped chocolate. Remove the gelatin leaves from the water and add them to the warm sugar solution.
4. Mix with a stick blender and chill in an ice cold water bath. Pour into a tray with high edges, and place in the freezer.

ESPRESSO GRANITE

1 gelatin leaf (2 g)
500 g (2 cups) freshly brewed espresso
80 g (⅖ cup) sugar

1. Soak the gelatin in cold water for at least 10 minutes.
2. Remove the gelatin leaf from the water and add it to the espresso, add the suga, and stir until it has dissolved.
3. Mix with a stick blender and chill the solution in a ice cold water bath. Pour into a tray with edges and place in the freezer.

Parfaits are easy to make, and you don't even need an ice cream machine to freeze them. In Italy, the dessert is called *Semifreddo*, which means "half-frozen." Due to the high sugar content, the egg yolks, and the airy cream, they never freeze to a firm ice cream. They also don't get as cold as ice cream and sorbet. Parfait is often used as filling in ice cream bombs.

If you want to make a two-colored parfait, you could line the bomb molde with banana parfait, and stick down a plastic cone that is filled with chocolate parfait, and fill the mold with it.

Semifreddo parfaits are often filled with liquor marinated macaroons, chocolate macaroons, or meringue, and candied fruits that have been dipped in alcohol, chopped chocolate, and caramelized nuts and almonds. Mocca or coffe are the original parfait flavors, usually served with various sides and sauces. Parfaits are often used as filling in ice cream cakes, in biscuit glacé, soufflé ice cream, and cassata.

There are many different ways to make parfait. In classic Swedish recipes, where you beat egg yolks with sugar, the result is usually a heavy and rich parfait, because it contains too little water. A parfait should be light and airy. The old Swedish recipes lack the art of cooking chemistry, which is one of the most important knowledge in cuisine.

I don't recommend mixing fruit purée into the parfait, because the fruit purée and the egg yolks make the dessert runny, where the fruit purée usually seeps through to the bottom. You can add gelatin if you want to improve the texture on the frozen parfait, and it prevents sedimentation, but only add a little bit, otherwise you'll end up with mousse instead. Nowadays, I add gelatin to all my parfaits. Freeze parfaits immediately, to prevent them from crystallizing.

Use warm beaten meringue, or Italian meringue as base for your fruit parfait. Then the parfait will turn out refreshing, with a more stable structure, as it is based on egg whites. This type of parfait is referred to as mousse glacé in technical jargon. It should freezed for at least 6 hours. When you beat foam based on egg yolks, it is important to used the medium speed on the whisk, so that you don't beat the air out of the yolks. The same rule applies to the meringue for the mousse glacé.

Whipped cream is also a type of foam. During the 1600s, Fritz Karl Vatel, was the first person to whip cream with sugar. Prince de Condé hired him to be his master chef at the castle of Chantilly. Hence, whipped cream with vanilla is called crème Chantilly.

Whipped cream turns out perfect if you beat it cold, at 39.2°F, in a chilled bowl. When you beat cream, you are beating it full of air bubbles which stabilizes the protein casein, and the butterfat is crystallized. During low temperatures, the fat molecules attach to each other into little crystals so that the cream becomes supple, light, and airy, which are important qualities when making parfait and mousse. The cooling process prevents the cream from getting too heavy and buttery. Beat the cream until it is fluffy, and store in the fridge.

Good to Know
The egg yolk stabilizes when the yolk protein denatures and partially coagulates during heating. One would think that the yolk fat would prevent foam formation, but because the fat is emulsified, the foam reducing activity is prevented.

A classic parfait base is the pâte à bomb, which is made with 3.5 oz egg yolks, and 7 oz sugar syrup, at 32° Baumé or 64° Brix. The name derives from the fact that it is often used as filling in ice cream bombs and ice cream cakes. Below, are the classic methods that I use daily.

Vanilla Parfait According to the Pâte à Bomb Method
1 gelatin leaf (2 g)
300 g (9/10 cup) simple sugar syrup (p. 44)
500 g (2 cups) whipping cream
2 vanilla pods
200 g (4/5 cup) egg yolks

1. Soak the gelatin in cold water for at least 10 minutes.

2. Cook the sugar syrup. Beat the cream until frothy in a chilled metal bowl, and place in the fridge.
3. Cut the vanilla pods into small pieces. Place the pieces, the sugar syrup, and the yolks in a 3 liters metal bowl, and place it in a simmering water bath (don't exceed 194°F, otherwise the yolks may coagulate).
4. Beat vigorously until the mass gets a creamlike texture, and patterns begin to form from the whisk. It should be ready at 185°F. Use a thermometer, or do a rose test or a ladle test (p. 25).
5. Transfer the gelatin leaf from the water to the egg batter. Stir until the gelatin has dissolved.
6. Strain the batter through a chinois or a fine-meshed sieve. Whisk it cold, light, and airy.
7. Fold the batter into the whipped cream. Pour the batter into a baking pan, or several small molds, and freeze.

Vanilla Parfait According to the Cooked Pâte à Bomb Method
This approach is quicker and more modern, but it produces a slightly lighter parfait that doesn't taste as creamy as the one above.

1 gelatin leaf (2 g)
500 g (2 cups) whipping cream
160 g (3/4 cup) egg yolks
2 vanilla pods
80 g (1/3 cup) water
200 g (1 cup) sugar

1. Soak the gelatin in cold water for at least 10 minutes.
2. Beat the cream to foam in a chilled metal bowl, and place it in the fridge.
3. Beat the yolks frothy.
4. Cut the vanilla pods into small pieces. Mix them with water and sugar in a small pan. Bring to a boil. Occasionally, brush the interior walls with a brush that has been dipped in water, until the temperature reaches 239°F.

5. Pour the sugar solution evenly into the beaten egg yolks, while beating the egg batter continuously.
6. Transfer the gelatin leaf from the water to the egg batter. Stir until the gelatin has dissolved.
7. Beat the egg batter cold and fold it into the whipped cream. Pour the batter into a baking pan, or several small molds, and freeze.

Vanilla Parfait According to the Crème Anglaise Method
This is a classic method, and it produces parfait with a dense and smooth texture. Use it if you want to make a rich and potent coffee parfait, or a full and soft chocolate parfait. You can infuse the milk with spices like cinnamon, cardamom, tonka beans, tea, herbs, or flowers. This is also a great base for licorice parfait.

250 g (1 cup) heavy cream
1 gelatin leaf (2 g)
1 vanilla pod, split and scraped
250 g (1 cup) milk
120 g (1/2 cup) egg yolks
200 g (1 cup) sugar

1. Beat the cream foamy in a chilled metal bowl, and store in the fridge.
2. Soak the gelatin leaf in cold water for at least 10 minutes.
3. Put the vanilla pods and seeds in a pan, add the milk, and bring to a boil. Set aside, and let it sit for at least 5 minutes.
4. Beat the egg yolks lightly with the sugar and add to the vanilla milk. Heat to 185°F, while continuously stirring. Use a thermometer, or do a rose test or a ladle test (p. 25).
5. Transfer the gelatin leaf from the water to the crème Anglaise. Stir until the gelatin has dissolved.
6. Strain the batter through a chinois or a fine-meshed sieve, into a bowl. Chill it in a water bath with ice cubes until the thermometer displays 68°F.
7. Fold the crème Anglaise into the whipped cream with a ladle, until you have a light and fluffy parfait. Pour the batter into a baking pan, or several small molds, and freeze.

PISTACHIO PARFAIT

Add 100 g (¾ cup) pistachio paste (p. 229), 50 g (⅓ cup) caramelized pistachios (p. 228), 1 drop essence of bitter almond, 1 drop orange blossom water to any of the vanilla parfait recipes. Optional: add 2 cl (1½ tbsp) kirschwasser (cherry brandy) or rum.

ALCOHOL PARFAIT

Add 50 – 100 g (⅕ cup – ⅖ cup) liqueur, or any other type of alcohol to any of the parfait recipes. You will need to lessen the amount of sugar, or the parfait won't freeze. Lessen it by 1.8 oz sugar for the cooked pâte à bomb, and the anglaise method. Lessen the amount of sugar syrup by 50 g (2½ tbsp) for the classic pâte à bomb method.

Some delicious additions are Grand Marnier, Pernod, Maraschino, whisky, cognac, Benedictine liqueur, Kahlua, Pisco, Tequila, and many others.

COFFEE PARFAIT

Add 25 g (¼ cup) crushed French espresso beans, instead of the vanilla pod, to the crème anglaise batter. Let the coffee blend to sit and marinate for at least 15 minutes.

COFFEE PARFAIT WITH RUM

Use the vanilla parfait batter according to the pâte â bomb method, and add 6 g (3⅓ tsp) Nescafé instant coffee that has been dissolved in 2 cl (1½ tbsp) arrak or rum.

TEA PARFAIT

Add 20 g (⅕ cup) tea to the crème anglaise batter. Allow to settle for 5 minutes.

GIANDUJA PARFAIT

Add 150 g (⅗ cup) melted (113–122°F) gianduja (p. 229) to the parfait batter.

PRALINÉ PARFAIT

Add 150 g (1 cup) crushed praline (p. 229).

HAZELNUT PARFAIT

Add 100 g (⅖ cup) hazelnut crème (p. 229), and 100 g (¾ cup) crushed caramelized almonds (p. 228).

CHOCOLATE PARFAIT

Add 200 g (⅘ cup) melted (122–131°F) dark chocolate.

ORANGE/LEMON PARFAIT

Add 100 g (⅖ cup) citrus concentrate from each fruit. Optional: add a little bit of Cointreau, or Grand Marnier if you are making the orange parfait.

FRUIT/BERRY PARFAIT

If you want to add fruits or berries in parfait, the same rules apply as for ice cream: they should be lightly candied, or the water in the berries and fruits will freeze to ice.

LIGHT CHOCOLATE PARFAIT

This type of chocolate parfait has a summer feel to it with its lightness.

400 g (1¾ cups) whipping cream
120 g (½ cup) egg whites
5 g (1 tsp) fresh lemon juice
200 g (1 cup) sugar
420 g (2 cups) dark chocolate, i.e. Valrhona Grand Cru Pur Caribé

1. Beat the cream foamy in a chilled metal bowl and place it in the fridge.
2. Bring water to a boil. Beat egg whites, lemon juice and sugar in a clean metal bowl.
3. Place the bowl over a water bath (make sure that the water temperature doesn't exceed 194°F, otherwise the egg whites tend to coagulate). Beat vigorously with an electric whisk until the batter is at a temperature between 131°F and 140°F. Remove from the water bath, and beat the meringue cold (medium speed on the whisk).
4. Finely chop the chocolate and transfer to a plastic bowl. Heat it in the microwave while stirring occasionally, until it is 131°F-140°F.
5. Stir a third of the whipped cream into the chocolate. Make an elastic, shiny emulsion with a plastic ladle. Add it to the meringue. Mix with a spatula into a smooth batter. Fold the rest of the cream into the batter so that you end up with a smooth and fluffy parfait. Fill molds, and freeze.

CHAMPAGNE PARFAIT

2 gelatin leaves (4 g)
500 g (2 cups) whipping cream

140 g (⅗ cup) egg yolk
100 g (⅓ cup) simple sugar syrup (p. 44)
100 g (⅖ cup) of a good, dry champagne
25 g (1¾ tbsp) cognac

1. Soak the gelatin leaves in cold water for at least 10 minutes.
2. Beat the cream foamy in a chilled metal bowl and place it in the fridge.
3. Beat egg yolks, sugar syrup, champagne, and cognac in a clean metal bowl. Place it in a simmering water bath, and beat continuously until the cream begins to thicken and patterns form in the foam.
4. At 185°F, lift the gelatin leaf out of the water, and mix it into the egg batter. Beat the sabayon at a medium speed, until the temperature has lowered to 68°F.
5. Fold the whipped cream into the batter and freeze in molds.

ORANGE PARFAIT

This recipe can also be used to make a lemon parfait with gin, or a mandarin or lime parfait with tequila or Pisco.

2 gelatin leaves (4 g)
500 g (2 cups) whipping cream
about 3 oranges
100 g (½ cup) sugar cubes
250 g (1 cup) freshly squeezed orange juice
100 g (½ cup) granulated sugar
120 g (½ cup) egg yolks

1. Soak the gelatin in cold water for at least 10 minutes.
2. Beat the cream foamy in a chilled metal bowl, and place it in the fridge.
3. Clean the oranges thoroughly. Grate the sugar cubes against the oranges, until all the peel is absorbed.
4. Mix orange juice, granulated sugar, and sugar cubes with the egg yolks, in a metal bowl. Place it over a hot water bath (don't exceed 194°F, that's when the yolks begin to coagulate).
5. Beat vigorously until the batter begins to thicken and patterns are formed in it. At 185°F, it is ready. Use a thermometer to check it, or do a rose test, or a ladle test.

6. Remove from the stove. Lift the gelatin out of the water and add to the egg foam. Beat until the gelatin has dissolved. Strain through a chinois or a fine-meshed sieve.
7. Beat the egg batter until it is 68°F. Fold the egg foam into the whipped cream, so that you get a light and fluffy parfait. Fill a mold and freeze.

If you want to add 1 oz Grand Marnier, or Cointreau to enhance the orange flavor, you need to lessen the amount of sugar by 30 g (2 tbsp), or the parfait won't freeze.

Cinnamon Parfait

2 gelatin leaves (4 g)
500 g (2 cups) whipping cream
145 g (3/5 cup) egg yolk
4 g (2¼ tsp) freshly ground true cinnamon
200 g (1 cup) sugar
80 g (1/3 cup) water
100 g (4/5 cup) finely chopped candied orange peel (p. 228)
100 g (¾ cup) crushed caramelized hazelnuts (p.228)

1. Soak the gelatin in cold water for at least 10 minutes.
2. Beat the cream foamy in a chilled metal bowl, and place it in the fridge.
3. Beat the egg yolks and cinnamon foamy.
4. Bring sugar and water to a boil in a small pan, occasionally clean the interior walls with a brush that has been dipped in water.
5. At 239°F, take a sugar sample (p. 232). If you don't have a thermometer, pour the boiling sugar syrup evenly into the egg batter while continuously beating with a whisk. Lift the gelatin leaf out of the water and add it to the egg batter. Beat the egg foam at a middle speed until it is about 68°F.
6. Use a ladle to fold the whipped cream into the batter, with the orange peel and nuts. Pour the batter into molds, and freeze.

Fruit Parfait (Mousse Glacé)

You can use all sorts of berries and fruits in a mousse glace. Try raspberries, strawberries, wild strawberries, blueberries, cloudberries, lingonberries, cranberries, green apple, rose hips, blackberry, gooseberry, buckthorn, black and red currants, amarelle cherries, morello cherries, plums, pineapple, mango, papaya, kiwi, and melon.

Try adding liquor to enhance the fruit or berry parfait. 2 – 4 cl (1½-3 tbsp) is enough, and you won't need to lessen the sugar content, the parfait will still freeze.

I recommend kirschwasser (cherry brandy) with strawberries, pineapple, morello cherries, or plums. Eau de vie au framboise is excellent in raspberry parfait. Calvados in apple parfait and au de vie au poires Williams in the pear parfait. Cloudberry liqueur tastes great in cloudberry parfait, gin with lingonberry parfait, and use vodka to spike the cranberry parfait.

You have the option to add 25 g (5 tsp) freshly squeezed lemon juice if you want to add some acidity. This particular recipe calls for warm beaten meringue. If you want to use the Italian meringue instead, see page 230, and replace with 190 g (3 cups) Italian meringue. You can store it in the freezer, and thaw the amount that you need.

1 gelatin leaf (2 g)
500 g (2 cups) whipping cream
60 g (¼ cup) egg white
5 g (1 tsp) freshly squeezed lemon juice
125 g (1 cup) powdered sugar
300 g (1 1/5 cup) fruit purée with 10% sugar

1. Soak the gelatin leaf in cold water for at least 10 minutes. Beat the cream foamy in a chilled metal bowl, and place it in the fridge.
2. Beat egg whites, lemon juice, and powdered sugar in a small bowl. Place the mix over a little pan with boiling how water, and heat it while continuously stirring the mix until it reaches 104–122°F.
3. Remove the bowl from the water bath and beat the batter at medium speed, until the meringue is cold, 68°F. (Always use the medium speed, otherwise the meringue will get dense and smeary, and the parfait will be heavy instead of light and fluffy).
4. Transfer the gelatin leaf to a pan with 1/5 cup of the fruit purée, heat to 113–122°F. Use a ladle to fold the mix into the meringue and add the rest of the fruit purée. Add the whipped cream, and then the lemon juice, and alcohol, if you decide to use it.
5. Fill molds and freeze as quickly as possible.

Good to Know When Beating Egg Whites to Meringue

It is important to fill the egg whites with as much air as possible. Therefore, beat the eggs with large movements fairly slowly in the beginning. Once the egg whites turn elastic, you can increase the speed to distribute the air evenly.

If you lower the pH-value from about 9.3 to the protein's isolectrical level, 4.5, the surface tension in the egg white will decrease, which contributes to a more stabilized foam, even when heated. Therefore, I often add a little bit of lemon juice, vinegar, or cream of tartar when I beat the egg whites. If you add salt it will affect the foam stability in a negative way, and you will need to beat the egg whites for a longer time.

Sabayon Glacé Semi-Freddo

3 gelatin leaves (6 g)
500 g (2 cups) whipping cream
240 g (1 cup) egg yolks
250 g (1 cup) marsala wine
250 g (1¼ cups) sugar

1. Soak the gelatin leaves in cold water for at least 10 minutes. Beat the cream foamy in a chilled metal bowl, and place it in the fridge.
2. Beat the egg yolks with wine and sugar in a metal bowl. Place it over a simmering water bath, but don't exceed 194°F, because the egg yolks will begin to coagulate at that temperature. Beat until you have firm foam. The eggs begin to bind at 185°F. If you don't have a thermometer, do a rose test or a ladle test (p.25).
3. Remove the water bath, and lift the gelatin leaves from the water and add them to the sabayon, stir until they have dissolved completely. Beat the

sabayon until the temperature is lowered to 68°F.

4. Fold the whipped cream into the sabayon. Fill a pastry bag, and pipe into tall glasses. Freeze them for at least 6 hours before you serve the sabayon.

5. Temper the ice cream in the fridge and decorate with blue grapes.

Ice Cream Soufflé

Ice cream soufflé is a light and fluffy parfait. Fill a soufflé mold that is about 8 inches in diameter, 1.2 inches tall with a piece of paper that is 2 inches high around it, staple the paper together. The paper is removed right before you serve the dessert. Dust it with cacao powder so that it resembles a warm soufflé, to add a little surprise element, no one will expect that it is cold. Ice cream soufflé used to be really popular back in the day. If you make it correctly, it is easy to make this delicious dessert.

Cloudberry soufflé with cloudberry coulis, or lingonberries used to be popular when I was young, as were other classic combination with Grand Marnier, strawberries, and raspberries.

MANGO SOUFFLÉ WITH BLACK CURRANT RIPPLE

Mango coulis with 750 g (approx. 6 cups) mango (p. 227)
250 g (2 cups) black currants + 25 g (2 tbsp) sugar (200 g, approx. ⅘ cup purée)
1 batch of the strawberry soufflé ice cream (on this page), but replace the purée with mango purée
2 cl (1½ tbsp) light rum
6 biscuits (¼ batch biscuit cuiller, p. 225)
1 batch spun sugar (p. 232)
cacao powder

1. Make the mango coulis.
2. Mix currants with sugar, strain through a sieve.
3. Fill a soufflé dish, about 8 inches in diameter, with 2 inches high paper around it.
4. Make the soufflé ice cream and add rum. Add half of the black currant purée, and stir the batter haphazardly to create a marble pattern.
5. Dip the biscuits in the black currant purée. Layer parfait with broken

biscuits in the dish, and smooth the surface. Freeze for at least 6 hours.

6. Make the spun sugar. Temper the frozen soufflé in the fridge for 30 minutes.

7. Dust the soufflé with cacao powder, and decorate with spun sugar, just like in the photo. Serve with mango coulis.

SOUFFLÉ GLACÉ AU FRAISE

This ice cream soufflé is very light and delicious and it can be varied with various fruit purées, i.e. raspberry, mango, blackberry, etc.

1 gelatin leaf (2 g)
400 g (1¾ cups) whipping cream

250 g (1 cup) fruit purée out of ripe strawberries with 10% sugar
100 g (⅖ cup) egg whites
25 g + 225 g (2 tbsp + 1⅛ cups) sugar
15 g (1 tbsp) freshly squeezed lemon juice
100 g (⅖ cup) water
optional: 2 cl (1½ tbsp) kirschwasser (cherry brandy)
8 biscuits (¼ batch biscuit cuiller, p. 225)
100 g (⅖ cup) strawberry purée with 10% sugar
spun sugar (p. 232)
strawberries, dipped in caramel (p. 124)
strawberry coulis made with 500 g (4 cups) strawberries (see page 227)

1. Whether you are using a large soufflé dish, or several smaller molds, cover the edges with paper. Staple together.
2. Soak the gelatin leaf in cold water for at least 10 minutes.
3. Beat the cream foamy in a cold metal bowl. Place it in the fridge.
4. Mix the cleaned strawberries with sugar into a purée.
5. Beat the egg whites with 25 g (2 tbsp) sugar and the lemon juice, at a medium speed, until you have foam.
6. Boil water with 225 g (1⅛ cup) sugar in a little pan, while you brush the inside walls with a brush that has been dipped in cold water. When the sugar solution is 251.6°F (use a thermometer, or make a sugar sample, p. 232), pour it into the meringue in a thin stream, while you beat it with a whisk constantly, lower the speed and beat it cold, 68°F.
7. Heat ½ dl (⅕ cup) of the fruit purée with the gelatin leaf (after you drain off excess water) to 104–122°F. Add the rest of the purée, and stir. Beat it into the meringue. Then, add the whipped cream, and the optional alcohol (if you don't have kirschwasser (cherry brandy), leave the alcohol out, there is no good replacement for it).
8. Pour a little bit of the soufflé batter into the bottom of the dish/dishes, dip the biscuits in strawberry purée and place them in the batter haphazardly. Layer soufflé batter and biscuits until the dish/dishes are full. Freeze for at least 6 hours.
9. Decorate with spun sugar and caramel dipped strawberries. Serve with strawberry coulis.

Soufflé Glacé au Grand Marnier

This is a classic ice cream soufflé. This is how I make a soufflé that is extra light in texture.

600 g (2½ cup) whipping cream
1 gelatin leaf (2 g)
1 orange
100 g (⅓ cup) simple sugar syrup (p. 44)
100 g (⅖ cup) egg yolk
125 g (approx. ½ cup) Grand Marnier, red
8 biscuits (¼ batch biscuit cuiller, p. 225)
⅕ cup Grand Marnier to use for dipping the biscuits
cacao powder
fresh berries or fruit salad to serve with the soufflé

1. Cover the edges of the soufflé dish/dishes with paper. Staple together.
2. Beat the cream foamy in a chilled metal bowl, and place in the fridge. Soak the gelatin in cold water for at least 10 minutes.
3. Wash the orange, and grate the outermost layer of the peel. Beat sugar syrup, egg yolks, and orange zest in a metal bowl.
4. Place the bowl over a pot with simmering water (about 194°F), Beat vigorously until the batter turns creamy. Remove the pot from the stove and use a thermometer to check the temperature. It should be 185°F. If you don't have a thermometer, do a rose test or a ladle test (p. 25).
5. Lift the gelatin out of the water and add it to the batter. Dissolve the gelatin with half of the liquor to 104-122°F. Beat into the egg foam, and fold the whipped cream and the remaining liquor into a fluffy mass.
6. Pour a little bit of soufflé batter into the bottom of the dish/dishes, dip the biscuits in Grand Marnier, and place them into the batter haphazardly. Layer soufflé batter and biscuits until the dish/dishes are full. Freeze for at least 6 hours.
7. Carefully remove the paper, and dust the soufflé with cacao batter. Serve with fresh berries, or a delicious fruit salad. A fruit coulis will complement the soufflé as well.

Biscuit Glacé Vanilla

When I used to be a young *pâtissier*, biscuit glacé was a common dessert. It was usually made in square dishes. First one would add a strawberry soufflé with marinated biscuits or macaroons in the middle. Once it was frozen, the dish would be filled with ginger parfait, or any other matching flavor. After the biscuit glacé was frozen again, the soufflés were removed from the dishes, cut into slices, and they were served with fruit coulis that would complement the soufflé. This basic mass can be flavored with coffee, chocolate, nougat, gianduja, liqueur, or any other type of liquor, etc.

Pâte à Bomb:
1 gelatin leaf (2 g)
500 g (2 cups) whipping cream
120 g (½ cup) egg yolk
200 g (1 cup) sugar
80 g (⅓ cup) water
1 vanilla pod, split and scraped

Italian meringue (You'll have 125 g of meringue when it is done. You can also make a warm beaten meringue if you think it is too much work to create sugar syrup, but the meringue won't be as light and fluffy):

40 g (⅙ cup) egg whites
80 g (⅖ cup) sugar
5 g (1 tsp) freshly squeezed lemon juice
30 g (2 tbsp) water

1. Soak the gelatin leaf in cold water for at least 10 minutes.
2. Beat the cream foamy in a chilled metal bowl, and store it in the fridge.
3. Make the Italian meringue out of the egg whites, sugar, lemon juice, and water (p. 230).
4. Beat the egg yolks to light foam.
5. Bring sugar, water, vanilla pod, and seeds to a boil in a little pan, until the solution is 239°F. If you don't have a thermometer, do a sugar sample (p. 232). Remove the vanilla pods and set them aside.
6. Mix the egg yolks with the boiling sugar syrup while beating constantly with a whisk. Add the gelatin leaf to the egg foam. Beat at medium speed until the batter cools down to 68°F.
7. Fold the whipped cream into the yolk foam with a ladle. Then add the whipped cream and the meringue and any optional flavoring, according to the same principals as with the parfait, only this is a much lighter type of parfait. Freeze for at least 6 hours.

Biscuit Glacé for Fruits and Berries, Variations

Make the same way you make biscuit glacé with vanilla, but also add fruit purée.

Pâte à Bomb:
1 gelatin leaf (2 g)

120 g (½ cup) egg yolks
175 g (⁹⁄₁₀ cup) sugar
80 g (⅓ cup) water
250 g (1 cup) fruit purée with 10% sugar
500 g (2 cups) whipped cream

Italian meringue (p. 230):
60 g (¼ cup) egg whites
5 g (1 tsp) freshly squeezed lemon juice
125 g (⅗ cup) sugar
60 g (4 tbsp) water

There are many ways you can vary a biscuit glacé. Here are some classics:

Carème: orange, nougat, and Grand Marnier.
Bénédictine: strawberry, and Bénédictine liqueur.
Tortoni: vanilla and coffe.
Napolitaine: nougat, strawberry, and vanilla.

Cassata Mousse

Cassata is a semifreddo. It is mostly used as filling in various desserts. Cassata Napolitana is a classic, delicious combination. An ice cream bomb dish is filled with a 0.4 inch layer of vanilla ice cream batter, let it freeze. Then add a 0.4 inch layer of raspberry ice cream batter, and freeze. Then add another layer of pistachio or chocolate ice cream. Fill with cassata mousse. The bomb is removed from the dish, and it is then cut up into elegant pieces that are delicious to serve with amaretti biscuits. This is a huge hit in Switzerland.

Day 1
100 g (⅗ cup) candied fruit, cut into small cubes.
50 g (⅕ cup) light rum
60 g (⅗ cup) sliced almonds
10 g (4 tsp) powdered sugar
1 tsp rum
50 g (⅓ cup) caramelized pistachios (p. 228)

1. Soak the fruit in the liquor.
2. Preheat the oven to 400°F.
3. Mix the sliced almonds with powdered sugar, and moisten with a little bit of rum.
4. Roast the sliced almonds until they turn golden brown, while stirring occasionally.

Day 2
500 g (2 cups) whipping cream
90 g (⅖ cup) egg whites
30 g (2 ½ tbsp) sugar
5 g (1 tsp) fresh lemon juice
150 g (¾ cup) sugar
80 g (⅓ cup) water

1. Beat the cream foamy in a chilled metal bowl, and store it in the fridge.
2. Beat the egg whites, 30 g (2½ tbsp) sugar, and lemon juice until stiff peaks form.
3. Mix 150 g (¾ cup) sugar with water in a little pot. Bring to a boil, and occasionally brush the inside walls with a brush that has been moistened with water. Boil the sugar syrup to 249.8–251.6°F. Check with a thermometer, or take a sugar sample (p. 232).
4. Stir the sugar syrup into the firm meringue while continuously whipping it. Beat until it is 68°F. It has to be cold, or the mousse will cut.
5. First, fold the marinated fruit, the caramelized pistachios, and the sugar roasted almond into the batter, then fold the lightly whipped cream into the batter.
6. Use the mousse as filling in an ice cream bomb, or an ice cream cake.

Iced Coffee & Iced Chocolate

These delicacies are usually served year-round on the entire continent, and they should be available on Swedish menus as well. They should be thick in texture, and come served with a long spoon and a straw.

VIENNESE ICED COFFEE

This specialty coffee comes from Vienna, where people love whipped cream. Try one of these at the famous Hofzuckerbäcker Demel at Kohlmarkt in Vienna. At Piazza San Marco in Venice, people are often seen walking around with an iced coffee or iced chocolate in their hand.

The coffee:
500 g (2 cups) water
50 g (½ cup) espresso beans, preferably French
2 g (2 tsp) Nescafé, dark roast
60 g (⅓ cup) sugar

1. Brew the espresso with the freshly ground espresso beans and the water. Stir the Nescafé and sugar into the brew until they dissolve. Quickly cool the beverage to 39.2°F, cover with plastic wrap and place in the fridge. The coffee can be stored in the fridge for 3 days.
2. Place two big scoops of vanilla ice cream in 6 chilled glasses.
3. Fill up with the cold coffee blend and stir with a spoon until you have a thick texture.

4. Garnish with lightly whipped cream, dust some cacao powder over it, and place a few coffee beans on top.
5. Serve this refreshing summer drink with some sort of chewy almond cookie, or orange tuiles.

VIENNESE ICED CHOCOLATE

Make a classic French hot chocolate, just like at the French pastry shops:

500 g (2 cups) milk
50 g (⅕ cup) water
60 g (⅓ cup) sugar
115 g (approx. ½ cup) dark chocolate, preferably Valrhona Grand Cru Araguani 74% kakao, finely chopped

Day 1
1. Cook milk, water, and sugar in a pot. Beat the blend until the sugar has dissolved entirely. Remove the pot from the stove. Add the finely chopped chocolate, and stir until it dissolves.
2. Mix with a stick blender to an emulsion. If you want to serve classic hot chocolate, you can pour it into warm cups, and garnish with lightly whipped cream, consisting of 60 g (⅓ cup) of sugar per liter (4 ¼ cup) of whipped cream. The whipped cream makes it a Viennese hot chocolate.
3. Iced chocolate: Chill the drink to 39.2°F. Cover with plastic wrap, and store in the fridge. You can store the chocolate drink for 3 days in the fridge.
4. Make half a batch of the vanilla ice cream (p. 32).

Day 2
1. Freeze the batter in the ice cream machine.
2. Beat 250 g (1 cup) cream with 15 g (1 ¼ tbsp) sugar in a chilled metal bowl until you have smooth foam. Cover with plastic wrap, and store in the fridge. Always cover whipped cream, as it easily absorbs other flavors in the fridge.
3. Place two big scoops of vanilla ice cream into 6 chilled glasses, pour the cold chocolate over the ice cream, and stir with a spoon until the blend turns viscous and thick.
4. Garnish with whipped cream, dust with cacao, preferably Valrhona red-brown cacao powder, which is better than most other brands.

Ice Cream as an Appetizer

There is no rule that says that ice cream has to be served at the end of a course. Add some salt, spices, and "foody" flavors, and surprise your guests with a delicious ice cream they never had before.

Foie Gras Ice Cream

1 gelatin leaf (2 g)
250 g (1 cup) milk
60 g (¼ cup) egg yolk
50 g (¼ cup) sugar
125 g (approx. ½ cup) duck liver terrine (buy it ready)
2 cl (1 ½ tbsp) cognac
2 cl (1 ½ tbsp) red port
fleur de sel and ground white pepper

1. Soak the gelatin leaf in cold water for at least 10 minutes.
2. Make a traditional crème anglaise with milk, egg yolks, and sugar (p. 32).
3. Lift the gelatin out of the water and add it to the crème, stir until it dissolves.
4. Add the terrine, and alcohol, a pinch of salt, and freshly ground white pepper. Mix until you have a smooth blend, and strain through a chinois or a fine mesh sieve.
5. Rapidly chill the mass to 39.2°F. Store in the fridge for at least 12 hours.
6. Freeze the ice cream in an ice cream machine. Don't freeze it for too long or it will crystallize.

Lobster Ice Cream

Use the same crème anglaise recipe as for the foie gras ice cream, but replace the duck liver terrine with 150 g (approx. ⅗ cup) of lobster coulis (p. 78), and replace the port with Madeira. Add some extra spice with cayenne pepper.

Truffle Ice Cream

2 gelatin leaves (2 g)
350 g (1 ½ cups) whipping cream
350 g (1 ½ cups) milk
10 g chopped truffle, preferably fall truffle
20 g (3 tsp) honey
2 cl (1 ½ tbsp) red port
200 g (⅘ cup) egg yolk
100 g (½ cup) sugar
optional: a drop of fine truffle oil
salt, and a pinch of freshly ground white pepper.

1. Soak the gelatin in water.
2. Bring cream, milk, the chopped truffle, salt, white pepper, and honey to a boil. Cover with a lid, and allow the blend to sit for 15 minutes, before you strain it to remove the truffle. Save the truffle, and soak it in port wine overnight.
3. Beat egg yolks and sugar, and add the milk blend, beat and pour back into the pot.
4. Heat the batter to 185°F, while continuously stirring it. If you don't have a thermometer, do a rose test or a ladle test (p. 25).
5. Add the gelatin leaves to the ice cream batter, stir until they dissolve. Mix vigorously with a stick blender.
6. Strain through a chinois or a fine mesh sieve.
7. Rapidly chill the batter to 39.2°F. Allow it to stand in the fridge overnight.
8. The next day, freeze the batter in an ice cream machine. Stir the marinated truffle into the frozen ice cream.

White Asparagus Ice Cream

White asparagus is a lovely spring vegetable. You can also use green asparagus in this recipe. It will turn out delicious, but the flavor will be very different than if you use white asparagus.

500 g (approx. 2 cups) asparagus purée made with about 1000 g (7 ½ cup) of fresh asparagus
2 gelatin leaves (4 g)
120 g (½ cup) egg yolks
200 g (1 cup) sugar
100 g (¾ cup) peeled sweet almonds
350 g (1 ½ cups) whipping cream
150 g (⅗ cup) milk
1 lemon
50 g (2 ½ tbsp) orange blossom honey
5 g (1 tsp) fleur de sel
15 g (1 tbsp) fresh lemon juice

1. Peel the asparagus and cut off a good chunk of the bottom part.
2. Boil the asparagus soft in 2 liters (8 cups) of water with 20 g (4 tsp) salt, 6 sugar cubes, and the juice from one lemon. Strain them, and mix in a blender, then strain the purée through a fine mesh sieve.
3. Soak the gelatin in cold water for at least 10 minutes.
4. Lightly beat the egg yolks with the sugar. Bring water to a boil and blanch the almonds, then rinse them with cold water, and remove the peels.
5. Place the almonds in a pot with the milk, cream, and the salt.
6. Add the peel from a clean lemon, and the honey. Bring everything to a boil, and remove the lemon peel from the blend to prevent the flavor from becoming too potent. Pour the blend over the egg yolks and heat to 185°F, or do a rose test or a ladle test (p. 25). Mix the batter vigorously with a stick blender. Strain it through a chinois or a fine mesh sieve.
7. Lift the gelatin leaves out of the water and mix into the ice cream batter, stir until it dissolves. Add the asparagus purée, the lemon juice, and mix vigorously with a stick blender. Rapidly chill to 39.2°F. Allow to sit in the fridge overnight.
8. The following day, freeze the batter in the ice cream machine.

Corn Ice Cream

1 gelatin leaf (2 g)
250 g (1 cup) milk
60 g (¼ cup) egg yolks
80 g (⅖ cup) sugar
500 g (approx. 3 cups) canned corn
about 5 g (1 tsp) fleur de sel
15 g (1 tbsp) fresh lemon juice

1. Soak the gelatin in cold water.
2. Make a crème anglaise with milk, egg yolks, and sugar (see vanilla ice cream base, p. 32).
3. Remove the gelatin leaf from the water and add to the cream, stir until it dissolves. Strain the cream through a chinois or a fine mesh sieve.
4. Mix corn, salt, and lemon juice into the cream. Strain through a chinois,

or a fine mesh sieve. Rapidly cool the batter to 39.2°F. Store in the fridge overnight.

5. The following day, freeze the batter in an ice cream machine.

POTATO ICE CREAM

600 g (almond potatoes (500 g, approx. 2 cups purée)
about 5 g (1 tsp) fleur de sel
5 g (1 tsp) fresh lemon juice

1. Peel and boil the potatoes soft, and allow the steam to dissipate.
2. Press the potatoes through a ricer, and mix them with the same amount of crème anglaise as is used in the corn ice cream. Add salt and lemon juice, and strain through a chinois or a fine mesh sieve.
3. Rapidly chill to 39.2°F. Store in the fridge overnight.
4. The following day, freeze the batter in an ice cream machine.

CAULIFLOWER ICE CREAM

750 g cauliflower (500 g, approx. 2 cups purée)
about 5 g (1 tsp) salt
about 5 g (1 tsp) freshly squeezed lemon juice

1. Wash the cauliflower and remove the leaves and core. Cut into little cauliflower florets.
2. Boil the florets soft in lightly salted water. Drain the water through a colander. Mix the cauliflower into purée.
3. Mix the purée with the same amount of crème anglaise as in used in the corn ice cream. Add salt and lemon juice. Strain through a chinois, or a fine mesh sieve.
4. Rapidly chill to 39.2°F. Store in the fridge overnight.
5. The following day, freeze the batter in an ice cream machine.

FENNEL ICE CREAM

750 g fresh fennel (500 g, approx. 2 cups purée)
2 whole star anise
about 5 g (1 tsp) salt
about 5 g (1 tsp) freshly squeezed lemon juice

1. Clean the fennel and boil it soft in lightly salted water with the star anise. Drain off the water through a strainer. Mix to a purée, and weigh it so that you have 17.6 oz of it.
2. Mix the purée with the same amount of crème anglaise as is used in the corn ice

cream. Add salt and lemon juice. Strain through a chinois, or a fine mesh sieve.
3. Rapidly chill to 39.2°F. Store in the fridge overnight.
4. The following day, freeze the batter in an ice cream machine.

AVOCADO ICE CREAM

750 g ripe avocado (500 g, approx. 2 cups purée)
30 g (6 tsp) freshly squeezed lime juice
salt
green Tabasco

1. Cut the avocados in half and remove the pits, release the pulp from the peel with a spoon.

2. Mix the avocado pulp with lime juice (to prevent oxidation, and to prevent it from turning brown). Mix with the same amount of crème anglaise as is used in the corn ice cream. Add lime juice, salt and drop of green Tabasco. Strain through a chinois, or a fine mesh sieve. Rapidly chill to 39.2°F. Store in the fridge overnight.
3. The following day, freeze the batter in an ice cream machine.

Tip!
If you want to serve the avocado ice cream as a dessert, leave out the Tabasco and salt.

LOBSTER ICE CREAM WITH HERBS

This exclusive appetizer is delicious and is excellent when you want to surprise a group of good friends.

Serves 8 people

Day 1

Lobster Coulis:

2 small lobsters (alive), each 250 g
20 g (4 tsp) sea salt
50 g (approx. ⅕ -⅖ cup) chopped shallots
50 g (approx. ⅕ -⅖ cup) finely chopped carrot
50 g (approx. ⅕ -⅖ cup) chopped cerery root
10 g (approx. 1 tbsp) crushed garlic
50 g (⅕ cup) rapeseed oil
⅖ cup cognac
125 g (approx. ½ cup) pulp from canned cherry tomatoes
125 g (½ cup) dry white wine
cayenne pepper

1. Immerse the lobsters in boiling hot water, and cook for 1 minute. Chill in ice cold water.
2. Break off the claws and remove the heads.
3. Bring 68 oz of water and the salt to a boil. Boil the bodies for 6 minutes, and boil the claws for 5 minutes. Remove them from the water and allow them to cool off a little bit. Remove the shells from the bodies, it is easier if they are still a little bit warm. Crack the claws with a knife and get the meat out. Place all the lobster meat in a plastic bag and store in the fridge.
4. Mix the lobster shells, shallots, carrots, celery root, and garlic into purée.
5. Heat the oil in a big pot and sauté the purée for 5 minutes while stirring it continuously. Add cognac, light a match and flambé the shells (be careful when you set them on fire). Add the tomatoes, and keep frizzling the blend until all the water has evaporated. Add the wine, and allow the blend to simmer, covered, for 20 minutes.
6. Strain through a sieve and press vigorously with the backside of a spoon to press out as much fond as possible.
7. Boil the fond until about 150 g remain (⅗ cup), add cayenne pepper.

Ice Cream:

1 gelatin leaf (2 g)
100 g (½ cup) sugar
100 g (⅖ cup) egg yolks
150 g hummer coulis
250 g (⅗ cup) whipping cream
fleur de sel
cayenne pepper
5 – 10 g (1 -2 tsp) fresh lemon juice

1. Soak the gelatin leaf in cold water for at least 10 minutes.
2. Beat yolks and sugar fluffy. Bring lobster coulis and cream to a boil. Pour the boiling coulis blend over the egg yolk and sugar and mix thoroughly.
3. Heat the blend to 185°F, while stirring it continuously. If you don't have a thermometer, do a rose test or a ladle test (p. 25).
4. Add the gelatin leaf to the ice cream batter. Add salt, cayenne pepper, and lemon juice, until you are satisfied with the taste.
5. Strain through a chinois or a fine mesh sieve, and mix the ice cream smooth with a stick blender. Rapidly chill the batter to 39.2°F, cover with plastic wrap and store in the fridge overnight.

Day 2

1. Freeze the batter in an ice cream machine.
2. You can serve this ice cream in cocktail glasses, and place about 50 g of fresh herbs (cleaned) in the bottom of each glass.
3. Use a spoon that has been dipped in hot water to shape the ice cream into eggs. Sprinkle with a little bit of fleur de sel and freshly ground black pepper.

Beet Carpaccio with Beet Sorbet and Grated Horseradish

Serves 6-8 people

1 batch of the beet sorbet (p. 56)
200 g (1½ cup) fresh beets
1 bunch of chives
about 100 g horseradish

Vinaigrette:
6 tbsp virgin olive oil
2 tbsp balsamic vinegar
salt and freshly ground white pepper

1. Make the beet sorbet and store it in the freezer. Put it in the fridge for 10 minutes before you serve it, if it is too hard.
2. Peel and slice the beets as thinly as possible, and spread them into a lovely pattern on chilled plates.
3. Make vinaigrette with oil, vinegar, salt, and pepper, and brush it over the beets on the plates.
4. Spread some finely chopped chives and a little bit of grated horseradish over the beets.
5. Use a spoon that has been dipped in hot water to shape the ice cream into beautiful eggs. You can serve this nice vegetarian appetizer right away with delicious bread and butter.

Almond Potato Ice Cream with Fried Anchovies and Fried Egg

This creation constitutes a nice contrast between the loose, crispy egg, the salty anchovies, and the refreshing ice cream.

Make the ice cream at least 4 hours before freezing it, or make it the day before.

Serves 8 people

1 batch of the potato ice cream (p. 75)
grated white bread, so called mie de pain
32 anchovy filets, authentic, not herring
fillets
flour
2 eggs
1 baking potato
1 liter (4¼ cups) cooking oil
fleur de sel
1 bunch of garden parsley
8 absolutely fresh eggs
1 pot of basil
1 lemon

1. Freeze the ice cream in an ice cream machine, until it has a smooth texture, and store the ice cream in the freezer. You may need to place it in the fridge for a few minutes before you serve it, if it is too hard.

2. Grate a day old white bread on grater, and sieve it through a fine mesh sieve. Drain off excess liquid from the anchovy fillets, and cover them in flour.

3. Beat the eggs, dip the fillets in them, then turn the fillets in the bread until they are covered in it. Place the fillets on a chilled plate and allow them to stiffen a bit.

4. Clean, and cut the potatoes into strips as thin as matches (pommes allumettes in technical jargon) and rinse them in running water for 5 minutes, to rinse away the starch.

5. Dry the potato strips thoroughly, and fry them in oil (356°F) until they are golden brown. Place them on paper towel that will soak up grease, and sprinkle with fleur de sel.

6. Rinse and dry the parsley. Cut it and fry for a moment, but make sure that it doesn't turn brown. Place on paper towel, and sprinkle with fleur de sel.

7. Crack each of the 8 eggs into individual cups.

8. Fry the anchovy filets in batches so that the oil doesn't get cold. Rapidly fry the basil leaves until they become transparent. Place the anchovies and basil on paper towels in the heated oven (167°F), and leave the oven door ajar, so that they are warm when you serve them.

9. Pour one egg at a time into the oil, and turn them back and forth with two spoons, for 1 minute until they have a nice color (don't let them get thoroughly cooked, they should be loose inside). Place them on paper towels and sprinkle with fleur de sel.

10. Place the potato strips on plates, and use a spoon that has been dipped in hot water to shape the ice cream into beautiful eggs. Place a basil leaf on top, then the anchovies, the fried basil, a lemon wedge, and the fried egg with som fleur de sel.

Asparagus Ice Cream with Strawberry Jelly

This is the ultimate way to enjoy white asparagus, beautifully presented as an ice cream with fresh strawberry jelly.

Christer Alfredsson at Olof Viktors bakery in Glemminge has a true passion for asparagus, and he is willing to drive many miles to Germany, just to get a hold of the very best asparagus.

You can use the recipe below to make delicious jellies with other fruits and berries.

Serves about 8 people

1 batch of white asparagus ice cream (p. 74)
1 organically grown, beautiful red rose

Strawberry Jelly, about 3 cups:
6 gelatin leaves (12 g; always count on one leaf per ⅓ cup of juice)
900 g (7¼ cups) ripe strawberries
70 g (⅓ cup) sugar

1. Strawberry Jelly: Soak the gelatin leaves in cold water for at least 10 minutes.
2. Remove any leaves from the strawberries, and rinse them, before you mix them with sugar in a bowl. Place it in a simmering water bath for 45 – 60 minutes.
3. Strain the juice through a fine straining cloth. Measure the juice.
4. Add the gelatin leaves, and stir until they dissolve.
5. Fill 8 glasses with jelly, and place them in the fridge until the jelly has a firm texture.
6. Remove the glasses from the fridge about 15 – 20 minutes before you serve the jelly, so that it isn't too cold.
7. Use a spoon that has been dipped in warm water to shape the ice cream into a beautiful egg that you serve with the jelly. Garnish with a rose petal.

FOIE GRAS ICE CREAM WITH PINK CHAMPAGNE JELLY

Serves 8 people

1 batch of foie gras ice cream (p. 74)
1 batch of apple chips (page 227)
fleur de sel
White pepper

Pink champagne jelly:
4 gelatin leaves (about 8 g)
370 g (approx. 1½ cups) pink champagne
150 g (¾ cup) sugar

1. Soak the gelatin leaves in plenty of cold water for at least 10 minutes.
2. Boil ⅖ cup of wine with the sugar. Lift the gelatin leaves out of the water and add to the wine and sugar blend. Stir until the gelatin has dissolved.
3. Add the remaining wine, and mix well, remove any foam with a teaspoon.
4. Pour the jelly into 8 glasses and place in the fridge so that it solidifies.
5. Remove the jelly from the fridge 15 – 20 minutes before you serve it, so that it isn't too cold. The same goes for the ice cream; if it is too hard, place it in the fridge until it softens.
6. Shape a beautiful egg out of the ice cream with a spoon that has been dipped in warm water.
7. Sprinkle the ice cream with a little bit of fleur de sel, freshly ground white pepper, and decorate with apple chips.
8. Serve with warm brioche.

Truffle Ice Cream on a Bed of Duck Liver Terrine

If you don't want to make your own duck liver terrine, buy one ready-made, but I always prefer to make my own. However, you will need to marinate it for 24 hours, bake it on day 2, and then allow the flavors to mature until day 3 before you serve it.

Serves 8 people

500 g fresh or frozen duck liver
5 g (1 tsp) fleur de sel
5 g (1 tsp) sugar
2 g (approx. ½ tsp) freshly ground white pepper
1 cl (2 tsp) Armagnac or cognac
2 cl (1½ tbsp) red port

Day 1
1. Use a small knife to remove any unwanted parts from the liver, such as possible blood vessels or tendons. Pick it into pieces.
2. Marinate the liver for 24 hours in the liquor, wine, and the spices.

Day 2
1. Preheat the oven to 225°F, and place a warm water bath (bain marie) inside.
2. Pack the duck liver into a 34 oz dish, preferably ceramic. Press firmly, and cut a piece of parchment paper to place over it, then cover with a lid.
3. Bake for exactly 20 minutes in the water bath in the oven.
4. Remove the dish from the water bath and allow it to cool off, with a weight on top of the paper. Place in the fridge for 24 hours before serving it.

Day 3
(If you don't have store bought terrine).
500 g duck liver terrine
fleur de sel, white pepper
1 batch of the truffle ice cream (p. 74)
truffle, 1 small can

1. Use a knife that has been dipped in warm water to cut the duck liver terrine into slices (1 slice per person). Sprinkle the slices with fleur de sel and freshly ground white pepper. Allow to stand for 10 minutes.
2. Soften the ice cream in the fridge if it is too hard when it comes out of the freezer. Shape it into beautiful eggs with a warm spoon.
3. Decorate the ice cream with a thin slice of truffle. Serve with warm brioche.

Melon Granite with Serrano Chips

My friend, Jan Theander, served this light, refreshing appetizer at Bullen in Malmö in the '70s when I was part of creating the menu. This succulent appetizer is a lovely marriage between the sweet granite and the delicate, salty chips. Perfect as a starter for a light summer meal, or works as a delectable snack.

Serves 8 people

200 g (approx. ¾ cup) Serrano ham, leaf-thin
    slices
1 batch of the melon granite (p. 63)

1. Preheat the oven to 175°F.
2. Place the ham slices on two trays covered with parchment paper, and dry them in the oven for 45 – 60 minutes.
3. Place 8 glasses in the freezer, fill them with granite, and stick Serrano chips into each glass.

Cucumber Granite with Fresh Smoked Salmon & Poached Egg

This is a wonderful and refreshing summer appetizer that is quick to make.

Serves 8 people

1 batch of the cucumber granite (p. 63)
200 g (approx. ¾ cup) freshly smoked salmon
    of high quality
8 eggs for poaching (see cauliflower ice cream
    with bleak roe and Poached Egg, p. 94)
chives

Place slices of salmon on plates, and use a spoon to the spread granite in the middle of the plate. Decorate with the egg and chives.

Kvibille Ice Cream with Caramelized Walnuts and Beet Chips with Cloudberry Compote

I created this cheese dessert during a guest appearance at the beautiful restaurant, Sundmans, in Helsinki. Sundmans is located steps away from the market hall, and it boasts a Michelin star. Serve small portions of this ice cream

Serves 8 – 12 people

Beet Chips:
2 large beets
⅔ cup simple sugar syrup (p. 44)

Slice the beets as thinly as possible, and soak them in the sugar syrup for a moment. Dry them in the oven on a nonstick silicone baking mat, or on a baking sheet on a tray at 175°F for 90 minutes, until they are dry.

Cloudberry Compote:
1 gelatin leaf (2 g)
375 g (1½ cups) milk
125 g (⅗ cup) sugar
25 g (3½ tsp) honey
175 g (¾ cup) Kvibille gräddädel
*   (a type of Swedish blue cheese,*
*   similar to the French Roquefort)*
125 g (approx. ½ cup) plain yogurt
30 g (6 tsp) fresh lemon juice
100 g (¾ cup) of caramelized walnuts
*   (page 228)*

1. Soak the gelatin leaf in plenty of cold water for at least 10 minutes.
2. Bring milk, sugar, and honey to a boil. Remove the saucepan from the heat. Lift the gelatin leaf out of the water and add to the milk blend. Stir until the gelatin has dissolved.
3. Add the remaining ingredients and mix with a stick blender until you have a smooth ice cream batter.
4. Make sure that the ice cream is soft and smooth when you serve it. You may need to place it in the fridge for a few minutes before serving it, in case it is too hard right out of the freezer. Pour a spoonful of compote into each bowl, and shape a beautiful egg out of the ice cream with a spoon that has been dipped in warm water. Garnish with beet chips.

OLIVE OIL ICE CREAM WITH SERRANO CHIPS AND
TOMATO TARTAR ON TOASTED PEASANT BREAD

Serves 8 people

Olive Oil Ice Cream:
2 gelatin leaves (4 g)
200 g (1 ⅗ cups) powdered sugar
250 g (1 cup) extra virgin olive oil
100 g (½ cup) fresh lemon juice
30 g fresh basil, preferably Genoese
about 10 g (2 tsp) fleur de sel, or according to
*   preference*
500 g (approx. 2 cups) Greek yogurt, plain

1. Soak the gelatin in plenty of cold
   water for at least 10 minutes.
2. Mix all the ingredients, except for
   the yogurt and gelatin leaves, into a
   fine purée.
3. Mix the yogurt into the batter with a
   whisk. Take about 2 dl (⅘ cup) of
   the batter and heat to 122°F.
4. Lift the gelatin leaves out of the
   water, and drain them from the
   water.
5. Add the gelatin leaves to the warm
   yogurt and stir until they has
   dissolved. Reheat to 122°F, and mix
   into the ice cream batter with a
   whisk. Rapidly cool to 39.2°F.
6. Freeze the batter in an ice cream
   machine.

Make the Serrano chips (p. 89)

Tomato Tartar & Bread:
8 plum tomatoes
1 red chili
1 shallot
25 g (2 tbsp) sugar
fleur de sel and freshly ground black pepper
8 slices of high quality peasant bread
4 cloves of garlic
basil oil
1 bunch basil
100 g (approx. ¾ cup) black and green olives
*   with pits*

1. Blanch the tomatoes in boiling water,
   and chill them in ice water. Remove
   the peels with a small, sharp knife.
   Remove the core, and dry the
   tomatoes thoroughly. Cut them into
   little cubes. Place in a strainer to get
   rid of excess water.
2. Remove the core from the chili, and
   chop it finely. Finely chop the
   shallot, and mix with the chili and
   the tomato pulp. Season with sugar,
   salt, and pepper.
3. Toast the bread slices. Crush the
   peeled garlic cloves with a knife and
   finely chop them. Rub the bread

slices in the garlic. Sprinkle with
basil oil.

4. Distribute the tartar in little
   cookie cutters, lift the ring and
   place the ham next to them. Make
   sure that the ice cream is soft and
   supple.
5. Shape the ice cream into beautiful
   eggs with a spoon that has been
   dipped in water. Decorate with
   fresh basil, olives, and some fleur
   de sel.

CAULIFLOWER ICE CREAM WITH BLEAK ROE AND POACHED EGG

Serves 8 people

1 batch of the cauliflower ice cream (p.75)
200 g fish roe
⅘ cup white wine vinegar
10 eggs
1 liter (4¼ cups) water
1 large baking potato
2 cups canola oil
fleur de sel
1 red onion
1 bunch chives

1. Pour the roe into a sieve to get rid of liquid; this will make it easier to shape them into eggs later.
2. Pour the vinegar into a bowl and carefully crack the eggs into the vinegar. Let them sit in the vinegar for 30 minutes.
3. Bring water to a boil in a large pot, carefully add the eggs in the vinegar and simmer for about 1 minute, until they float to the surface. Don't let them become hardboiled. Immediately rinse them with cold water in the pot, until they have cooled off. Store them in the water until you serve them.
4. Peel and slice the potato thinly in a cutting machine, or use a cheese slice. Rinse the slices in cold water for at least 5 minutes to get rid of the starch. Dry them between sheets of paper towel. Fry the potato slices in the oil (356°F) until they turn golden brown. Place them on paper towels again, and sprinkle with fleur de sel (carefully, because the roe is salty). Place the potato chips on plates.
5. Finely chop the peeled red onion, and cut the chives into small pieces (save a few straws to decorate with).
6. Add an egg shape of the ice cream (shape with a spoon that has been dipped in warm water). Add a spoonful of roe and the poached egg next to it, then sprinkle with a little bit of fleur de sel. Spread red onion and chives over and decorate with a few chive straws.

Yellow Corn Ice Cream with Guacamole

This delectable vegetarian appetizer literally melts in your mouth. Guacamole and corn ice cream are both very popular in Mexico.

Serves 6 people

1 batch of the corn ice cream (p. 74)

Guacamole:
1 lime
1 red chilli
about 5 g (approx. ⅓ cup) fresh coriander
2 plum tomatoes
3 ripe avocados
salt and ground white pepper
2 tbsp extra virgin olive oil

1. Roll the lime back and forth before you squeeze it, it will make it easier for you to extract more juice.
2. Remove the core from the chili. Finely chop the chili and the coriander.
3. Blanch the tomatoes in boiling water and immediately soak them in ice water. Remove the peels, cut them in half and remove the seeds. Cut them into fine cubes.
4. Cut the avocados in half, remove the pits, and use a spoon to release the pulp from the peel. Mash the pulp with a fork with the other ingredients, and at the tomato pieces at the end. Carefully season with salt.
5. Shape 6 tartars with a little circle on the plates; rinse it in water in between each one.
6. If the ice cream is hard when you remove it from the freezer, place it in the fridge for a few minutes before you serve it so that it softens.
7. Shape the ice cream into beautiful eggs with a spoon that has been dipped in warm water. Place them on the tartars and sprinkle with salt flakes.

Strawberry and Tomato Bruschetta with Basil Yogurt Ice Cream

This refreshing appetizer can also be served as a dessert if you add a little bit of extra sugar. Make sure that the tomatoes and the strawberries are really ripe for best possible flavor. It will complement the basil ice cream well on a warm summer day.

Serves 6 people

1 batch of the basil yogurt ice cream (p. 42)
6 slices of peasant bread, the continental kind with air bubbles, preferably sourdough
⅔ cup olive oil, regular, use it for sautéing the bread
250 g (1⅓ cup) plum tomatoes
500 g (4 cups) strawberries
1 lemon, the juice
50 g (¼ cup) sugar
fleur de sel
⅕ cup of a high quality extra virgin olive oil
1 pot of basil, preferably Genoese
black pepper

1. Sauté the bread slices in olive oil, and place them on plates.
2. Remove the seeds from the tomatoes and cut them into fine cubes. Clean the strawberries and cut them into small pieces.
3. Mix tomatoes and strawberries with lemon juice, sugar, salt, olive oil, and a few basil leaves. Season with black pepper.
4. Place the bruschetta mix on top of the bread slices, and shape beautiful eggs out of the ice cream with a spoon that has been dipped in warm water. Garnish with basil leaves.

TOMATO SORBET SERVED IN A GLASS WITH A CELERY STALK LIKE A BLOODY MARY

Serves 8 people

Place 8 tall tumbler glasses in the freezer.
Make a batch of tomato sorbet (p. 60),
with a lot of spices, and place two scoops
of the sorbet in each glass. Use an ice
cream baller that has been dipped in
warm water. Pour 2 cl
(1½ tbsp) cold vodka into each glass,
sprinkle with freshly ground black pepper,
and stick a celery stalk into the sorbet.

Desserts

Beignet with Elderflower or Meadowsweet with Scented Geranium Ice Cream

This crispy dessert with its lightly scented ice cream is a pleasant surprise to the taste buds.

Serves 6 people

½ batch of the flower ice cream with geranium (p. 43)
12 elder flowers or meadowsweet
50 g (⅕ cup) cognac
25 g (2 tbsp) sugar
15 g (approx. 2 tbsp) vanilla sugar
1 batch of the quick fry batter (p. 111, beignet with zucchini flowers)
1 liter (4¼ cups) cooking oil
½ batch of the butter streusel (p. 224)
geraniums (citronella) to use as garnish
powdered sugar

Day 1
Make the ice cream batter.

Day 2
Freeze the batter in an ice cream machine.

1. Marinate the flowers in cognac, sugar, and vanilla sugar for about 30 minutes. Then place them on paper towels to dry off.
2. Make the fried batter. Heat the oil to 356°F. Coat the flowers in the batter, fry them golden brown, and place them on paper towels.
3. Spread a bed of butter streusel on the plates.
4. Form the ice cream into beautiful egg shapes with a spoon that has been dipped in warm water. Decorate with a flower.
5. Place the ice cream eggs on top of the butter streusel, and add the beignets. Dust with powdered sugar and serve right away.

BLACK CURRANT GRANITE WITH VANILLA POACHED PEACH

This delicious, flavorful dessert is very refreshing, and the contrast between the black currant granite and the soft, vanilla flavored peaches is exquisite. Unfortunately, we don't use black currants too often in Sweden.

Serves 6 people

1 batch of black currant granite (p. 64)
6 beautiful, ripe peaches
mint leaves to garnish with

Sugar Syrup:
1 vanilla pod, split and scraped
150 g (¾ cup) sugar
300 g (1¼ cups) water
300 g (1¼ cups) sweet dessert wine
100 g (⅔ cup) fresh lemon juice

1. Blanch the peaches in boiling water, immediately transfer them to ice water, and use a small knife to remove the peel.
2. Split the vanilla pod lengthwise and scrape out the seeds with a little knife.
3. Bring the vanilla pod, sugar, water, wine, and lemon juice to a boil in a pot, and simmer for 5 minutes. Add the peaches, bring to a boil, and set the pot aside, and let the peaches soak until they are completely soft when you insert a knife.
4. Chill the peaches in the solution in a cold water bath, allow them to sit in room temperature for at least 6 hours. You can even poach them a day earlier.
5. Remove the pits with pliers so that the peach looks intact.
6. Fill martini glasses with granite, and place the drained, cored peaches on top, and garnish with peppermint.

WHITE COFFEE ICE CREAM WITH ESPRESSO GRANITE

This luscious coffee dessert offers an explosive contrast between the aggressive espresso granite, and the mild, soft coffee ice cream. It's delicious to serve with an almond cookie, such as a vanilla macaroon.

Serves 6 people

Make a batch of the espresso granite (p. 64), and ½ batch of the white mocha ice cream (p. 39). Fill large frozen martini glasses with espresso granite, and press the granite towards the edges. Dip an ice cream baller in warm water and shape a large ice cream scoop, and place it in the center of the martini glass. Serve immediately.

TAHITIAN VANILLA ICE CREAM SERVED IN A CHOCOLATE TULIP

This is a simple, yet sophisticated way to serve good vanilla ice cream. You can also add warm chocolate sauce with it.

Serves 6 people

Day 1

Make half a batch of the vanilla ice cream with Tahitian vanilla pods (p. 32).

Day 2
1. Make a batch of chocolate tulips (p. 224).
2. Freeze the ice cream in the ice cream machine, and store it in the freezer.
3. Beat 100 g (⅖ cup) cream with 5 g (1 tsp) sugar until you have supple foam in a chilled bowl. Fill a paper cone with the whipped cream. Cut a small hole at the bottom.
4. Pipe a ball of cream onto each plate, and place the chocolate baskets on the plates, make sure that they are standing up.
5. Make sure that the ice cream is soft and supple, if you need to place it in the fridge a few minutes beforehand. Shape nice big scoops of it with an ice cream baller that has been dipped in warm water. Place the scoops in the chocolate tulips.

Piña Colada Sorbet with Pineapple Chips

This light and refreshing dessert is an excellent way to end a heavy meal, or just serve it as a refreshment on its own.

Serves 6 people

12 pineapple chips (p. 227)
1 batch of the piña colada sorbet (p. 49)
fresh peppermint

1. Make the pineapple chips a few hours beforehand, so they are dry and crispy.
2. Place 6 tall glasses in the freezer for a moment.
3. Fill the glasses with the freshly frozen sorbet (if it has been in the freezer for a long time, place it in the fridge for 30 minutes until it softens in texture) with an ice cream baller that has been dipped in warm water.
4. Decorate with chips and peppermint. Garnish with a vanilla pod if you want. Serve immediately.

BEIGNET WITH ZUCCHINI FLOWERS, AND LAVENDER & TAPIOCA SORBET

I tried my very first fried zucchini flowers from a street stand in Nice. It tasted yummy in the sunny city. Carefully open the flowers with a small knife and cut off the stem inside, about 0.6 inch from the mount, so that you have a piece to hold on to. Make little incisions on the flower all around so that it is ready to be fried. You can also use elderflowers, or meadowsweet.

Serves 6 people

Day 1
Make half a batch of the tapioca sorbet with tonka beans (p. 58), but replace the tonka beans with 20 g (approx. 5 tbsp) fresh lavender, or 5 g (1 tbsp) dried lavender.

Day 2
Make half a batch of the butter streusel (p. 224). Freeze the ice cream in the ice cream machine, and store it in the freezer.

18 small, fresh zucchini flowers
25 g (1¾ tbsp) Cointreau
25 g (1¾ tbsp) freshly squeezed orange juice
10 g + 25 g (4 tsp + 3⅓ tbsp) confectioners' sugar
1 liter (4¼ cups) cooking oil
fresh lavender flowers for decoration

Quick Fry Batter:
1 lemon, the zest
250 g (2 cups) plain flour
200 g (⅘ cup) water (95°F)
100 g (⅖ cup) pale ale
40 g (⅙ cup) egg yolk
5 g (1 tsp) salt
15 g (1 tbsp) rapeseed oil
5 g (1 tsp) vanilla sugar
60 g (¼ cup) egg whites
5 g (1 tsp) fresh lemon juice
25 g (2 tbsp) sugar

1. Mix the liqueur with the orange juice and 10 g (1½ tbsp) powdered sugar, marinate the zucchini flowers in the liqueur marinade for about 30 minutes.
2. Mix lemon zest with flour, tepid water, and the ale, until you have a smooth batter. Add egg yolks, salt, oil, vanilla sugar, and beat the batter with a whisk.
3. Beat the egg whites and lemon juice foamy, add 25 g (2 tbsp) sugar, and beat the foam firm.
4. Fold the fry batter into the egg whites with a ladle, until you have a light and fluffy mass.
5. Heat the cooking oil to 356°F.
6. Dry the zucchini flowers on paper towels until they are completely dry. Dip them in the batter and fry them golden brown, in two batches. Remove them from the cooking oil with a perforated ladle and place them on paper towels. Keep them warm in the oven at 200°F, on a tray with parchment paper.
7. Place the zucchini flowers on plates, and generously dust them with confectioners' sugar. Shape beautiful eggs out of the soft ice cream, and place them on a little bit of butter streusel, and decorate with lavender flowers.

Meadowsweet Sorbet with Strawberry Coulis and Fresh Berries

This light and refreshing ice cream dessert is a hit in the summer. Pair it with strawberry compote, and you'll have an excellent winter dessert.

Serves 6 people

About 500 g (4 cups) fresh berries (seasonal)
¼ batch of the butter streusel (p. 224)
if possible, fresh flowers to garnish with

1. Make a batch of the meadowsweet sorbet (p.55)
2. Make a batch of the strawberry coulis with 250 g (2 cups) strawberries (p.227).
3. Make a bed of butter streusel in the center of each plate.
4. Drizzle the plate with strawberry coulis, and serve the remaining coulis in a sauceboat.
5. Decorate the plates with berries.
6. Dip an ice cream scoop in warm water, and use it to shape beautiful eggs out of the sorbet. Place them on top of the streusel, and decorate with a flower (like in the photo) if you want.

Noisette Chocolate Cake with Vanilla Ice Cream

This exclusive dessert is elegant, yet seductive with its various layers and textures. The nutty chocolate bottom is a decadent contrast to the chocolate jelly, and the creamy vanilla ice cream. You don't need to add the gold leaf, but it will improve the aesthetic. Gold leaf (can be bought at frame stores) is edible, and has been used for garnishing exclusive chocolates for several hundred years.

Serves 12 people

Day 1

½ batch of the vanilla ice cream (p. 32)

Chocolate Hazelnut Biscuit:

55 g (approx. ⅓ cup) raw hazelnuts
110 g (½ cup) sugar
120 g (½ cup) eggs
40 g (⅖ cup) flour
40 g (⅖ cup) cocoa, preferably Valrhona
135 g (⅗ cup) butter
180 g (approx. ⅗ – ⅘ cup) egg whites
5 grams (1 tsp) fresh lemon juice
60 g (⅓ cup) sugar

1. Preheat the oven to 350°F.
2. Mix the hazelnuts with 55 g (¼ cup) of the sugar in a blender until you have a fine powder, a so called tpt *(tant pour tant)*.
3. Beat the eggs with the remaining sugar and the hazelnut flour until foamy, about 10 minutes.
4. Sift flour and cocoa onto a paper. Melt butter carefully, and allow it to cool down to 95°F.
5. Beat egg whites, lemon juice and a third of the sugar at medium speed, until it forms meringue, add another third of the sugar, and increase the speed on the whisk, add the remaining sugar, and beat to a firm meringue.
6. Use a ladle to carefully fold the egg foam into the batter, and then the cocoa flour blend. When everything is mixed, stir a large spoon of the mass into the butter and mix well. Beat the butter into the mass and carefully stir everything into a fluffy blend.
7. Spread the batter on a baking sheet on a tray with high edges. Bake for about 12 minutes, or until the mass springs back when you press on it. Transfer to a wire rack, and allow it to cool off. Cover in plastic wrap and place in the freezer.

Sugar Syrup for the Marinade:

125 g (⅗ cup) sugar
175 g (¾ cup) water
5 g (1 tsp) Nescafé, dark roast
40 g (approx. ⅕ cup) cognac

Bring water, sugar, and Nescafé to a boil, and allow the blend to cool off. Add the liquor.

Cooked milk chocolate mousse with caramel:

2 gelatin leaves (4 g)
250 g + 250 g (2 cups + 2 cups) whipping cream
75 g (⅖ cup) sugar
5 g (1 tsp) freshly squeezed lemon juice
175 g (approx. 9/10 cup) milk chocolate, preferably Valrhona Jivara Lactée 40%

1. Soak the gelatin leaves in plenty of cold water for at least 10 minutes.
2. Bring 250 g (2 cups) of whipping cream to a boil in a pot, and set aside.
3. Melt the sugar and lemon juice to a golden yellow caramel, while stirring continuously. Add the warm cream, and boil until the sugar has dissolved completely.
4. Add the gelatin leaves into the cream and stir until they dissolve. Add the chopped chocolate, and mix with a stick blender into an emulsion. Add the remaining cream (cold), and mix.
5. Cover with plastic wrap, and store in the fridge until the following day.

Continued on the next page.

Day 2
1 batch of the chocolate jelly (p. 225)
120 g (approx. ⅗ cup) dark chocolate,
preferably Valrhona Grand Cru
Manjari 64.5%
1 sheet of gold leaf
2 sheets of plastic, preferably with Valrhona
print, or 2 sheets of overhead transpa-
rency film.

The Assembling Process:

1. Place the hazelnut chocolate bottom on a tray and brush with the sugar syrup until it is soaked up by the cake bottom. Cut into two cake bottoms with a sharp knife.

2. Beat the cold chocolate mousse in a cold bowl until it is a smooth foam (don't beat it for too long).

3. Spread the mousse over one of the bottom halves, and place the other one on top, press it down evenly with a tray. Freeze for at least 3 hours.

4. Cut the bottom in the center with a knife that has been dipped in warm water, and cut out 6 individual cakes from each half. Place the cakes on a wire rack and use a measuring cup to pour the chocolate jelly (that has been cooled to 95°C) over the cakes.

Shake the wire rack so that excess glaze is drained off.

5. Finely chop and temper the chocolate (p. 234). Spread it over the plastic film in a very thin layer, by using a pallet. When the chocolate begins to solidify, cut small round plates with a smooth, round cookie cutter (press hard). Place the plates in the fridge with a weight on top; otherwise they will bend in the fridge.

6. Spread the remaining chocolate on the overhead transparency film, and quickly stroke with a glue scraper to form spirals (p. 234). Transfer them to plates once they have solidified, and place little plates of dark chocolate around them. Decorate with chocolate spirals. Use a knife to take a little piece of gold leaf and attach it to the chocolate jelly.

7. Before you serve this dessert, make sure that the ice cream is soft and supple; otherwise place it in the fridge for a few minutes.

8. Shape beautiful ice cream eggs with a spoon that has been dipped in warm water, and place them on the cakes.

CHOCOLATE CYLINDER WITH CARAMEL ICE CREAM AND CHOCOLATE CRÈME

The chocolate crème filled delicate cylinder makes for an exquisite dessert. Try it with a dollop of refreshing whipped cream.

Serves 6 people

Day 1
Make half a batch of the caramel ice cream with fleur de sel (p. 34)

Day 2
Freeze in the ice cream machine. Make a batch of the chocolate tulips (p. 224). Use a sharp knife to cut thick card stock into a stencil that is about 2.8 inches long and 2.8 inches wide. Bake the same way as the baskets, but lift the discs and roll them around a wooden stick and press at the seam so the rolls are held together. Continue until you have 6 rolls. If you want to store them, place them in an airtight jar, to prevent them from softening.

Caramelized Hazelnuts:
100 g (¾ cup) hazelnuts
20 g (5 tsp) sugar
5 g (1 tsp) fresh lemon juice
(See page 228)

Chocolate Crème:
1 gelatin leaf (2 g)
75 g (⅔ cup) muscovado sugar
60 g (¼ cup) egg yolks
125 g (½ cup) heavy cream
125 g (½ cup) milk
4 g (2 ¼ tsp) instant Nescafé, dark roast
110 g (approx. ½ cup) chopped dark chocolate, preferably Valrhona Grand Cru Guanaja 70.5%

1. Soak the gelatin sheet in plenty of cold water for at least 10 minutes.
2. Whisk sugar and yolks lightly. Boil the cream, milk and Nescafé, add it to the egg yolk batter and mix well. Pour back into the pot and heat to 185°F, while stirring continuously. If you don't have a thermometer, do a rose test, or a ladle test (p. 25).

3. Lift the gelatin leaf out of the water and stir it into the cream blend until it has dissolved. Pour half of the cream over the chopped chocolate and stir until you have thick mass, add the remaining cream in small doses so that it becomes an emulsion. Mix it vigorously with a stick blender and place in the refrigerator to cool.

7 oz whipping cream
0.4 oz sugar

Beat the cream and sugar in a cold bowl until a loose foam forms.

Caramel Sauce:
100 g (½ cup) sugar
50 g + 50 g (⅕ + ⅕ cup) water
2 g (approx. 1 tsp) instant Nescafé, dark roast

Cook the sugar with 1.8 oz water to 356°F, until the sugar turns into a golden yellow caramel sauce. Add 1.8 oz of water and the Nescafé, and boil until half of the water has evaporated.

Cocoa

Serving Suggestion:
1. Place the cylinders onto cold plates, and use a pastry bag to pipe the chocolate cream into the cylinders. Garnish with caramelized hazelnuts.
2. Shape ice cream eggs with a spoon that has been dipped in warm water. Place them inside of the cylinders.
3. Sprinkle with more nuts. Pipe the lightly whipped cream just like in the photo, and dust with a little bit of cocoa. Drizzle some caramel sauce onto the plates. Serve immediately.

PISTACHIO ICE CREAM WITH BUTTER STREUSEL AND FRESH SWEET CHERRIES

The combination between the creamy pistachio ice cream and the succulent cherries is absolutely mouthwatering!

Serves 6 people

Day 1
Make half a batch of the pistachio ice cream (p. 34).
Make half a batch of the butter streusel, but replace the almond meal with finely ground pistachios (p. 224).

Day 2
Freeze the ice cream in the ice cream maker.

25 g (approx. ⅕ cup) pistachios
750 g (approx. 4 cups) ripe & beautiful sweet cherries

Serving:
1. Place the pistachio streusel in the middle of the plates, and garnish with cherries all around.
2. Crush the pistachios with a rolling pin.
3. Dip a spoon in warm water, and shape beautiful ice cream eggs that you place on top of the streusel.
4. Garnish with the crushed pistachios.

RASPBERRY ICE CREAM IN TULIP BASKETS WITH
RASPBERRY COULIS AND FRESH RASPBERRIES

Is there anything more delicious than a crispy, buttery basket filled with creamy raspberry ice cream and fresh raspberries?

Serves 6 people

Raspberry coulis made with 250 g (2 cups) of
*   raspberries (p. 227)*
6 crispy baskets (p. 224)
1 batch of the raspberry ice cream (p. 40)
500 g (4 cups) fresh raspberries
confectioners' sugar
fresh peppermint

1. Drizzle plates with a little bit of raspberry coulis, and use a spoon to create a pattern, just like in the photo (it is easier than it looks). Place the crispy baskets on top.

2. Dip an ice cream scoop in warm water and place a large scoop of raspberry ice cream in each basket.

3. Decorate with raspberries, and dust with some confectioners' sugar, and top it off with a peppermint leaf.

STRAWBERRY ICE CREAM SERVED IN CRISPY BASKET WITH FRESH BERRIES AND STRAWBERRY COULIS

This delectable dessert leaves everyone in awe.

Serves 6 people

Strawberry Coulis made with 250 g (2 cups) of ripe strawberries (p. 227)
6 crispy baskets (p. 224)
1 batch of the strawberry ice cream (p. 40)
500 g (4 cups) mixed fresh berries (seasonal)
confectioners' sugar

1. Drizzle plates with strawberry coulis. Place the crispy baskets on top.
2. Dip an ice cream scoop in warm water and place a large scoop of strawberry ice cream in each basket.
3. Decorate with mixed berries, and dust with some confectioners' sugar.

Strawberry Yogurt Ice Cream in Tulip Baskets with Fresh Strawberries, Black Currant Coulis and black Currants, and Caramelized Strawberry

A refreshing and delicious dessert with an exquisite contrast between black currants and the strawberries.

Serves 6 people

6 crispy baskets (p. 224)
half a batch of the strawberry yogurt ice
    cream (p. 42)
black currant coulis made with 250 g
    (2 cups) black currants (p. 227)
150 g (1⅕ cups) black currants for garnish

Caramelized Strawberries:
250 g (1¼ cups) sugar
100 g (⅖ cup) water
50 g (2½ tbsp) glucose
500 g (4 cups) strawberries

1. Bring sugar, water, and glucose to a boil, while you brush the interior walls of the pot with a brush, to prevent crystallization. When the solution is 311°F, place the pot in a cold water bath to stop the water from boiling, and to prevent the caramel from turning brown. If you don't have a thermometer, do a sugar sample (p. 232).
2. Place 6 large, fresh strawberries on forks and dip them in caramel, one at a time, then allow the caramel to solidify. Rinse the remaining strawberries and let them dry on paper towels. Cut them in half, but leave the hull on.
3. Pour black currant coulis onto the plates and decorate with black currants. Place the baskets on top.
4. Place a large scoop of ice cream in each basket. Decorate with strawberries and place a caramelized strawberry in the middle of the dessert.

Vanilla Ice Cream Served with Fresh Berries in Tulips and Sugar Dome

This refreshing dessert is just as beautiful as it tastes. Making sugar domes is not that hard, you just need be persistent.

Serves 6 people

Day 1
Make half a batch of the vanilla ice cream (p. 32)

Day 2
Freeze the ice cream in the ice cream maker.

Black currant coulis made with 8.8 oz black currants (p. 227)
6 crispy baskets
500 g (4 cups) mixed fresh berries to use for garnishing
6 yellow pansies

1. Sugar Domes: Cook the caramel the same way as in the recipe for caramelized strawberries (p. 124).
2. Oil the backside of a soup ladle. Spin a thin mesh of sugar threads on the dome (see p. 233), and carefully remove it from the ladle and allow it to cool off. Repeat this process until you have 6 domes. If you need to reheat the caramel, spin the pan over the heat until the caramel turns liquid. Never stir the caramel, it will "kill" the sugar, it will crystallize and become useless.
3. Serving: Pour black currant coulis on the plates and use a spoon to create a pattern, like in the photo. Place the baskets on top.
4. Dip an ice cream scoop in warm water, so that you can shape the ice cream into scoops that you place in the baskets. Decorate with berries (after you wash and dry them).
5. Carefully place the sugar domes over the baskets and decorate with pansies.

Risotto Ice Cream with Thin Pistachio Biscuits, Orange chips, and Raspberries

This light and fluffy ice cream combination has all the colors and flavors of Italy. It will be a favorite with your guests.

Serves 6 people

1 batch of the risotto ice cream (p. 36)

Pistachio Hippenflarn (crispy biscuits):
75 g (½ cup) pistachios
75 g (⅗ cup) confectioners' sugar
75 g (⅗ cup) flour
75 g (⅓ cup) milk
1 drop of bitter almond oil, and optional: 1 drop orange blossom water
30 g (2 tbsp) egg whites
25 g (3 tbsp) pistachios for decoration
200 g (1⅗ cups) raspberries for decoration
orange chips (page 227)

Nougat:
50 g (¼ cup) sugar
5 g (1 tsp) lemon juice
peppermint

1. Freeze the ice cream.
2. Mix pistachios and icing sugar in a blender to a fine powder and add flour, milk, bitter almonds, and possibly orange blossom water. Blend to a paste.
3. Scrape out the mixture and work in half of the egg white firs, then add the rest until you have blend that is absolutely smooth. Cover with plastic wrap and set aside to rest for 2 hours. Never beat the crispy batter (hippen) with a whisk, it should only be mixed; otherwise the baskets will become too porous and crack during the baking process. When you allow the mixture to rest, the get rid of possible air bubbles and the batter will become smoother.
4. Use a sharp knife to cut out a stencil that is 0.4 × 0.3 inches out of paper that is 0.04 inches thick. Place it on a baking sheet and use a pallet to spread the mass into 18 stencil shaped plates. Spread some whole pistachios over them, and bake at 350°F until they are golden brown, about 5 minutes. Once they are cold, immediately place them in a jar and cover with a lid so that they don't soften.
5. Dry orange chips in the oven at 175°F, about 2 hours. Place two a little bit on top of each other, so that you get two chips stuck together, as in the photo. As soon as they have cooled off, transfer them to a jar and cover with a lid so that they don't soften.
6. Make sure that the ice cream is soft and supple; otherwise place it in the fridge for 30 minutes before you serve it.
7. Melt the sugar with the lemon juice in a little saucepan, until you have a yellowish brown nougat. Dip the orange chips in the nougat, and attach them to the pistachio biscuits with the pistachios on top. Also dip stem from the peppermint in the nougat, so that you can attach the peppermint leaves behind the chips.
8. Place the pistachio biscuits on the plates and place a beautiful ice cream egg on top. Press another pistachio biscuit on top of the ice cream, and add another ice cream egg. Carefully press another pistachio biscuit on top. Make sure that it is straight.
9. Decorate with a few raspberries.

Black Currant Sorbet Served in Tulips with Black Currant Coulis and Crème Anglaise with Lemon Verbena

Black currant sorbet always tastes delicious, but it is extra yummy when served in the delicate tulip basket.

Gustav Vi Adolf always craved black currant sorbet as an entremets whenever he visited Malmö, and for dessert he would have lemon soufflé with sabayon sauce. I remember that for starters, he would always pick the clear oxtail soup with sherry and cheese pastries.

Serves 6 people

½ batch of caramel (p. 232)
1 batch of the tulip batter (p. 224)
25 g (3 tbsp) pistachios

1. Cook the caramel in a little saucepan and immediately place the pot in a cold water bath to stop the boiling process. Allow to cool for 5 minutes.
2. Dip a tablespoon in the caramel and try to make a butterfly shape with it on a baking sheet. Let the butterfly cool a little bit before you lift it with a pallet, and bend it. Make 8 butterflies so that you have extra ones.
3. Preheat the oven to 400°F.
4. Spread the tulip batter on baking sheets, shape into 6 bottom discs that are as big as dessert plates, about 7 inches in diameter. Spread pistachios on top. Bake them in the oven, one tray at a time, about 5 minutes, until the edges have a nice brown color.
5. Shape the bottom discs into cones, and immediately place them in glasses so that they retain their shape while they solidify. Store in an airtight jar so that they don't soften.

Crème Anglaise:

10 g (⅕ cup) lemon verbena
100 g (⅖ cup) whipping cream
100 g (⅖ cup) milk
60 g (¼ cup) egg yolks
40 g (⅕ cup) sugar

Nougat:

50 g (¼ cup) sugar
5 g (1 tsp) fresh lemon juice

½ batch of the black currant sorbet (p. 47)
100 g (⅘ cup) black currants to decorate with
black currant coulis made with 125 g (1 cup)
black currants (p. 227)

1. Blanch the lemon verbena by dipping it in boiling hot water and immediately chill it in ice water.
2. Bring cream, milk, and lemon verbean to a boil, remove the pot from the heat and cover with plastic wrap. Let the infusion sit for 5 – 10 minutes.
3. Beat egg yolks and sugar, and beat the egg mix into the infusion. Heat it to 185°F while stirring continuously. If you don't have a thermometer, do a rose test, or a ladle test (p. 25). Strain the sauce through a chinois, or a fine mesh sieve, and immediately chill it in an ice cold water bath. Store in the fridge.
4. Serving: Make sure that the sorbet is soft and supple, you may need to place it in the fridge until it softens if it is too hard.
5. Place the cones on plates and melt the sugar with lemon juice until you have a golden brown nougat. Dip a knife into the nougat, and use it to attach a butterfly to each cone.
6. Pour a little bit of crème anglaise, and some black currant coulis on the side. Decorate with a few black currants.
7. Dip an ice cream scoop in warm water, and use it to shape the sorbet into scoops. Fill the cones with scoops of the sorbet.

RHUBARB TARTE WITH STRAWBERRY ICE CREAM, OR BLUEBERRY TARTE WITH MASCARPONE ICE CREAM

René Qurin and I worked together at Savoy Hotel in Malmö when we were boys. He moved to Malmö from Alsace, France, in 1970. René never returned, instead he married the cold-buffet manageress, Eva. Today, he is a pastry chef in Båstad, and he creates beautiful specialties from his home region. Alsace is one of my favorite regions in France. René always mixed his shortcrust pastry and pie dough on a baking table, and he was a specialist at baking beautiful pastries with puff pastry. Begin making the dough at least 2 hours, or an entire day before you begin the process.

Serves 6 people

1 batch of the strawberry ice cream (p. 40), or ½ batch mascarpone ice cream (p. 35), depending on if you are going to use rhubarb or blueberries.
6 tart dishes, 0.8 inch high edges, about 4.7 oz in diameter
500 g (4 cups) blueberries or 600 g rhubarb (500 g, approx. 4 cups netto)

This is the classic pie dough that Réne used to make:
250 g (2 cups) flour
125 g (½ cup) butter
5 g (1 tsp) salt
60 g (4 tbsp) water

1. Spread the flour into a circle on the baking table. Place the soft butter and the salt in the middle of the circle. Pinch the dough until you have a crumbly mass, add the water and quickly work the dough together. Wrap the dough in plastic wrap and store it in the fridge for 2 hours.
2. Place the tarte dishes together. Use a rolling pin to roll the dough until it is 0.1 inch thick. Place it on top of the dishes. Lightly flour the dough on top. Take a piece of dough, dip it in flour, and use it to press the dough into the dishes.
3. Use the rolling pin to roll over the dishes, press firmly, cut off excess dough with a knife. Prick the bottoms with a fork. Store the dishes in the fridge for at least 30 minutes.
4. Preheat the oven to 375°F.
5. Bake the pie dough in the oven until they are light brown, about 10 minutes. Remove them from the oven and add blueberries, or the peeled and cut rhubarb (sugar cube size pieces), mixed with sugar.

Egg Batter:
25 g (1¾ tbsp) unsalted butter
250 g (1 cup) whipping cream
100 g (⅔ cup) eggs
40 g (⅙ cup) egg yolks
50 g (¼ cup) sugar
5 g (1 tsp) pure vanilla sugar

1. Melt the butter and set aside. Bring cream to a boil and set aside.
2. Beat eggs, egg yolks, sugar, and vanilla sugar, and add the warm cream and the melted butter. Mix well. Pass through a chinois, or a fine mesh sieve.
3. Fill the dishes with the egg batter, and bake until golden brown, about 30 minutes. If you make one big pie, count on 45 – 50 minutes.
4. Allow the pies to cool and carefully release them from the dishes.
5. Serve lukewarm, with ice cream.

ICE CREAM CAKE WITH APPLE AND CALVADOS

This delicious apple cake is an excellent way to finish off a fall meal. Great after a main course that consists of fried goose or duck. Perhaps serve it on St. Martin's Day, it instead of the traditional Scandinavian apple cake. As a Scandinavian, St. Martin's Day is very important to me.

If you are more used to fast food, and don't want to bother with all the steps in this recipe, you could just do a triple burger with only apple chips and ice cream.

Serves 14 – 16 people

Two circular foil dishes, about 8 inches in diameter
A ring shape, about 9.5 inches in diameter

½ bath of the tulip dough (p. 224)
1 green apple for decoration
1 batch of fruit jelly (page 226)

Calvado Parfait:
1 gelatin leaf (2 g)
250 g (1 cup) whipping cream
80 g (⅓ cup) egg yolk
95 g (approx. ½ cup) sugar
65 g (approx. ¼ cup) water
50 g (⅕ cup) calvados

1. Soak the gelatin sheet in plenty of cold water for at least 10 minutes.
2. Whip the cream to foam and store it in the fridge.
3. Beat the egg yolks to foam.
4. Boil sugar and water to 239°F, and use a brush, that has been dipped in cold water, to brush the interior walls of the pot. If you don't have a thermometer, do a sugar test (Page 232).
5. Pour the syrup in an even stream into the whipped egg yolks. Transfer the gelatin leaf to the egg yolk foam.
6. Beat the egg foam really cold. Fold the whipped cream and the calvados into the egg foam and whisk it into a light a fluffy parfait.
7. Pour the parfait into a foil dish that is lined with plastic wrap and freeze it for at least 6 hours, but preferably overnight.

Green apple purée for the coulis and ice cream:
4 gelatin leaves (8 g)
1000 g green apples
juice of 1 lemon
sugar

1. Cut each apple into 4 wedges and place them in 34 oz of boiling water with the lemon juice. Cover, and boil them until soft.
2. Let the apples drain in a sieve. Weigh the pulp, add 10 percent sugar and blend to a smooth purée. Strain it through a sieve.

Apple coulis to put in the middle of the cake:
4 gelatin leaves (8 g)
250 g (1 cup) apple purée
100 g (⅓ cup) glucose
25 g (5 tsp) lemon juice
25 g (5 tsp) calvados

1. Soak the gelatin leaves in plenty of cold water for at least 10 minutes.
2. Mix the apple purée with glucose, lemon juice, and calvados.
3. Take the gelatin leaves out of the water, and add them to a pot. Melt the gelatin at a temperature between 113° F and 122°F. Mix into the coulis.
4. Pour into a foil shape lined with plastic wrap and place it in the freezer.

Green apple ice cream:
4 gelatin leaves (8 g)
250 g (1 cup) water
250 g (1¼ cups) sugar
300 g (1⅕ cups) apple purée
500 g (2 cups) milk

1. Soak the gelatin leaves in plenty of cold water for at least 10 minutes.
2. Boil a sugar syrup with the water and sugar, remove the saucepan from the stove. Lift the gelatin leaves out of the water and add them to the syrup, stirring until the gelatin dissolves.
3. Allow to cool to 95°F. Add apple purée and milk, and mix.
4. Freeze the ice cream in an ice cream machine.

Apple chips:
1 green apple, i.e. Granny Smith (see the recipe for fruit chips, p. 227)

Continued on page 136.

Lemon Dacquoise Bottom:
1 lemon
10 g (2½ tsp) sugar
60 g (¼ cup) egg whites
10 g (2 tsp) fresh lemon juice
20 g (5 tsp) sugar
85 g (9/10 cup) almond flour
85 g (approx. ⅔ cup) sugar

1. Preheat the oven to 350°F.
2. Draw a circle that is about 9 inches in diameter, with a pen on a baking paper.
3. Wash the lemon and grate the zest from half the lemon. Sprinkle the zest with 10 g (2 ½ tsp) of sugar and rub it with a pallet until it starts to flow.
4. Beat the egg whites, lemon juice, and 10 g of the sugar to a solid meringue in an absolutely clean metal or copper bowl.
5. Mix the almond flour, and 85 g of sugar, making a tant pour tant.
6. Carefully fold the almond meal and the lemon zest into the meringue.
7. Use a pallet to spread the meringue evenly inside the circle on the baking sheet. You could also use a pastry bag to pipe the meringue like a spiral inside of the circle. Just make sure that you cut a fairly big hole at the bottom of the bag.
8. Bake for 12 – 15 minutes until the surface is brittle, the meringue should be soft inside.

Assembling the cake:
1. Place the lemon bottom in the bottom of the circle shape, and place it in the freezer.
2. Fill it with half of the apple ice cream, and make sure to even it out. Hit the dish against the table so that the ice cream sinks into the bottom. Use a spoon that has been dipped in warm water to stroke ice cream along the edge of the circle shape. Place in the freezer for 30 minutes.
3. Release the apple coulis from the foil dish and press it firmly into the ice cream. Place it in the freezer again.
4. Release the frozen parfait from the foil dish and place it on top of the apple coulis. Press firmly.
5. Remove the remaining ice apple ice cream from the freezer and store it in the fridge for 30 minutes, or until it is soft and supple.
6. Remove the circular dish from the freezer and spread the remaining ice cream over it. Smoothen the surface, and put it back into the freezer. Cover with plastic wrap.
7. Make the tulip dough, and preheat the oven to 400°F. Use a pallet to spread the dough into a thin, round disc, about 8 inches in diameter. Bake it golden brown, remove it from the oven, and lift it, bottom down into a bowl so that it bends beautifully.
8. Core the apple, and cut it into large cubes, and mix them with a tiny

amount of the fruit jelly.
9. Remove the circle dish from the freezer, heat it with your hands, and carefully release the cake from the circle.
10. Place the cake on a jar. Heat the apple jelly to 95°F, pour it over the cake and glace it with a pallet in one fell swoop, so that the ice cream doesn't melt.
11. Remove any potential drops around the cake. Use a pallet to carefully transfer the cake to a cake stand, and put in the fridge for 30 minutes to allow it to thaw a little bit.
12. When you serve the cake, decorate with apple chips all around it, and garnish with the tulip basket and the apple pieces, as shown in the picture.

SUMMERY ICE CREAM CAKE

This delicious ice cream cake is a favorite with all family members, young and old, and you don't even need an ice cream machine to make it.

Serves 12 people

A springform pan, 9.5 inches in diameter
2 sheets of plastic film, preferably with
    Valrhona print, or 2 sheets of overhead
    transparency film
1 lemon dacquoise bottom (page 136)
80 g (⅔ cup) dark chocolate, preferably
    Valrhona Grand Cru Manjari 64.5%
½ batch of the vanilla parfait according to
    the pâte à bomb method (page 65)
½ batch of strawberry mousse glacé
    (raspberry mousse glacé, see Gateau
    glacé Georgette,
page 143, but replace the raspberry purée
    with strawberry purée)
½ batch of strawberry jelly (see Bomb
    Sylvestre, page 206)
about 250 g (2 cups) of fresh berries for
    garnish
peppermint
confectioners' sugar
coulis made with 500 g (4 cups) strawberries
    (page 227)

1. Begin by baking the lemon dacquoise bottom, about 9 inches in diameter. Let it cool before you remove the baking sheet.
2. Finely chop 40 g (⅓ cup) of the chocolate, and melt it in the microwave while stirring it occasionally until it has a temperature between 113°F and 131°F.
3. Brush the bottom with the melted chocolate, and place it in the fridge so that the chocolate solidifies.
4. Place the cake bottom inside a springform pan, that you have lined with plastic wrap to ease the process of removing the parfait later.
5. Make the vanilla parfait, and the strawberry mousse glacé, and layer them in the springform pan until it is full. Carefully stir with a spoon to create a marble pattern. Cover the cake with plastic wrap, and freeze it for at least 6 hours before you serve it.
6. Temper the remaining chocolate (p. 234), and spread it thinly on the plastic film. When it begins to solidify, use a ruler and a sharp knife to cut the chocolate into strips that are about 1.2 inches wide. Cut the strips into squares. Place them between weights in the fridge, so that they don't bend as they solidify.
7. Heat the strawberry jelly to 95°F. Place the cake in the springform pan on the table. Pour jelly over the cake, and stroke away any excess jelly with a pallet.
8. Once the jelly has solidified, release the cake from the springform pan. Place the cake on a jar, and rub the ring with your hands until it releases and falls down. Transfer the cake to a cake plate.
9. Place the chocolate squares so that they wrap around the cake, and decorate with mixed fresh berries and peppermint, just like in the picture. Dust with a little bit of confectioners' sugar. Store in the fridge for at least 30 minutes before you serve the cake.
10. Serve with strawberry coulis on the side in a sauceboat.

Nougatine Palette with Ice Cream Fruits

This particular ice cream structure is common in France. Nougatine baskets and pots filled with ice cream fruits can be found in every pastry shop in France and Switzerland.

1 batch of nougatine (p. 225)
100 g (½ cup) dark chocolate, preferably
  Valrhona Grand Cru Guanaja 70.5%
50 g (2½ tbsp) honey, firm
cocoa for modeling

1. Cut a stencil in the shape of a painter's palette. Use paper that is 0.04 inch thick, and make sure that that palette is about 9.5 inches in diameter.
2. Preheat the oven to 300°F. Quickly roll the nougatine with a rolling pin, place it in the oven on a baking sheet on a tray, and let it soften.
3. Remove it from the oven, and place the stencil on top, and cut a hole with a plain cookie cutter, about 1.2 inches in diameter. Use a knife to cut away any excess nougat around the stencil.
4. Chocolate brushes: Finely chop the chocolate and melt it in a plastic bowl in the microwave, or over a water bath, stir occasionally. Temperature should be about 122 - 131°F. Stir the honey into the chocolate and allow the mass to solidify in room temperature.
5. Cut the mass into 3 pieces, and shape them into brushes with a little bit of cocoa. Allow the brushes to solidify in room temperature.
6. Place the palette on a plate with the brushes inserted in the hole. Freeze the palette.
7. Decorate with sorbet fruits (see the right). If you don't have ice cream fruit molds, you can decorate the palette with scoops of sorbet instead. It will taste just as good, and look almost as good.

Ice Cream Fruits

Fill fruit molds with freshly frozen ice cream or sorbet, and press them together, to get rid of any excess ice cream. Freeze the ice cream fruits.

When you want to serve them, dip the molds in cold water, release the fruits from the molds, and place them on a chilled baking sheet. Color them with an airbrush, or a very soft brush that has been dipped rapidly in food coloring, and that you brush lightly onto the fruits. Don't cover the fruits in too much food coloring, or it won't look good once they thaw. Freeze them again, until you want to use them again. If you want to, you can dip them in cold milk while they are frozen. Then they will be covered in a thin film. This is popular especially if you make large fruits, or ice cream swans.

ICED GEORGETTE CAKE

This delectable ice cream cake used to be a specialty at Savoy Hotel in Malmö, and it would be a classic dessert in the banquet room. It is hard to beat the lovely combination of chocolate, raspberries, and crispy almond. It used to be garnished differently back then. I have modernized the look to our times.

Serves 14-16 people

2 springform pans, 10.2 inches in diameter
raspberry coulis made with 500 g (4 cups)
    raspberries (p. 227)
1 batch chocolate jelly (p. 225)
500 g (4 cups) fresh raspberries for
    garnishing
powdered sugar
lemon balm

Raspberry mousse glacé:
1 gelatin leaf (2 g)
250 g (1 cup) whipping cream
30 g (2 tbsp) egg whites
65 g (½ cup) confectioners' sugar
5 g (1 tsp) lemon juice
150 g (⅗ cup) raspberry purée with 10%
    sugar

1. Soak the gelatin sheet in plenty of cold water for at least 10 minutes.
2. Whip the cream to a light foam and place it in the fridge.
3. Mix egg whites, sugar, and lemon juice in a clean metal bowl, and beat lightly with an electric mixer. Place the bowl in a water bath on the stove and heat to 140°F while beating the mix continuously. (Be sure not to heat the water bath above 194°F, because the egg whites will coagulate).
4. Remove the bowl from the water bath and whisk the meringue until it is really cold on medium speed.
5. Heat 50 g (⅕ cup) of the raspberry purée, add the drained gelatin leaves and stir until they have dissolved. Add to the remainder of the purée, and mix.
6. Beat the raspberry purée and fold it into the whipped cream.
7. Fill a spring form that has been lined with plastic wrap with the mousse. Cover with plastic wrap and freeze for at least 6 hours.

Chocolate parfait:
275 g (1⅛ cup) whipped cream
160 g (⅘ cup) dark chocolate, preferably
    Valrhona Grand Cru Pur Caribe 66.5%
100 g (⅖ cup) egg yolk
125 g (⅗ cup) sugar
40 g (2¾ tbsp) water

1. Whip the cream into loose foam and set it in the fridge.
2. Finely chop the chocolate and melt it in microwave, stirring occasionally (be careful not to overheat it).
3. Beat yolks, sugar, and water in a metal bowl, and place it in a simmering water bath (don't exceed 194°F, to prevent the eggs from coagulating). Heat to 185°F (use a thermometer), the mass will begin to thicken when it is ready.
4. Pass the mass through a chinois or a fine mesh sieve, and beat the egg foam cold on a medium speed with an electric whisk, or by hand.
5. Heat the chocolate to 122 - 131°F. Add a third of the whipped cream into the melted chocolate and mix into a smooth, homogeneous blend.

Use a spatula to mix in the remaining cream.
6. Fold the chocolate cream into the egg yolk so that you get a light and airy parfait.
7. Fill a circular baking pan that is about 10 inches in diameter, and that is lined with plastic wrap, with the chocolate parfait, and smoothen the surface. Hit the pan on the table to flatten the parfait. Freeze at least 6 hours, or until the next day.

Caramelized almonds:
Almonds are especially delicious when they
    are really crisp.
100 g (1 cup) sliced almonds
15 g (2 tbsp) powdered sugar
40 g (2¾ tbsp) water

1. Preheat the oven to 356°F. Mix almonds and powdered sugar on a silicone baking mat, or a sheet of baking paper, moisten with water and stir without crushing almonds.
2. Roast them golden brown, stirring occasionally (don't leave the oven unattended).
3. When the almonds are golden brown, transfer them to a bowl to cool.

Japonaise bottoms:
200 g (2 cups) finely ground, unpeeled almonds
200 g (1 cup) sugar
200 g (⅘ cup) egg whites
15 g (1tbsp) lemon juice
75 g (⅖ cup) sugar

1. Preheat the oven to 350°F.
2. Draw two circles that are 10 inches in diameter on two sheets of baking paper.
3. Mix the almonds and sugar creating a tant pour tant.

Continued on page 144.

4. Beat the egg whites, lemon juice, and sugar to a firm meringue in an absolutely clean metal bowl with an electric mixer or a hand whisk.
5. Fill a disposable plastic piping bag with the meringue and cut a hole at the tip. Pipe two cake bottoms inside of the circles. Start in the middle and pipe in a spiral all around until you cover the space inside the circles. You can also spread the meringue as evenly as possible in the circles.
6. Bake for 20-30 minutes; occasionally open the oven door to allow the water to evaporate from the meringue mass. When the bottoms are golden brown, place them on a baking sheet and turn them bottom side up. If it is easy to pull the paper off from the bottoms, they are dry enough. Otherwise, you will need to bake them in the oven for a little bit longer. Turning them makes them cook flatter. Leave them to cool off.

Brushing the bottoms:
80 g (⅖ cup) dark chocolate, preferably Valrhona Grand Cru Guanaja 70.5%

1. Finely chop the chocolate and melt them in a bowl in the microwave. Stir occasionally until the temperature is about 122 - 131°F.
2. Use a small brush to brush the underside of the bottoms with the chocolate, in order to isolate the bottoms so that the parfait doesn't make them soggy when they are thawing.

Chocolate filigree:
100 g (½ cup) dark chocolate, preferably Valrhona Grand Cru Manjari 64.5%

1. Finely chop the chocolate and melt it in the microwave, or in a water bath, stirring occasionally.
2. Draw a circle that is 9.5 inches in diameter on a sheet of baking paper.
3. Temper the chocolate (page 234).
4. Fill a paper cone with the chocolate, and cut a small hole at the tip. Pipe the chocolate as a maze, or filigree inside the of circle. Allow to solidify on the paper.

Assembling the cake:
1. Place an almond cake bottom, chocolate side up, on the table.
2. Release the chocolate parfait from the circular form, by rubbing the sides with your hands until it releases.
3. Place the cake on top of the almond base and press gently.
4. Release the raspberry parfait and place it on top.
5. Add another almond circle with the chocolate side facing the parfait; use a tray to press gently so that the cake is level. Place the cake on a sheet of baking paper on a wire rack.
6. Heat the chocolate jelly to 95°F; pour the frosting on the middle of the cake and around the cake edges and glaze the top with a pallet. Allow to solidify for 2 minutes.
7. Use your right hand and a pallet to carefully lift the cake.
8. Sprinkle almonds all around the cake so that the edge is covered.
9. Place the cake on a beautiful plate and decorate with fresh, dry raspberries.
10. Cover half of the chocolate filigree and sprinkle with powdered sugar, remove the paper.
11. Lift the chocolate filigree and place it on top of the raspberries, and garnish the chocolate plate with raspberries and lemon balm.
12. Serve with raspberry coulis on the side.

The classic croquembouche used to be a permanent feature at Swedish weddings until the 1970s. Nowadays they have been replaced by the wedding cake; however, they are still the ultimate test for aspiring pastry chef students.

The croquembouche should be three levels high, with a top. They are made with almond paste and a little bit of egg whites, and the pieces are held together with caramel sauce. The decoration usually consists of grapes, pulled caramel flowers, dark chocolate truffles, and the crown at the top; the blown caramel swans that are symbolizing the bride and the groom.

Vanilla Parfait with Caramelized Macadamia Nuts and Cherry Jubilée

Cherry Jubilée is a classic side with vanilla parfait and baked Alaska, or as we call it, *glace au four*. The cherries should be flambéed at the table and served with ice cream and a good almond cake. If you don't have a baking dish that looks like a pyramid, and if you don't want to get, just bake it in different shape, it will taste just as good. If you don't want to bother with the complicated decoration, it will taste almost as good with just the parfait.

Serves 8-10 people

1 pyramid baking pan that can hold about 1 ½ liter
150 g (approx. 1 cup) of caramelized macadamia
(See caramelized nuts, page 228),
allow them to cool off
1 batch of vanilla parfait according to the crème anglaise method (page 65)
An almond cake bottom (see Bomb à l'Opéra, page 214), let it cool off, and freeze
¼ batch of the chocolate jelly (page 225)

Spraying chocolate for cakes, ice cream, and pastries:
175 g (approx. ⁹⁄₁₀ cup) dark chocolate, preferably Valrhona Grand Cru Guanaja 70.5%
75 g (⅓ cup) cocoa butter

1. Melt the cocoa butter to 113 - 122°F.
2. Melt the chopped chocolate to at the same temperature as the cocoa butter.
3. Mix the chocolate with the cocoa butter. Strain the chocolate through a fine sieve before filling the syringe. Spray with and olive oil syringe with a pump, for great pressure, or use an electric paint gun.

Parfait:
1. Crush the caramelized macadamia nuts with a rolling pin and fold them into the vanilla parfait. Fill the baking mold with the parfait, and shake the table so that it is distributed evenly.
2. Place the frozen almond base on top and press on it firmly so that it attaches. Cover with plastic wrap and freeze it for at least 6 hours, or overnight.
3. Release the parfait by dipping the mold in tepid water, put it back into the freezer.
4. Place the parfait on top of a can with a baking sheet under. Spray the parfait all around with the chocolate mixture until it is covered. Put it back into the freezer.
5. Heat the chocolate jelly to 95°F and fill a small paper cone with it, cut a small hole in the tip.
6. Remove the parfait from the freezer again, and stripe it with the jelly in an irregular pattern, as shown. Place it in the fridge for 30 minutes so that the parfait becomes tempered. (You can make the decoration several hours in advance, so that you don't need to rush it at the last minute).

Cherry Jubilée:
750 g (approx. 4- 5 cups) sour cherries, like morello (you can use frozen cherries too)
185 g (approx. 2 cups) sugar
150 g (⅗ cup) red wine
1 ½ inch true cinnamon stick
75 g (approx. 4-5 tbsp) red currant jelly

9 cl (6 tbsp) kirschwasser (cherry brandy), or cognac

Thickener:
2 cl (1½ tbsp) kirschwasser (cherry brandy), or cognac
7 ½ g (1 tbsp) corn starch

1. Wash the cherries well and allow them to dry, or thaw the frozen cherries.
2. Boil sugar and red wine with the cinnamon until the solution reaches a temperature between 233° F and 237.2°F. Use a thermometer, or take a sugar sample (page 232).
3. Strain the solution over the cherries in a flambéing pan and bring to a boil. Add the jelly.
4. Dissolve corn starch in a little bit of liquor and whisk into a thickener. Boil everything with the thickener.
5. Carry the flambéing pan to the table, add the alcohol, and set alight. Serve with the parfait.

Classic Swedish Glace au Four

Sometimes on the continent the Norwegian omelet (also known as the Baked Alaska) is made. It is a type of meringue with egg yolks.

In our country, we usually make the classic French meringue, but preferably warm whipped to get rid of sugar granules in the meringue.

At Cunard Line we always used to serve baked Alaska at Captain's Dinner with burning Cherry Jubilée, and the guests were delighted when the ice cream rockets burned and the servers marched in with the flaming desserts.

In Sweden it was usually served with warm chocolate sauce. If the guests saw a *glace au four* being served in the dining room, they would order the dessert, especially when it was a Vesuvius with burning alcohol on top. The head waiter would then pour chocolate sauce like lava around while the alcohol was burning in egg shell half on top.

Serves 8-10 people

Day 1

½ batch of vanilla ice cream (page 32)
½ batch of strawberry ice cream (page 40)
1 batch of biscuit à la cuiller (p. 225)

1. Preheat the oven to 450°F.
2. Spread the mass over a baking paper with a pallet and bake it golden brown for 7-8 minutes.
3. Remove it from the oven and sprinkle with a little bit of sugar. Place a sheet of baking paper on top, and turn it upside down and transfer it onto a wire rack to cool.
4. Put it in the freezer covered in plastic wrap.

Day 2

1 batch chocolate sauce (see page 214, Bomb à l'Opéra)

Sugar syrup:

135 g (approx. ⅗ – ¾ cup) sugar
100 g (⅖ cup) water
1 lemon
8 cl (7½ tbsp) Cointreau, or Grand Marnier, or any other liqueur that you love

Fruit salad:

1 small fresh pineapple
1 green apple
1 ripe pear
2 oranges
1 banana
4 passion fruits

Meringue:

180 g (¾ cup) egg whites
15 g (1 tbsp) fresh lemon juice
350 g (1¾ cups) sugar
10 g (2 tsp) pure vanilla sugar
1 lemon, finely grated zest

1. Create sugar syrup by boiling the water and sugar, and allow it to cool. Add the freshly squeezed lemon juice to prevent the fruit salad from becoming soft.
2. Peel the pineapple, cut it into wedges, and cutting away the tough stem. Dice the pulp.
3. Peel the apple and the pear and cut them into beautiful wedges. Cut away the peel on the oranges and fillet them.
4. Peel the banana and cut it into slices. Halve the passion fruits and scrape out the pulp. Mix the fruit salad with a spoon, cover with plastic wrap and place in the fridge.
5. Freeze the ice cream in the ice cream machine, and place them in the freezer, covered with plastic wrap.
6. Remove the biscuit cake bottom from the freezer. Remove the baking paper and halve it lengthwise. Transfer one half to an oven-safe dish and use a knife to cut it into an oval shape.
7. Let the fruit salad drain until it is dry. Save the sugar syrup.
8. Mix ⅘ cup of the fruit salad syrup with the liqueur and brush the cake bottom with half of the solution. Spread the fruit salad on top.
9. Remove the ice creams from the freezer and make sure that they are creamy. Dip an ice cream scoop in warm water and add the mixed ice cream scoops on top of the cake bottom with the fruit salad until all the ice cream is used up.
10. Cut to the second cake bottom into an oval, put it on top of the ice cream layer and shape it with your hands as an omelet, (oval).
11. Brush the rest of the liqueur syrup over the top bottom until it is juicy. If you don't have enough of the sugar syrup, just take some from the fruit salad. Place in the freezer for 30 minutes.
12. Keep the chocolate sauce warm in a water bath that does not exceed 95 – 104°F. Mix the sauce vigorously with a hand blender before serving it.
13. Preheat the oven to 475°F. Whisk together egg whites, lemon juice, sugar and vanilla sugar in an absolutely clean metal bowl and place it in a simmering water bath, never exceeding 194°F, otherwise the egg whites will coagulate. Beat the mixture the entire time until it reaches a temperature of 131- 140°F. Immediately remove it from the water bath and whisk it cold at a medium speed until you have a stiff meringue. Add the lemon peel with a spatula. Fill a plastic piping bag with a star tube with the meringue.
14. Remove the ice cream from the freezer, pipe the meringue around on all the sides and spread it evenly with a pallet, so that the ice cream is completely covered. Decorate it the classic way, as in the picture. Back in the day this cake used to be garnished with candied red cherries, candied green pears, or candied garden angelica, but it doesn't really add anything to the taste. I think it is beautiful as it is.
15. Place it on a cold tray in the oven and bake it golden brown. Serve immediately with the warm chocolate sauce.

Tip!

Don't burn it with a gas flame, like many people tend to do, because it kills the finesse of this dessert.

It is important to have a soft baked meringue shell around the ice cream. The contrast between warm and cold always arouses delight. Even something as simple as freshly baked, crispy pancakes with whipped, cold cream, and jam serves a delightful taste experience.

PISTASCHIO PARFAIT WITH FLAMBÉED PINEAPPLE

When I was young, flambéing used to be a common culinary technique; and it is beginning to come back again. This dessert with caramelized pineapple and creamy parfait is both beautiful and delicious. Serve with almond tuiles with anise, or any good almond cake. Kirschwasser (cherry brandy) always tastes good with flambéed fruit.

Serves 8 people

A silver plate
A round cake pan with a hole in the middle, called a savarin pan (1½ - 2 liter).
1 batch of the lemon dacquoise (page 136) with the same diameter as the bottom of pan
1 batch of the pistascho parfait with cooked pate à bomb (Page 67)
100 g (¾ cup) sliced caramelized almonds (See Gateau Glacé Georgette, page 143)
2 large fresh pineapples, preferably Del Monte, extra sweet
25 g (1¾ tbsp) unsalted butter
100 g (½ cup) sugar
10 cl (approx. ⅖ cup) kirschwasser (cherry brandy), or amber rum or brandy for flambéing

1. Bake the bottom and let it cool, freeze it for about 1 hour. Remove it from the baking sheet.
2. Fill the baking pan with the parfait, place the bottom on top and press it firmly. Freeze it for at least 6 hours, or make the day before.
3. Cut off the top and the shell on the pineapple with a sharp knife so that no black spots remain.
4. Preheat the oven to 475°F. Grease a large oven-proof dish with butter.
5. Roll the pineapple in the sugar and place in the dish.
6. Bake the pineapple until it starts to caramelize on the surface and turn brown, 8-10 minutes.

Structure:

1. Dip the baking pan in warm water, release the parfait gently and place it in the middle of the plate. Decorate one side with the most beautiful pineapple crown.
2. Heat the liquor and pour it into a hot sauceboat.
3. Quickly place the hot pineapple pieces on the plate, set the hot liquor on fire, and pour it over the pineapple pieces so that they are burning beautifully when you serve this dessert. Sprinkle the pineapple with the sliced almonds. Serve immediately, while the contrast between warm and cold is at its best.

LEMON CHARLOTTE WITH RASPBERRIES

For 12 people

Marie Antonin Carême created the charlotte russe dessert when he was head chef for the Russian czar, and he used to flavor it with caraway liqueur. This dessert can be varied in many different ways. Here I have lined the mold with spoon macaroons, and I have piped a cover with the same batter. The filling is the same lemon parfait that we used to make at Savoy Hotel in Malmö when I was young commis Patissier there. This dessert pairs best with raspberry coulis and a nice glass of chilled muscat Beaume de Venise.

Day 1
raspberry coulis made with 500 g (4 cups)
frozen raspberries (page 227)
250 g (approx. 2 cups) candied raspberries,
or frozen raspberries (See preserving
berries, page 228)

Day 2
1 set of biscuit à la cuiller batter (page 225)

Lemon Parfait
If you rub sugar cubes against citrus fruits, the flavor will be more potent, then when you grate the peel with a grater. So take the time to do this, it will be well worth it. I remember how we used to stand for hours in Switzerland, rubbing sugar cubes for the Christmas tangerine sorbet that would be served inside the peel. We had thousands of orders for Christmas.

Sugar syrup for soaking:
2 lemons
50 g (⅔ cup) confectioners' sugar

Parfait:
3 gelatin leaves (6 g)
2 lemons, yellow and ripe with thin peels
50 g (approx. ¼ cup) sugar cubes
⅕ cup dry white wine

80 g (⅓ cup) egg yolks
150 g (¾ cup) granulated sugar
25 g (5 tsp) water
500 g (2 cups) whipping cream

1. Draw two round circles, 9.5 inches in diameter, on a baking paper and pipe tongue-like peeks with the batter towards the center of the circle with plain tube, nr. 12. This will be the cover. Pipe the other circle as a spiral, starting in the middle; this will later be the cake bottom. Pipe the remaining batter diagonally on baking tray that has been covered with parking paper. Sprinkle sugar over the bottoms.

2. Bake the bottoms in the same manner as the spoon macaroons but extend the baking time with 7-8 minutes until they are golden brown. Immediately transfer the bottoms to a wire rack, and let them.

3. Squeeze the juice out of the lemons and mix together with confectioners' sugar until it melts into a syrup.

4. Parfait: Soak the gelatin in plenty of cold water for at least 10 minutes.

5. Wash and dry the lemons. Rub the sugar cubes against them until all the peel is gone and the sugar cubes are soaked. Heat the wine with the sugar cubes to 122°F, until the sugar has dissolved completely. Remove the gelatin leaves from the water and add them to the wine and stir until the gelatin has dissolved.

6. Beat the egg yolks airy. Boil sugar and water and pour over the yolks while constantly whisking. Beat the mass cool, to about 68°F.

7. Squeeze the juice from the lemons and stir down into the gelatin solution. Beat the cream to light, airy foam in a chilled metal mixing bowl. Fold the gelatin solution into the cream; make sure that the temperature is about 95°F. Fold the egg foam

into the batter with a spatula so you get a light and airy parfait batter.

8. Turn the bottoms upside down and pull off the paper. Brush the diagonal bottom with the lemon sugar syrup and cut out strips that are as wide as the ring is high. Line the baking dish with the strips, with the baked side facing outward. Trim the edges so that they are sticking out as little as possible.

9. Place the spiral bottom in the bottom of the ring and brush lightly with lemon syrup. Fill with half of the parfait using a plastic piping bag with a high plain tube, or cut a large hole in the tip. Spread pickled raspberries over the parfait. Fill up with the remaining parfait and smoothen the surface with a pallet. Hit the dish on the table to get rid of any air pockets in the batter. Place in the freezer for at least 3 hours.

10. Before serving, place the parfait in the fridge so that it isn't too hard. Brush the backside of the lid with the lemon syrup and place it on top. Dust with confectioners' sugar; decorate with a few raspberries and peppermint leaves. Serve with raspberry coulis.

Tip!
If you want to serve a classic lemon fromage, reduce the sugar by 50 g (¼ cup) and put the mixture in a 1 liter dish that you have dusted with confectioners' sugar. Place in the freezer for 1 hour. Dip the dish in tepid water, remove the fromage from the mold and place it in the fridge to thaw for up to 1 hour. Serve with fresh raspberries and raspberry coulis for the best possible dessert after a Sunday meal, perhaps consisting of veal roast, cream sauce, cucumber salad, and black currant jelly. Guaranteed to make anyone my age nostalgic.

Violet Ice Cream with Fresh Violets

This delicious ice cream has a slight tone of violet, and it is a perfect as pre-dessert before you serve the main dessert when you treat your guests to a fancy dinner. Or, you could garnish it with more fresh berries and combine it with violet ice cream, if you want to serve it as the main dessert.

Serves 8 people

1 batch of the violet ice cream (page 43)
½ batch of butter streusel (p. 224)
fresh violets

Day 1
Boil the ice cream mass and let it stand in the refrigerator until the next day.

Day 2
1. Bake butter streusel and let it cool.
2 Freeze the ice cream. Temper it in the refrigerator if it is too hard.
3. When serving, remove the ice cream from the freezer and use a spoon that has been dipped in warm water to form a beautiful ice cream egg, and place it on the butter streusel.
4. Garnish with a few violets.

STRAWBERRIES FÉMINA

A refreshing dessert after a good dinner, or a cooling treat during a hot summer day.

Serves about 6 people

½ batch of the strawberry granite (page 64)
1 batch orange sorbet (page 57)
1 batch orange chips of 1 orange (page 227)
3 oranges
⅓ cup simple sugar syrup (page 44)
600 g (5 cups) strawberries
75 g (⅓ cup) Cointreau
75 g (⅗ cup) confectioners' sugar

1. Make the granite and freeze the sorbet in an ice cream machine.
2. Make orange chips and allow them to dry in 175°F for about 2 hours or until they are dry. Store them in an airtight jar as soon as they have cooled, to prevent them from getting soft.
3. Wash an orange and cut the peel as thinly as possible with a sharp knife. Blanch the peels in boiling water for 5-10 minutes to get rid of any bitterness. Drain in a sieve.
4. Boil the syrup with the peels and let them simmer until they are clear. Cool and store in the fridge.
5. Place 6 tall glasses in the freezer.
6. Use a small, sharp knife to cut away the peels on the oranges and cut the oranges into thin, peel free wedges. Rinse and hull the strawberries and cut each strawberry into 4 pieces.
7. Drain the candied orange peels in a sieve. Marinate strawberries, orange fillets and candied orange strips in Cointreau and confectioners' sugar for one hour.
8. Put some marinated strawberries and orange fillets in the glasses. Shape beautiful eggs out of the orange sorbet with a spoon that has been dipped in hot water and put them on top. Fill with marinated strawberries and add a spoonful of sorbet, and cover with the remaining strawberries.
9. Spread the strawberry granite on top, stick two orange chips into the dessert and serve with some sort of almond pastry.

Serves 8 people

1 springform pan, 8 inches in diameter

1 batch lemon sorbet (page 57)
1 pot of peppermint
200 g (1 ⅗ cups) fresh raspberries
confectioners' sugar

Pâte à cigarette:
100 g (7 tbsp) unsalted butter
100 g (⅖ cup) egg whites
20 g (4 tsp) pure vanilla sugar
80 g (¾ cup) confectioners' sugar
100 g (¾ cup) plain flour
bitter almond oil

1. Make sure that the butter and egg whites have a room temperature. Preheat the oven to 400°F.
2. Sift vanilla sugar, confectioners' sugar, and flour together. Mix butter with the sifted ingredients, add the egg white in small portions until you have a smooth batter. Season with a few drops of bitter almond oil (better to add too little than too much).
3. Draw 4 saucer-sized circles on a parchment paper. Add a tablespoon of batter into the center of each circle and spread out as fine as possible until the batter is slightly larger than the circle.
4. Bake about 4 plates per tray at a time, about 5 minutes or until they are beautifully golden brown around the edges. As soon as you remove the tray from the oven, transfer the bottoms to upside down turned glasses and allow to solidify. Continue this process until you run out of batter. Store the bottoms in a dry place, you can even make them a few days ahead.

Almond short crust pastry, extra firm:
60 g (½ cup) flour
175 g (1½ cups) flour
120 g (8½ tbsp) butter, unsalted (room temperature)
90 g (¾ cup) confectioners' sugar
2 g (⅓ tsp) fleur de sel
30 g (⅓ cup) of almond meal
50 g (⅕ cup) eggs

The bottom glaze:
50 g (⅕ cup) eggs
40 g (⅙ cup) egg yolks

1. Sift 60 g (½ cup) flour onto a baking paper, and sift 175 g (1⅖ cups) onto another sheet of baking paper.
2. Mix the soft butter with confectioners' sugar, salt, almond meal, 60 g (½ cup) flour, and the egg into dough. Gently work the remaining flour into the dough without overworking it. Cover in plastic wrap and store in the refrigerator for at least 1 hour.
3. Work the pastry dough smooth with your hands at first, then roll it into a round bottom, about 0.12 inch thick. Occasionally flour and lift the dough so that it does not stick to the table. Flour it on top and roll the dough onto the rolling pin.
4. Place a 2 inches high springform pan that is about 8 inches in diameter onto a baking paper. Take a little piece of dough, dust it in flour and use it to press the dough in the pan to get rid of any air pockets. Prick the dough with a fork, and leave it to rest for 30 minutes in the refrigerator or in freezer.
5. Preheat the oven to 350°F. Cut a baking sheet so that it is slightly larger than the pan, place it inside the pan and fill it with dried peas or beans. Bake the dough for about 20 minutes until it is golden brown. Remove from the oven and remove peas or beans.
6. Whisk together the eggs and egg yolks and brush the entire crust surface. Return to the oven again, and bake for about 2 minutes. Remove from the oven and allow the crust to solidify.

Lemon Cream:
4 yellow ripe lemons with thin peels
165 g (approx. ⅘ cup) sugar
300 g (1¼ cups) eggs
350 g (1½ cups) whipping cream

1. Wash the lemons, grate the zest from two of the lemons, and squeeze the juice out of all four.
2. Create a syrup with the sugar and the strained lemon juice.
3. Beat the eggs lightly with the lemon zest, add the boiling syrup and whisk until well blended.
4. Boil the cream, and add the boiling cream to the batter and mix well.
5. Preheat the oven to 350°F, fill the form with the cream and bake for about 40 minutes. Remove from the oven and let it cool. Let it stand in the refrigerator until it has solidified.

Coulis:
250 g (2 cups) raspberries
250 g (approx. 2 cups) red currants
75 g (⅗ cup) confectioners' sugar
1 lemon, the juice

1. Mix berries and confectioners' sugar in a blender, pass through a sieve and season with lemon juice. Keep cold.
2. Dust the lemon tart surface with confectioners' sugar and caramelize it with a gas flame until it is golden brown.
3. Dip a sharp knife in warm water and cut into pieces. Make sure the sorbet is soft. If it is too hard, temper it in the fridge until it has softened.
4. Place a piece of tart on the plate, and place a tulip shape next to it. Form a large ball of sorbet with an ice cream scoop and put inside the tulip. Add the coulis and garnish with a few raspberries. Decorate with a little bit of peppermint.

Chocolate Meringue Cake with Vanilla Ice Cream

This dessert is so delicious that it usually becomes every chocolate lover's favorite. Even the kids will love this flavorful cake, and it can be stored in the fridge for several days.

Serves 8 people

Day 1
½ batch of vanilla ice cream (page 32)

Chocolate Meringue:
120 g (½ cup) egg whites
125 g (⅗ cup) granulated sugar
5 g (1 tsp) lemon juice
125 g (1 cup) confectioners' sugar
55 g (⅗ cup) high quality cocoa, preferably Valrhona

Chocolate Cream:
225 g (approx. 1⅓ cups) dark chocolate, preferably Valrhona Grand Cru Guanaja 70.5%
125 g (½ cup) unsalted butter
40 g (⅙ cup) egg yolks
120 g (½ cup) egg whites
70 g (⅙ cup) sugar
15 g (1 tbsp) lemon juice
cocoa to dust the cake

1. Preheat the oven to 200° F. Draw three circles on a baking paper, 8.5 inches in diameter. Place the paper on a baking tray.
2. Beat the egg whites with one third of the granulated sugar and lemon juice in an absolutely clean metal bowl. Whisk until you have light foam. Add another third of the sugar and increase the whipping speed. Add the remaining sugar and whisk to a stiff meringue.
3. Sift confectioners' sugar and cocoa onto a paper. Fold the cocoa-sugar into the meringue with a pallet until you have a light and airy mass.
4. Fill a piping bag (with a smooth tube nr. 12) with the meringue or cut a hole in the tip of the bag. Inside the marked circles, pipe the meringue from the center outward. Next pipe 2 inch long meringues with the remaining meringue batter on another baking sheet with parchment paper. Bake for 60-90 minutes until they are dry and airy. Let cool on a rack.
5. Chocolate cream: Finely chop the chocolate and melt it in microwave while stirring occasionally to 113°F. Set aside, add the cold butter and the egg yolks and whisk to a smooth paste.
6. Boil some water in a saucepan. Whisk together egg whites, sugar, and lemon juice in an absolutely clean metal bowl. Place it over the saucepan and whisk vigorously until it reaches a temperature of 131 – 140°F (make sure the water does not exceed 194°F. because then the egg white will coagulate).
7. Remove from the heat and beat the meringue cold. Fold the chocolate cream into the mixture and stir until fluffy.
8. Place a meringue bottom on the table, spread a third of the cream over the bottom with a pallet. Place another bottom over the cream, and cover it on top and all around with cream. Place the cake in the fridge overnight.

Day 2
1. Freeze the ice cream.
2. Remove the cake from the fridge and let it stand for 30 minutes in room temperature, press the meringue in place, and dust with cocoa and a little bit of confectioners' sugar.
3. Serve the cake with freshly frozen vanilla ice cream and strong coffee.

Meringue Roll with Cassata Mousse and Strawberry & Peppermint Coulis

Serves 12 people

1 batch cassata mousse (page 71)
2 batches of the strawberry coulis (page 227)
    with 20 g (approx. ⅓ cup) peppermint
confectioners' sugar
cocoa
600 g (5 cups) mixed fresh red berries

tpt (tant pour tant):
100 g (¾ cup) roasted peeled hazelnuts
90 g (approx. ½ cup) sugar
10 g (2 tsp)   pure vanilla sugar
70 g (8¾ tbsp) corn starch

Meringue Roll:
200 g (⅘ cup) egg whites
15 g (1 tbsp) lemon juice
50 g + 150 g (¼ cup + ¾ cup) sugar

1. Preheat the oven to 350°F.
2. First, make a tpt by mixing nuts, sugar, vanilla sugar, and corn starch into a fine powder in a food processor.
3. Whisk the egg whites on medium speed with the lemon juice and 50 g (¼ cup) sugar. Add 150 g (¾ cup) sugar while constantly whipping the batter into a solid meringue.
4. Fold the tpt into the meringue with a spatula. Fill a plastic piping bag (with a plain tube nr. 12) with the meringue.
5. Place a sheet of baking parchment paper on a baking tray and pipe the meringue lengths side by side, lengthwise. Bake for about 20 minutes, open the oven door a few times to air out the oven. When the meringue is firm but still springs back when pressed on, and it is golden brown it is ready. If you bake it for too long, it will crack when you roll it up. Let cool on a wire rack.
6. Spread the cassata mousse over the meringue and roll together with a greaseproof paper to a tense roll. Store in the freezer for at least 6 hours.
7. Make the strawberry coulis and add the peppermint, mix, and pass through a sieve.
8. When serving, cut beautiful oblique discs out of the meringue roll with a sharp knife and dust with confectioners' sugar and cocoa. Place on a plate and garnish with mixed red berries and fresh mint. Serve with strawberry coulis on the side.

Wild Strawberry Ice Cream

For 6-8 people

Day 1
Make a batch of the strawberry ice cream
(page 40), but replace the strawberries
with wild strawberries.

Day 2
Make half a batch of the French meringue
(page 230), pipe small oblong meringue
shapes and bake them at 200°F for about
90 minutes, or until they are dry. Crush
the meringue in your hand and sprinkle a
little bit onto each plate. Freeze the ice
cream and form a beautiful egg out of it
with a spoon that has been dipped in
warm water. You can decorate it with
some fresh wild strawberries if you want.

Tip!
If you have enough wild strawberries, you
can enhance the flavor by making a wild
strawberry coulis (page 227) and serve it
with the ice cream. Any sort of sweet
pastry, like the orange tuiles (page 226),
will also complement this dessert.

An authentic pastry chef that specializes in ice cream should also be able to carve beautiful ice sculptures.

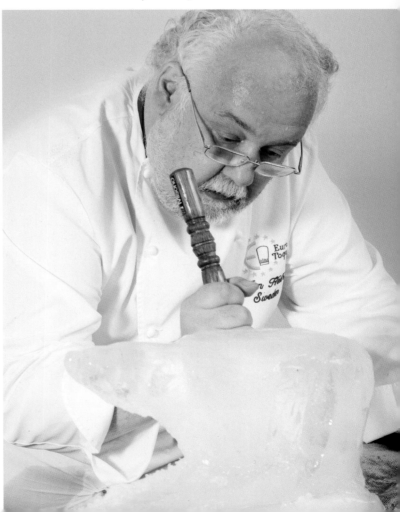

Polar Bear Sculpture in Ice with Ice Cream Fruits

During my years working on cruise ships, I created many ice cream sculptures, which was one of the fun tasks for the Captain's dinner.

This polar bear is carved with a chisel out of an ice block that weighs about 55 lbs. In the front you see painted ice cream fruits, filled with ice cream and sorbet.

I freeze the ice by mixing ice cubes with water and freezing the mass in a plastic box. When you remove the box from the freezer, cover it with a bag, and allow it to stand in room temperature for 2 hours to thaw.

Next, I carve the polar bear out of the ice block with a chisel. You won't need any other tools, because the ice will be soft enough.

You can illuminate the underside of the ice block with a flashlight.

ORANGE TUILES WITH VALRHONA ICE CREAM

Everyone loves this delicious dessert. The combination with the brittle orange tuiles, and the soft and smooth chocolate ice cream is bound to be good. Make sure to get hold of the right chocolate. Valrhona has a superior quality, I think, and you can get a hold of it almost everywhere nowadays.

For 6 people

Chocolate Rolls:
80 g (⅖ cup) dark chocolate, preferably Valrhona Grand Cru Guanaja 70.5%

Day 1
Make half a batch of dark chocolate ice cream (page 37) with Valrhona Grand Cru Guanaja 70.5%.

Day 2
1. Freeze the ice cream in and ice cream machine and place it in the freezer.
2. Make a batch of orange tuiles (page 226).
3. Chocolate Rolls: Chop and melt chocolate in microwave or water bath at 122 - 131°F. Apply it thinly on the marble slab or tray and stroke it back and forth with a pallet until the chocolate hardens. Metal table scrapers work well for scraping out rolls. (see page 234, chocolate techniques).
4. Place a tuile on each plate and make sure that the ice cream is soft and smooth, temper it in the fridge otherwise until it softens.
5. Shape big beautiful eggs out of the ice cream with a spoon that has been dipped in hot water. Garnish with a chocolate roll.

RED TEA ICE CREAM WITH CHOCOLATE

Tea ice cream is not that well known in Sweden, but using different kinds of tea as flavoring in ice cream is bound to taste good. Iced tea with lemon has found its way to Sweden, so perhaps tea ice cream will become popular as well.

The garnish in the image is made with sugar-based dough that is called pastillage. I used it to make the exotic flowers in the photo, then I painted them with an airbrush. I am not including that recipe, it is too complicated. However, I couldn't help myself from making something beautiful on the plate

For 6 people

Day 1
Make half a batch of tea ice cream (page 37) with red (rooibos) tea.

Day 2
1. Make a batch of almond tuiles with anise (page 226). Freeze the ice cream in an ice cream machine and store it in the freezer.
2. Chop 150 g (¾ cup) of dark chocolate, preferably Valrhona Grand Cru Manjari 54.5%, and melt it to 122 - 131°F in the microwave while stirring occasionally, or in a water bath.
3. Temper the chocolate (see page 234, chocolate techniques).
4. Fill a paper cone with the chocolate, and cut a small hole in the tip. Pipe a chocolate net inside six round dishes that hold ⅔ cup, and that have been polished with cotton inside so that the chocolate will release and so that it does not crack as it settles. Place them in the refrigerator for 60 minutes.
5. Carefully remove the nets from the molds. Place them in deep plates, and shape beautiful eggs out of the smooth ice cream and serve this delicious dessert with anise tuiles.

ICE BLOCK WITH NOUGATINE PLATE AND ROSE ICE CREAM

This beautiful dessert is quite simple to make but has a great impact with small means. Ice cream with roses tastes a lot better than one might imagine. Serve with vanilla macaroons (page 226) and raspberry jam (page 227).

For 6 people

6 ice block plastic molds, that each hold 1⅓ cups, empty cream packets will suffice as well. You can also use plastic rose molds (some stores with soap molds will have them).

1 batch rose ice cream (page 43)
1 batch nougatine (p. 225)
250 g (2 cups) fresh raspberries
rose petals from organically grown roses

Day 1

1. Cook the rose ice cream and let it settle in the refrigerator until the next day.
2. Fill half of the ice blocks with water and freeze for 2 hours.
3. Place 6 small shot glasses on the ice blocks in the molds and fill up with water around the glasses. Freeze until the next day.

Day 2

1. Freeze rose ice cream, and if you are using rose molds, fill them and freeze the ice cream in the molds. Alternatively, you can shape the ice cream into beautiful eggs with a spoon dipped in hot water, it is also beautiful.
2. Preheat the oven to 300° F. Make the nougatine. Quickly roll it out by using a rolling pin and a silicone baking mat to roll it as thin as possible. Put into the oven on a baking sheet to soften.
3. Cut out round plates in nougatine with cookie cutter that is slightly larger than the ice cubes (press hard). Remove any excess nougat from them. If you want to, can you make a hole in the center with a smaller cookie cutter, but it is not necessary.
4. Pour hot water into the whiskey glasses so that they release from the molds and remove them so that a hole remains in the ice.
5. Place the ice blocks on napkins, put a few raspberries in the holes, and place a nougatine disk on top.
6. Dip the ice cream molds in cold water, release the ice cream and place it on top of the ice blocks. Garnish with a few rose petals.

Manjari Chocolate Parfait

This chocolate lover's dessert should be served well tempered, so that the parfait is creamy and soft inside, and creates a subtle contrast with the thin chocolate shell.

Serves 8 people

8 strips of overhead transparency film, 2 inches wide and 8.2 inches long, stapled into rings
½ batch light chocolate parfait with dark chocolate, preferably Valrhona Grand Cru Manjari 64.5% (page 67)

Manjari chocolate biscuit:
18 g (2⅓ tbsp) flour
105 g (approx. ½ cup) dark chocolate, preferably Valrhona Grand Cru Manjari 64.5%
60 g (4¼ tbsp) unsalted butter
100 g (⅔ cup) egg whites
5 g (1 tsp) lemon juice
55 g (approx. ¼ cup) sugar
50 g (approx. ⅓ cup) egg yolks (about 3)

Syrup to soak the layers:
15 g (2 tbsp) confectioners' sugar
15 g (1 tbsp) water
20 g (4 tsp) Cointreau

1. Preheat the oven to 350°F. Sift the flour onto a baking paper.
2. Melt the chopped chocolate and butter in a plastic bowl in the microwave. Heat to 122 - 133°F.
3. Whisk the egg whites, lemon juice, and sugar to a rigid meringue. Beat on medium speed so that you get a stable meringue.
4. Whisk the egg yolks and a ladleful of meringue batter into the chocolate butter. Mix with a spatula to a smooth and airy mass. Sift the flour into the mass, and fold it in gently with a spatula.
5. Use a pallet to spread the batter evenly over a sheet of baking paper. Bake it golden brown for 16-18 minutes, immediately transfer it to a wire rack.
6. Dissolve powdered sugar in the water and the liquor with a whisk.
7. Place the plastic film rings on a baking sheet with baking paper, cut out 8 round bottoms out of the biscuit, that are slightly smaller than the rings in diameter, and put them inside the rings. (Freeze the remaining biscuit for another occasion). Brush the biscuits with the syrup until they have absorbed all of the liquid.
8. Use a plastic piping bag (with a plain tube) to fill the rings with the parfait, smoothen the surface with a pallet. Freeze rings for at least 6 hours, or overnight.

Assembling the cake:

8 strips of soft plastic film, 2.8 inches wide, and long enough to reach around the rings exactly.
200 g (1 cup) dark chocolate, preferably Valrhona Grand Cru Manjari 64.5%

1. Release the parfaits from the rings and put them back into the freezer.
2. Finely chop the chocolate and melt it in the microwave in a plastic bowl, or in a water bath to 122 - 133°F.
3. Temper the chocolate (see page 234). Apply an even layer of chocolate on one plastic film strip at a time.
4. Remove a parfait from the freezer, wrap it in a chocolate strip (chocolate facing inward) and squeeze at the top so that it looks like in the photo, this can be done quickly when the parfait is frozen. Make sure that the seam is on top so that the plastic can be easily removed without ruining the dessert. Store in the fridge. Continue until all the parfaits are wrapped. If the chocolate thickens while you are working with it, heat it only to 87.8 – 89.6°F, and continue.
5. Place the parfaits on plates, carefully remove the plastic and let them stand in room temperature until they are soft before you serve them.

LOVE HEARTS

Perhaps the perfect dessert to serve at the engagement party, or wedding?

Serves 8 people

fresh organically grown roses
8 heart molds in plastic

½ batch of parfait according to the crème anglaise method (page 65)
1 batch classic French meringue (p. 230)
1 batch fruit jelly (page 226)

Day 1
1. Make the parfait with 20 g (approx. ⅓ cup) of flavorful rose petals that you let soak in the cream. Optionally, add a little bit of rose water to enhance the flavor.
2. Preheat the oven to 250°F. Fill a plastic piping bag (with a plain tube, nr.12, or cut a hole in the tip) with the meringue.
3. Pipe 2 inches long oval meringues on a baking sheet, baking mat, or silpat mat. Sprinkle sugar over them so they become brittle. Put them in the oven with open throttle for 10 minutes and then lower temperature to 200°F. Dry them until they feel dry, about 90 minutes.
4. Make the fruit jelly.

Day 2
½ batch of biscuit à la cuieller (p. 225)
granulated sugar
red food coloring
1 drop of rose water

Sugar syrup:
30 g (4 tbsp) confectioners' sugar
20 g (4 tsp) water
1 drop of rose water

1. Preheat the oven to 450°F. Use a pallet to spread the biscuit mass like a jelly roll and bake it golden brown for 7-8 minutes. Sprinkle with lots of sugar, add a baking paper on top and turn it upside down on the baking tray. Transfer the roll cake to a wire rack to cool.
2. Cut bottoms out of the roll cake, slightly smaller than the heart molds. Use a plain cookie cutter, or a heart shaped cookie cutter if you have one.
3. Stir together sugar and water until dissolved, and flavor with the rose water.
4. Use a plastic piping bag to fill the molds with the parfait. Spread it with a pallet and hit the molds against the table so that no air pockets remain in the batter.
5. Place the bottoms that have been brushed with the syrup on top and press carefully. Freeze for at least 6 hours.

Assembly:
1. Heat the jelly to 95°F and mix with some food coloring and rose water.
2. Remove the parfaits from the plastic molds by dipping them in warm water. Transfer them onto a wire rack with baking paper underneath.
3. Fill a plastic piping bag with the jelly, and cut a small hole in the tip. Pipe the jelly over the hearts so that they are completely covered.
4. Crush some meringues with a rolling pin, transfer the crumbs onto plates and gently lift the hearts with a spatula and place them on top. Garnish each heart with a rose leaf. Serve with a bowl of mixed red berries on the side.

Raspberry Ganache Spiral with Vanilla Ice Cream

Photographer Klas Andersson contributed to the idea behind this elegant dessert. Raspberries with chocolate is always a successful combination. When you dry the raspberries you intensify the aroma with the Manjari chocolate, which is also acidic. Confiserie Brändli in Basel were first to make the raspberry ganache and the recipe used to be secret. It consisted of 35.3 oz raspberry purée with 10% of sugar that was brought to a boil, and poured over 53 oz of chopped milk chocolate, and this was stirred into a ganache. Finally, we added 10.6 oz of unsalted butter.

It was good, I promise!

Serves 8 people

Day 1
½ batch of vanilla ice cream (page 32)
250 g (2 cups) fresh raspberries to the drying

1. Cook the ice cream.
2. Preheat the oven 175°F.
3. Spread the raspberries over a tray that has been covered with parchment paper and dry them in the oven for about 8 hours. When they are light and dry, they are ready. Store in airtight container once they have cooled.

Ganache:
160 g (approx. 1⅓ cups) raspberries
15 g (1½ tbsp) sugar
150 g (¾ cup) dark chocolate, preferably Valrhona Grand Cru Manjari 64.5%
30 g (approx. 2 tbsp) unsalted butter
25 g (2 tbsp) of sugar to make the raspberry powder

1. Mix the raspberries and sugar with a stick blender to a purée and pass through a fine sieve. Finely chop the chocolate and put it in a bowl.
2. Bring the raspberry purée to a boil, and pour it over the chocolate and stir with a spoon until the chocolate has dissolved. Mix with a stick blender into an emulsion. Insert a thermometer. When the temperature has dropped to 95 – 104°F, add the butter and mix to a nice ganache with mayonnaise-like consistency. Cover with plastic wrap and store the ganache at room temperature until the next day.

Day 2
1. Freeze the ice cream.
2. Fill a plastic piping bag (with plain tube nr. 10, or cut a small hole in the tip) with the ganache.
3. Place a sheet of baking parchment paper on a tray and pipe 8 spirals on it, like in the photo. Let them solidify in the fridge for about 1 hour.
4. Place a baking sheet on top of the spirals, turn them upside down and carefully remove the paper.
5. Mix the dry raspberries with sugar to a powder. Sprinkle raspberry powder over the spirals and gently transfer them to dessert plates. Let them stand in room temperature for at least 1 hour so that the ganache softens.
6. Dip a tablespoon in warm water to shape a beautiful ice cream egg and place it next to the spiral. Garnish with a thin piece of vanilla pod and some mint. Serve right away with the remaining vanilla ice cream on the side.

Orange Parfait with White Chocolate Coating

This delicious and refreshing parfait embedded in white chocolate is delicious with the warm chocolate sauce. The flavors of chocolate and orange complement each other.

Serves 8 people

2 sheets of soft overhead transparency film
1 batch of chocolate biscuit Manjari (Page 175, chocolate parfait Manjari)
1 batch Cointreau sugary syrup (Page 175, chocolate parfait Manjari)
½ batch orange parfait (page 67)
300 g (1½ cups) white chocolate, preferably Valrhona Ivoire, or Lindt
1 batch of the warm chocolate sauce (Page 214, Bomb à l'Opéra)
cocoa powder, preferably Valrhona

1. Bake chocolate biscuits and let them cool on a wire rack.
2. Stir the syrup until the sugar dissolves.
3. Cut the overhead transparency film into 8 pieces that are 2 inches wide and 8.3 inches long. Staple them into circles, and place them on a tray with baking paper.
4. Cut bottoms out of the chocolate biscuits with a plain cookie cutter, about 3 inches in diameter, and place them inside rings. Brush the bottoms with syrup until they are completely soaked.
5. Make the orange parfait, and fill a plastic piping bag with the parfait, and cut a hole in the tip. Fill the circles with the parfait, and use a pallet to smoothen the surface. Freeze for at least 6 hours, or overnight if you want to make them a day before.
6. Loosen the parfaits from the rings, set them on a tray with baking paper and set them in the freezer again.
7. Use a sharp knife to cut 8 pieces, 2.4 inches wide and 8.3 inches long, out of the soft plastic.
8. Finely chop the chocolate and melt it in a plastic bowl in the microwave while stirring occasionally, or in a water bath.
9. Temper the chocolate (see page 234). Spread a thin layer of chocolate over the plastic sheets, and place around the parfaits, with the chocolate layer facing the parfait. Gently press and carefully remove the plastic film. Press towards the center, so that it looks like in the picture, place in the freezer and continue to cover all eight parfaits and store them in the freezer.
10. Heat the remaining chocolate and be careful not to exceed 84.2°F, because then you will need to temper the chocolate again. Spread half of the chocolate thinly on a piece of marble or metal and make huge rolls out of the white chocolate by scraping them with a metal table scraper of metal (See illustration page 235).
11. Make the chocolate sauce and keep it warm in a water bath.
12. Temper the parfaits for 15-30 minutes in the fridge before you serve them. Use a knife to check if they are soft. Place them on plates, and garnish with chocolate rolls like in the picture. Dust with cocoa and serve with warm chocolate sauce.

This elegant dessert is nice to serve with a little surprise inside.

Serves 8 people

8 semi-round individual molds in metal or plastic
1 sheet of gold leaf (can be found in framing stores)
½ batch of mango sorbet (page 50)
250 g (¾ cup) dark chocolate, preferably Valrhona Grand Cru Guanaja 70.5%
200 g (1⅗ cups) mixed red berries
cocoa powder, preferably Valrhona

1. Make the sorbet and store it in the freezer.
2. If you are using metal molds, polish them with cotton inside so that the chocolate does not crack when it pulls itself together. Melt chocolate in the microwave in a plastic bowl at 122-131°F while occasionally stirring, or in water bath.
3. Temper the chocolate (see page 234). Fill a paper cone with it, and cut a small hole in the tip. Pipe a fine chocolate net inside the molds, pipe the chocolate extra thick around the edge. Place the chocolate in the refrigerator until the chocolate contracts, which usually takes about 30 minutes.
4. Remove the chocolate nets gently by pressing on one side. Let the molds return to room temperature and rub them with cotton again. Temper the chocolate again and make 8 additional chocolate nets.
5. Make sure that the sorbet is smooth, temper it in the fridge otherwise.
6. Sprinkle the underside of the eight glasses with cocoa powder and place a chocolate half onto each glass.
7. Shape little beautiful sorbet eggs with a dessert spoons that has been dipped in warm water, and place one egg into one chocolate net.
8. Add a few mixed berries and gently add another chocolate net on top, that has been decorated with a little bit of gold leaf (placed there with the tip of a knife). Serve this spectacular chocolate dessert right away.

Banana Split

All Americans, and most Swedes, love this classic dessert. I remember when I worked for Cunard Line that as soon as we had banana split on the lunch menu, 75 percent of the guests ordered it for dessert. Many ice cream parlors serve a scoop of vanilla ice cream, and a scoop of strawberry ice cream between the bananas, and sometimes melba sauce, and chocolate sauce. In my variation, I serve only vanilla ice cream and chocolate sauce, which I think tastes much cleaner. This dessert is "childishly delicious" if you use high quality chocolate, good vanilla ice cream, and well-ripened, sweet bananas.

For 4 people

Day 1
Make half a batch of vanilla ice cream (page 32)

Day 2
½ batch chocolate sauce (page 214, Bomb à l'Opéra)
banana chips from one banana (page 227)
50 g (½ cup) sliced almonds
250 g (1 cup) whipping cream
15 g (1½ tbsp) sugar
5 g (1 tsp) pure vanilla sugar
4 beautiful, ripe bananas

1. Freeze ice cream in ice cream machine and store it in the freezer.
2. Make chocolate sauce and banana chips.
3. Preheat the oven to 350°F. Spread the almonds on a baking sheet and toast them golden brown in the oven, stirring occasionally so they don't get burned.
4. Whip the cream to a smooth foam along with sugar and vanilla sugar in a well-chilled metal bowl.
5. When you want to serve this dessert, peel bananas and cut them lengthwise in half. Place them on plates, preferably oblong. Pipe cream around the bananas and sprinkle with sliced almonds.
6. Add a couple of big scoops of the smooth and soft vanilla ice cream. Pour chocolate sauce over the dessert, and stick a banana chip into the delicious combination.

MERINGUE PAVLOV WITH PASSION FRUIT SORBET AND FRESH FRUIT

Crispy meringue with fresh passion fruit sorbet and fresh berries is a great way to end a nice dinner.

Serves 8 people

*1 batch of the classic French meringue
(p. 230) but replace 10 g (4 tsp) powdered
sugar with 10 g (2 tsp) pure vanilla sugar,
to give the meringue an aroma of
vanilla.*
½ batch of passion fruit sorbet (p. 54)

Garnish:
*about 500 g (approx. 4 cups) fresh pineapple,
raspberry, red currants and strawberries*
peppermint
100 g mango coulis (p. 227)
100 g strawberry coulis (p. 227)
confectioners' sugar

1. Preheat the oven to 250°F.
2. Draw eight circles, 3.1 inches in diameter, with a pencil, on a sheet of baking parchment paper.
3. Put the meringue in a plastic piping bag with plain tube nr. 12, or cut a hole in the tip. Pipe a spiral of meringue within each circle, build on each pass creating a slightly conical shape. Sprinkle a little sugar on top to make them brittle.
4. Place them in the oven for 10 minutes with open throttle. Lower the temperature to 200°F and bake them until they feel dry, about 90 minutes.
5. Freeze the sorbet in an ice cream machine and store it in the freezer.
6. Structure: Place the meringue shells on plates and draw a line of strawberry and mango coulis next each other. Serve the remaining coulis on the side.
7. Make two scoops out of the smooth sorbet with an ice cream scoop that has been dipped in warm water. Decorate with fruits and berries, as shown, and garnish with a mint leaf or other appropriate herb, sprinkle with confectioners' sugar and serve immediately.

Ice Cream Meringue with Raspberries

Meringue Suisse is a common dessert at pastry shops in France and Switzerland. The simplest variation is a classic meringue Chantilly, which is filled with the whipped cream and served with warm chocolate sauce. It can also be filled with various ice creams and decorated with whipped cream, and berries or fruit. Sometimes the meringues are pushed into the ice cream to fill it out, but I don't think it is necessary.

Serves 8 people

1 batch of classic French meringue (p. 230)
1 batch of raspberry ice cream (page 40)
500 g raspberry coulis (page 227)
250 g (1 cup) whipping cream
15 g (1½ tbsp) sugar
5 g (1 tsp) pure vanilla sugar
500 g (4 cups) fresh raspberries
peppermint
confectioners' sugar

1. Preheat the oven to 250°F.
2. Put the meringue in a plastic piping bag with plain tube nr. 12, or cut a hole in the tip. Pipe 16 oval meringues, about the size of an egg, on a parchment paper, or a baking mat. Sprinkle with sugar so that the meringues become brittle.
3. Set the meringues in the oven with open throttle and lower the temperature to 200°F after 10 minutes. Dry them until they feel dry, it takes about 90 minutes.
4. Freeze raspberry ice cream in ice cream machine and store it in the freezer.
5. Make the raspberry coulis.
6. Whip the cream with sugar and vanilla sugar in a chilled metal bowl to a flexible foam.
7. Place two scoops of raspberry ice cream (formed with an ice cream scoop that has been dipped in hot water) on a plate. Press a meringue on each side of the ice cream, like in the photo. Pour a little bit of coulis over the ice cream and serve the rest on the side.
8. Decorate with piped cream by using a piping bag with a star tube. Garnish with raspberries and mint leaves, and dust with confectioners' sugar.

Strawberry and Mascarpone Ice Cream Rolled in Meringue Crumbs and Fresh Strawberries

I cannot describe the excitement I felt when I tried this excellent Italian ice cream for the first time in a small restaurant in Genoa. Their fried seafood was no joke either.

Serves 8 people

1. Make a batch of classic French meringue (Page 230). Preheat the oven to 250°F.
2. Fill a plastic piping bag (with a plain tube) or cut a hole in the tip. Pipe oval meringues on a baking sheet, or a silicone baking mat. Sprinkle with sugar to make it more brittle.
3. Place the meringues in the oven with open throttle and lower the heat after 10 minutes to 200°F. Dry them until they feel dry, about 90 minutes.

Ice Cream:
2 gelatin leaves (4 g)
20 g (approx. ⅓ cup) of lemon verbena
500 g (4 cups) cleaned and rinsed ripe strawberries
250 g (2 cups) confectioners' sugar
85 g (5½ tbsp) freshly squeezed orange juice
15 g (1 tbsp) lemon juice
250 g (approx. 1 cup) mascarpone

1. Soak the gelatin leaves in plenty of cold water for at least 10 minutes.
2. Add the lemon verbena to boiling water, immediately pick it up and put it in ice water.
3. Purée strawberries, lemon verbena, and confectioners' sugar, and pass through a sieve.
4. Lift the gelatin leaves out of the water, and put them in orange and lemon juice, heat it to 122°F and mix it into the strawberry purée.
5. Mix the mascarpone into the ice cream batter.
6. Freeze the ice cream in an ice cream machine and store it in the freezer.

500 g (4 cups) ripe strawberries for decoration
500 g strawberry coulis (page 227)
confectioners' sugar

1. Rinse, hull, and cut each strawberry into four pieces. Place them on 8 plates in the same pattern as in the image.
2. Crush 6 meringues gently into crumbs with a rolling pin. Add a little bit meringue crumbs in the middle of the plates so that the ice cream lies still.
3. Make sure that the ice cream is smooth and soft. Otherwise, temper it in the fridge for about 15 minutes.
4. Dip a large ice cream scoop in hot water, and use it to shape ice cream scoops, and roll them in the meringues crumbs and put them in the middle of the plates. Dust with confectioners' sugar and serve with strawberry coulis in a sauceboat on the side.

Sea Buckthorn Vacherin with Blackberries

I dedicate this delicious ice cream cake with its origins from Switzerland to the late Chef Werner Vögeli, who was chef and culinary manager at Opera Cellar, in addition to being a *hovtraktör*, an honorary title given by the Swedish royal family for excellence in the art of cooking. Werner loved meringue and Swedish berries, such as cloudberries, arctic bramble, and hawthorn. A few years ago, when I was awarded the Werner Prize and the Werner figurine, my diploma said that I had taught hundreds of cooks and pastry chefs to make desserts over the years. It made me think like Werner - to always be proud of my profession, but to remain humble, just like Werner always was despite his high position. Glory to Werner and his gastronomic achievements in Swedish cuisine, and let him rattle with the pots in heaven!

Serve this dessert after a classic game meal, perhaps saddle of hare, or saddle of venison, with a good red wine.

Serves 8 people

A spring form pan, about 10 inches in diameter

1 batch of classic French meringue (p. 230)
80 g (⅔ cup) dark chocolate, preferably Valrhona Grand Cru Manjari 64.5%
1 batch of sea buckthorn sorbet (page 54)
1 batch of fruit jelly (page 226)
250 g (2 cups) blackberries for garnish
500 g (4 cups) blackberries for the coulis (page 227)

Meringue:

1. Preheat the oven to 250°F. Draw a circle, 9.5 inches in diameter on a baking paper.
2. Fill a plastics piping bag (with a plain tube, nr. 12, or cut a hole at the tip) with the meringue batter, and pipe a meringue bottom in the circle as a spiral starting in the middle.
3. Use the remaining batter to pipe 2 inch long, oblong meringues, sprinkle some sugar over them so they become brittle.
4. Set the meringues in the oven with the damper open, and lower the heat after 10 minutes to 200°F. Dry them until they feel dry to the touch, about 90 minutes.

Assembling the cake:

1. Chop and melt the chocolate in a plastic bowl in the microwave while stirring occasionally, or in a water bath.
2. Brush the melted chocolate over the large meringue bottom. Put it down in a spring form pan and place it in the freezer.
3. Freeze the sorbet, fill the spring form pan with it, and even out the surface at the top. Cover with plastic wrap and freeze for at least 6 hours, or overnight.
4. Heat the fruit jelly to 95°F, quickly spread it over the ice cream cake and allow it to solidify.
5. Release the cake from the spring form pan by heating the edges with your hands until it releases.
6. Place the cake on a beautiful plate and garnish with meringues all around it, as shown in the image. Garnish with blackberries and serve with blackberry coulis on the side. In Switzerland, they used to serve this dessert with a pot of whipped cream on the side, but I don't think it is necessary.

Gianduja parfait with Green Apple Purée

This dessert looks gorgeous when presented in the classic seafood cocktail glasses, like in the image, but it will look just as beautiful in large wine glasses. The soft hazelnut flavored gianduja parfait is very smooth and creamy, because we use the crème anglaise method. The sour apple compote balances the sweetness to complete this dessert

Serves 8 people

16 ball molds that each hold ⅕ cup, out of plastic or silpat
plastic sheet with gold print
overhead transparency film

1 batch of the parfait according to the crème anglaise method (Page 65)
150 g (⅗ cup) gianduja mass (page 229)
100 g (¾ cup) caramelized hazelnuts (p. 228)
200 g (1 cup) milk chocolate, preferably Valhrona Jivara Lactée 40%
100 g (½ cup) dark chocolate, preferably Valhrona Grand Cru Pur Caribe 64.5%

Gianduja Parfait

1. Make a batch of parfait according to the crème anglaise method with vanilla and 150 g (⅗ cup) extra cream. Add the gianduja mass to the basic mass and stir it smooth.
2. Fill the molds with the mass, by means of a plastic piping bag with large plain tube, or cut a hole in the tip. Even out the molds with a spatula and hit them against the table to get rid of any air pockets. Freeze for at least 6 hours, or overnight.
3. Use a rolling pin to crush the caramelized hazelnuts in a clean kitchen towel so they don't fly all over the place.
4. Release the parfaits out of the molds by dipping them in warm water and put them together to form balls, joining them as evenly as possible. Roll the balls in the crushed hazelnuts and return them to the freezer.
5. Chop and melt the milk chocolate in a plastic bowl in the microwave while stirring occasionally, or in a water bath.
6. Temper the chocolate (page 234).
7. Remove balls from freezer and place them on a baking sheet. Put some chocolate in your hand and roll the balls quickly until they are covered in the chocolate. Let them settle on the baking sheet and put them back in the freezer.
8. Chop and melt the dark chocolate in a plastic bowl in the microwave while stirring occasionally, or in a water bath.
9. Temper the chocolate and spread it thinly over the plastic sheet with the gold print, or two sheets of overhead transparency film. As soon as it has solidified, cut out 8 round circles with a smooth cookie cutter that has the same diameter as the glass you are going serve the dessert in. Cut a little hole in the middle with a small cookie cutter so that you get a small chocolate ring. Put them in the fridge to solidify, with a weight on top, to prevent them from bending.

Green apple compote:

5 green apples
50 g (⅕ cup) lemon juice
90 g (approx. ½ cup) sugar

1. Core the apples and cut each apple into 8 pieces.
2. Cook the apples with lemon juice and sugar to a thick compote over high heat.
3. Pass through a vegetable mill, cover with plastic wrap, and let it cool. Store in the refrigerator.

Assembling the dessert:

1. Temper the parfait for 30 minutes in the fridge so that it's soft inside (test it with a knife).
2. Place the middle piece of the chocolate in the bottom of glass, add apple compote and place the larger chocolate ring on top.
3. Melt a little bit of leftover chocolate, use the tip of a knife with the chocolate to attach the gianduja parfait on top of the ring.

RED LOVE APPLES WITH APPLE SORBET

These apples are gorgeous and delicious, draped in red caramel, and with a refreshing apple sorbet filling. They are both stylish and decadent after a fall dinner with good friends. Classic roasted duck with red cabbage, apple sauce, butter fried potatoes, and a good red wine would be a perfect taste teaser to start off with.

Serves 8 people

8 beautiful, green, tart apples
1 lemon
½ batch of green apple sorbet (page 49)

Tosca:
50 g (3½ tbsp) butter
50 g (¼ cup) sugar
50 g (2½ tbsp) of honey
50 g (⅕ cup) whipping cream
50 g (½ cup) sliced almonds

Caramel:
500 g (2½ cups) sugar
200 g (⅘ cup) water
100 g (⅓ cup) glucose
red food dye

80 g (⅖ cup) white chocolate, preferably Valrhona Ivoire, or Lindt, for the chocolate whip

1. Tosca: Preheat the oven to 350°F. Boil all the ingredients except for the almonds in a small saucepan while stirring the solution continuously to 250°F. Occasionally brush the inside of the saucepan with a brush that has been dipped in water to prevent crystallization. Remove the saucepan from the heat, add the sliced almonds, and stir.

2. Use a pallet to spread the mass over a baking sheet, or a pastry mat. Bake in the oven until golden brown, about 8-10 minutes. Remove the tray from the oven and let the tosca solidify for a minute.

3. Use a plain, round cookie cutter to cut out round tosca bottoms, equal in size with the apple opening (see step 6). Store in an airtight jar because they become soft quickly at room temperature.

4. Chocolate rods: Chop and melt chocolate in a plastic bowl in the microwave while occasionally stirring, or in a water bath.

5. Temper the chocolate (page 234). Fill a paper cone with the chocolate and cut a small hole in the tip. Pipe thin streaks along the long side of a parchment paper, and allow to solidify. Cut 0.8 inch long pieces with a knife.

6. Cut off the top of the apples, and core them with a melon baller, and squeeze a little bit of lemon juice inside.

7. Cook a caramel with sugar, water, glucose and red food dye to 311°F, use a thermometer or do a sugar test (Page 232). Brush the inside of the saucepan with a brush and water occasionally to prevent crystallization. Dip the bottom of the pan in cold water to stop the caramel from boiling.

8. Dig a fork into the apples and dip them all the way up to the edge in the caramel, let them drain and place them on parchment paper to solidify.

9. Freeze the sorbet in an ice cream machine, and store it in the freezer.

10. Place the apples on inverted small glass bowls and use an ice cream scoop that has been dipped in hot water to fill them with sorbet. Place white chocolate rods all around and put the tosca on as a lid, as shown.

Coupe Romanoff is a classic when it comes to ice cream coupe, and it is huge on the continent. At the Savoy Hotel in Malmö, we used to have Fraises à la Romanoff on the menu.

The head waiters enjoyed making it at the table. Other popular strawberry desserts were Fraises à la Sarah Bernhardt, Fraises à la Ritz, and Fraises à la Geraldine Ferrar, which were also served iced. Back then, all menus were in French. Hippen rolls are classic with ice cream coupes. Of course you can buy them finished, but they won't taste as good as when you make them yourself. This is how the show rolled at the Savoy when we made Fraises à la Romanoff:

For 4 people

500 g (4 cups) strawberries, washed and hulled, and marinated in 50 g (⅖ cup) confectioner's sugar, 10 g (2 tsp) pure vanilla sugar, 2 cl (1½ tbsp) kirschwasser (cherry brandy) and 2 cl (1½ tbsp) maraschino liqueur over ice for 10 minutes.

Served with crème Chantilly:

250 g (1 cup) whipping cream, 15 g (1 ½ tbsp) sugar and the marrow of a vanilla pod, whipped to a lightweight foam in a chilled metal bowl and poured into a sauceboat. The strawberries were carried to the table iced in a bowl with a napkin, served in deep plates and the head waiter would coat them beautifully with crème Chantilly. A soft and supple scoop of vanilla ice cream was placed on the side and the whole dessert was sprinkled with crushed pistachios.

But let us get back to the Coupe Romanoff.

For 6 people

Day 1
1 batch of strawberry ice cream (page 40)

Boil the ice cream batter and place it in the fridge until the next day.

Day 2
strawberry coulis made with 8.8 oz of strawberries (see berry coulis, page 227)
250 g (2 cups) whipping cream
15 g (1½ tbsp) sugar
5 g (1 tsp) pure vanilla sugar
1 batch hippen batter (page 224)
250 g (2 cups) beautiful, ripe strawberries to garnish with

1. Freeze the ice cream in an ice cream machine and store it in the freezer. Make the strawberry coulis.
2. Whip the cream to a smooth foam in a chilled metal bowl with the different sugars. Make the hippen batter.
3. Make a template by drawing circles that are 4 inches in diameter. Use a regular size paper that is 0.4 inch thick. Cut the circles out and remove them. Place the stencil on a baking sheet, or a baking mat, spread the hippen batter with a pallet knife and carefully remove the stencil.
4. Bake in two rounds. Lift them up with a spatula immediately when they come out of the oven roll them around a pencil. You must be quick, otherwise they will solidify. Return them to the oven and continue. Repeat the procedure until you have used up all the hippen masse.

5. Structure: Always cool the coupe glasses in the freezer for a few minutes.
6. Put a few tablespoons of strawberry coulis in the bottom of the glasses and fill with two scoops of the smooth strawberry ice cream (with an ice cream scoop that has been dipped in warm water). Add one tablespoon of strawberry coulis on top, and garnish with whipped cream (with a piping bag with a star tube).
7. Brush the strawberries for the garnish with strawberry coulis and decorate as shown in the photo. Stick a hippen roll into the ice cream. Serve this delicacy right away.

There are many different classic ice cream coupes and I mention a few briefly here.

Coupe Denmark: Put vanilla ice cream in a bowl and press an indentation in the ice cream. Pipe cream bows around and decorate with toasted sliced almonds. Pour hot chocolate sauce into the indentation.

Coupe Pêche Nellie Melba: Vanilla ice cream and half a vanilla poached peach, with cream bows around it, and garnished with toasted sliced almonds. Pour melba sauce (Page 227) over the peach.

Coupe Belle Hélène: Vanilla ice cream, half a vanilla poached pear on top, cream bows around, and warm chocolate sauce.

Coupe Jacques: Fruit salad with kirschwasser (cherry brandy), strawberry and cream bows all around.

Strawberry Frappé

Frappées are ice cream shakes consisting of milk, cream, crushed ice with matching ice cream, and any fruit or berry coulis. Everything is mixed vigorously in a blender into a light and airy cocktail, served in tall, chilled glasses with a straw and a spoon. Frappées can be varied in infinite ways and are very refreshing in hot weather. In Switzerland, we had a whole menu of different frappées year round in the cafeteria: banana, pineapple, raspberry, chocolate, hazelnut, mocha, praliné, etc. Use the same basic recipe as here.

Serves 8 people

Day 1
1 batch of strawberry ice cream (page 40)
*1 batch strawberry coulis with 8.8 oz
    strawberries (page 227)*

Day 2
⅕ cup ice cubes
120 g (approx. ½ cup) whipping cream
6 dl (2½ cups) milk

1. Freeze the ice cream in an ice cream machine.
2. Put 8 large scoops of strawberry ice cream in a blender, add the crushed ice (crush it in a towel with a hammer). Add strawberry coulis, cream and milk.
3. Mix to a light and airy frappe, pour into tall, chilled glasses, and serve with a spoon and a straw.

ICE CREAM BOMBS

An ice cream bomb almost always consist of an ice cream shell, with a filling made with ice cream, sorbet, parfait, or a pâte à bombs glacé mousse, which is a kind of parfait. It always takes twice as much syrup, as it takes egg yolks to make a classic pâté à bomb, and then it becomes mixed down with whipped cream and flavoring.

Vanilla Bomb Filling or Pâte à Bomb

This filling is half frozen. It may be flavored the same way as the classic parfait. Reduce the amount of cream to 250 g (1 cup) if you want a type of parfait instead.

375 g (approx. 1½ cups) of whipping cream
1 vanilla bean, preferably Tahitian, split and scraped out
1 cup simple sugar syrup for the sorbet (page 44)
160 g (approx. ⅔ cup) egg yolks

1. Whip the cream to a smooth foam in a chilled metal bowl and place it in the fridge.
2. Put vanilla bean and seeds in a pot along with sugar syrup and yolk. Heat the mixture in a simmering water bath while constantly whipping, not exceeding 194°F, because then the yolks may coagulate. When the temperature is between 179.6 and 185°F, the mass is finished. If you don't have a thermometer, do a rose test or a ladle test (p 25).
3. Pass the mass through a chinois or fine sieve, whisk the egg foam cold, and fold it into the whipped cream.
4. Cover with paper, cover with a lid, and place in the freezer.

Fruit Mousse used as filling in ice cream bombs, so-called demi-glacé, or semi-frozen.

A simple and tasty filling

500 g (2 cups) whipping cream
⅕ cup fruit purée with 10% sugar
⅕ cup simple sugar syrup (page 44)
possibly the juice from a lemon

Whip the cream to a smooth foam in a chilled metal bowl, carefully mix the sugar syrup and fruit purée into the cream, and possibly add a little bit of lemon juice to balance acidity. Fill the molds, cover with a paper, and the lid, and freeze.

The bomb mold is easy to release, making it is easy to work with, but there are other useful molds. You should not use hot water when releasing the ice cream from the mold, because then the ice cream melts and the surface becomes uneven. The ice cream bomb has a stored temperature at about 46.4°F, and the water temperature should be about 42 - 50°F, which is sufficient to release the mold from the ice cream.

Parfaits can be varied in the same manner as ice cream bombs. You can fill half of the mold with a parfait, stick a cone inside of it with a different type of parfait and fill the mold all the way up so you get two different flavors in the same mold, with two different colors. You can make hundreds of ice cream bombs with different fillings, and some of them are classic. We had at least 50 variations on the menu depending on the season.

Here are some classics:

Américaine: The mold is dressed with strawberry ice cream and filled with orange ice cream.

Batavia: The mold is dressed with pineapple ice cream and filled with strawberry ice cream with strips of pickled ginger.

Aida: Covered with strawberry ice cream and filled with kirschwasser (cherry brandy) parfait.

Camargo: Covered with coffee ice cream and filled with vanilla parfait.

Printanier: Covered with strawberry ice cream and filled with maraschino parfait.

Madame Butterfly: Orange ice cream shell, filled with yellow chartreuse parfait with marinated yellow chartreuse prunes.

Marie-Louise: Covered with raspberry ice cream, and filled with vanilla parfait.

Tutti-frutti: Covered strawberry ice cream, and filled with lemon ice cream with maraschino marinated pickled fruit.

Tortoni: Covered with nougat ice cream, and filled with coffee parfait that is flavored with cognac.

Sarah: Covered with pineapple ice cream and filled with strawberry mousse ice cream.

Romanoff: Covered with peach ice cream and filled with vanilla parfait with pickled strawberries.

Portugaise: Covered with mandarin ice cream and filled with curaçao parfait.

Comtesse: Covered with raspberry ice cream and filled with apricot parfait flavored with maraschino liqueur.

BOMB FROU-FROU AS MADAME POMPADOUR

It used to be very common to make desserts as Madame Pompadour. The porcelain dolls used to be leased by the confectioner. If you want to get a hold of one, they are still available at cook-shops, or you could call Bakers at Lessebo so they can bring one home from France. If you don't want to make quite the dramatic impression, you could make the ice cream bomb without the doll. It will taste just as good, but it won't evoke the same nostalgia.

This delicious ice cream bomb should be served with the orange tuiles (page 226).

Serves 12 people

A 1½ liter (50 oz) ice cream bomb dish

Day 1
½ batch vanilla ice cream base (page 32)
A mazarin (almond) base (see Bomb à l'Opéra, page 214), let it cool, and freeze

Day 2
1. Freeze the ice cream in an ice cream machine and place it in the freezer along with the ice cream bomb mold for 10 minutes.
2. Line the mold with vanilla ice cream (see picture, page 203). Dip the ladle in warm water first. Place the mold in the freezer for 30 minutes.
3. Use the ladle to cover the mold again, if the ice cream has slipped down. Put it in the freezer for an additional 30 minutes.
4. Dip a ladle in warm water and use it to pull up the ice cream on the sides one last time and place it back in the freezer.

Filling
Rum Parfait with Candied Pineapple and Chopped Dark Chocolate:
2 slices candied pineapple (p. 228)
40 g (⅕ cup) dark chocolate, preferably Valrhona Grand Cru Araguani 72%
300 g (1¼ cups) whipping cream
1 gelatin leaf (1 g)
80 g (⅓ cup) egg yolk
100 g (½ cup) sugar
25 g (5 tsp) squeezed lime juice
40 g (2¾ tbsp) water
50 g (⅕ cup) of dark rum

1 batch of spun sugar (page 232) colored with a little bit of red food dye

1. Pick the candied pineapple out of the sugar syrup and allow it to drain properly. Wipe it on paper towels. Cut it into cubes.
2. Chop the chocolate into pieces that are the same size as the candied pineapple pieces.
3. Whip the cream to a foam in a cold metal bowl and place it in the fridge.
4. Soak the gelatin in plenty of cold water for at least 10 minutes.
5. Whisk egg yolks foamy by hand.
6. Boil sugar, lime juice, and water in a small saucepan and brush down the inside of the pan with a small brush. Boil to 239°F, use a sugar thermometer, or do a sugar test (page 232).
7. Beat well with mixer, pour the syrup into the egg foam, and add the gelatin, and whisk until the gelatin has dissolved. Continue beating the mixture until the egg foam is cold.
8. Stir the liquor into the blend, then fold the whipped cream into the mixture, and add the candied pineapple, and the chocolate.
9. Remove the ice cream mold from the freezer, fill with the parfait, and add the mazarin bottom on top and press it carefully into place.
10. Put it in the freezer, and keep it there for at least 6 hours before you serve the bomb.

Structure:
1. Dip the mold in warm water until the ice cream starts to release around the edges. Press on one side so that it spins around.
2. Place the ice cream on a beautiful plate and temper it in the fridge for 15-30. Check with a knife to make sure that it is soft.
3. Drape in spun sugar. Back in the day, the bomb was also decorated with a small porcelain doll.

BOMB SYLVESTRE - NEW YEAR'S EVE ICE CREAM BOMB

This evening should be festive all the way through. Why not start out with freshly boiled lobster with mayonnaise as the appetizer? Perhaps fillet of beef with truffle sauce and fried duck liver as the main course, and then finish off with this dazzling dessert. Perfect, before the fireworks begin. Decadent creamy strawberry, filled with tangy champagne sorbet, all draped in spun sugar. Could it be more festive?

If you find the caramel arch to be too tedious to make, stop right there. However, it is not as difficult as it looks. The bomb will taste just as good without the advanced garnish, but it sure looks good if you add it!

For 12-14 people

An ice cream bomb mold that holds about 68 oz.

Day 1
A double batch of orange tuiles (p. 226)
1 batch strawberry ice cream with crème anglaise (Page 40)
1 ½ batch champagne sorbet (page 60)
750 g strawberry coulis (page 227)

Strawberry Jelly:
5 gelatin leaves (10 g)
450 g (3⅗ cups) strawberries
50 g (¼ cup) sugar
juice of half a lemon
125 g (⅗ cup) sugar

1. Soak the gelatin leaves in plenty of cold water for at least 10 minutes.
2. Rinse and hull the strawberries. Mix 450 g (3⅗ cups) of strawberries with 50 g (¼ cup) of sugar to a fine purée in a mixer (should be 500 g, approx. 2 cups purée).
3. Bring to a boil, while stirring, and add the gelatin leaves. Stir until the gelatin has dissolved.
4. Pass through a fine sieve. Make a mazarin cake bottom (Bomb à l'Opéra, p. 214).

Day 2

1. Freeze the strawberry ice cream in an ice cream machine, and place it in the freezer. Freeze the sorbet, and store it in the freezer.
2. Place the mold in the freezer for 10 minutes.
3. Spread the strawberry ice cream in the dish. Dip a spoon in warm water and use it to spread the ice cream all the way to the brim. Put it back in the freezer for another 30 minutes.
4. Spread the ice cream up to the brim again and put it back in the freezer.
5. Spread the ice cream up to the brim again if it falls down.
6. Fill the mold with champagne sorbet and smooth it out with a spatula.
7. Place the mazarin bottom on top and put it back in the freezer for at least 6 hours, or overnight.

Decoration
1 batch of spun sugar (p. 232)
yellow food coloring

1. Dip the bomb mold in warm water and release the ice cream by pressing on one side, so that the ice cream spins around. Put it back in the freezer.
2. Place the ice cream bomb on a jar and place a piece of paper underneath.
3. Heat the strawberry jelly to 95°F. Pour the jelly over the ice cream, and allow to drain.
4. Carefully transfer the bomb to a tray, and put it back in the freezer.
5. Boil and spin the spun sugar, which is colored light yellow with food coloring (see the photo on page 232). Place it carefully in a tight plastic bucket with a lid and let it sit in room temperature, it will be good for several days if you place some type of dehumidifier on the bottom of the bucket. When I was a boy, we always used to put an un-extinguished limestone on the bottom.

Caramel Arch:
500 g (2½ cups) sugar
200 g (⅘ cup) water
125 g (approx. ⅓ cup) glucose
Red and green food coloring

1. Boil sugar, water and glucose to 311°F, use a thermometer or do a sugar test (page 232). Brush the inside of the pan every now and then with a brush that has been dipped in water to prevent the sugars from crystallizing. Dip the pan in a bowl with cold water to stop it from boiling.
2. Pour about ⅖ cup of the caramel into a strong glass, add a drop of red food color and stir with a spoon.
3. Pour the caramel into a paper cone surrounded by a cloth. Seal the cone well and lift it up with the towel around it to avoid any burns. Cut a small hole at the tip and pipe a few cascades on baking paper, as shown in the picture.
4. Dye the caramel in the pan with green food coloring. Pour about ⅘ cup of it into a paper cone and pipe the year numbers, and little cascades on the parchment paper.
5. Oil two 12 inches long rulers and place them on a baking sheet with 0.2 inch apart. Pour the caramel between the rulers and let semi-solidify. Remove the rulers and cut the caramel even with a sharp knife so that you are left with a small plaque that you can attach the arch to. Immediately Place the arch over the bomb shape and make sure that it is straight. Wait for it to solidify.
6. Heat the remaining caramel on the stove without stirring it, or it may crystallize and "die" as us pastry chefs call it.
7. Carefully dip the arch in the caramel, attach the feet to it and wait until they have solidified.
8. Lightly dip the feet in the caramel and attach it to a glass plate. Make sure that it really is attached before you let go.
9. Dip the cascades and the numbers in the caramel and place them around the bomb, use the image to guide you. I also decorated the cake with a few yellow moons and stars in marzipan that I rolled out and let dry. I made the bells with sugar that I shaped and moistened with water. Then, I let them dry overnight.

Serving:

1. Temper the ice cream bomb by placing it in the fridge for 30 minutes.
2. Carefully place it underneath the caramel arch, and drape the ice cream with spun sugar, like in the picture.
3. Stick down some sparklers all around and set them alight so that this creation is extra festive when served.
4. Serve orange tuiles on a beautiful plate, and strawberry coulis in a sauceboat to enhance the taste of strawberries.

BOMB SURPRISE

Serves 14-16 people

A 2 liters (68 oz) ice cream bomb mold
A mazarin (almond) cake bottom
(page 214, Bomb à l'Opéra)
125 g (⅘ cup) caramelized hazelnuts
(p. 228)
1 batch of the vanilla parfait according to
the pâté à bomb method (page 65)
80 g (⅔ cup) dark chocolate, preferably
Valrhona Grand Cru Manjari 64.5%
plastic sheet with Valrhona print, or
a sheet of overhead transparency film
¼ batch black currant sorbet (page 47)
¼ batch mango sorbet (page 50)

Fruit for decoration:
1 small ripe mango
1 passion fruit
black currant, fresh or frozen

1. Bake the almond cake bottom and freeze it as soon as has it cooled.
2. Make the caramelized hazelnuts and allow them to cool. Crush them inside a clean kitchen towel with a rolling pin so they don't fly all over the place.
3. Make the vanilla parfait. Fold the crushed nuts into the parfait. Fill the ice cream bomb mold with the parfait, and place the frozen almond bottom on top, put the lid on the mold, and store in the freezer for at least 6 hours, or overnight.
4. Finely chop the chocolate and melt it in a plastic bowl in the microwave while stirring occasionally, or in a water bath.
5. Temper the chocolate (see chocolate techniques on page 234) and spread it thinly over the plastic sheet. Once it almost has solidified, use a round cookie cutter that is 1.6 inches in diameter to cut the chocolate into little round plates. Put them on a tray with something heavy on top so that they won't bend, and put them in the fridge.
6. Make the sorbets, and store them in freezer.
7. Dip the bomb mold in lukewarm water and press on one side of the ice cream bomb so that it releases from the mold. Put it on a small plate, and return it to the freezer.
8. Fill a plastic piping bag (with plain tube nr. 12, or cut a hole at the tip) with the black currant sorbet. Pipe the sorbet at regular intervals from the bottom, and moving up towards the center of the ice cream dome.
9. Do the same with the mango sorbet to fill the gaps between the black currant sorbet, as in the picture. Store the bomb in the freezer again.
10. Cut a piece of mango away from the pit, cut a grid pattern in it and fold it out. Cut the passion fruit in half and place it on top.
11. Remove the bomb from the freezer and leave it to temper in the fridge for 5-10 minutes so that it softens, because it is covered in sorbet. Decorate the bomb with chocolate plates wrapping around the dessert. Garnish with fruit on top, and dust with a little bit of powdered sugar. Serve with a good cake of your choice.

A wedding bomb should always be filled with flavors that most people like, since so many different individuals will eat it. This beautiful ice cream is covered with a thin layer of white chocolate to enhance the flavors. Make sure that everyone gets a nougatine plat to nibble on. It goes so well with the ice cream.

Serves 12-14 people

A 2 liters (68 oz) ice cream bomb mold
1 mazarin cake bottom (page 214, Bomb à l'Opéra)
1 batch of strawberry ice cream (page 40)
½ batch mango sorbet (page 50)
1 batch nougatine (p. 225)

Caramel:
250 g (1¼ cups) sugar
100 g (⅖ cup) water
50 g (2½ tbsp) glucose
red food dye

Chocolate Spray:
150 g (¾ cup) white chocolate, preferably Valrhona Ivoire, or Lindt
100 g (approx. 7 tbsp) cocoa butter
A beautiful red rose with green leaves
750 g mango coulis (p. 227, carries and Fruit coulis)

Day 1
1. Bake the mazarin bottom, let it cool and freeze it until you need it again.
2. Make the strawberry ice cream.

Day 2
1. Place the bomb mold in the freezer for 10 minutes. Freeze the strawberry ice cream in an ice cream machine, and store it in the freezer.
2. Use a spoon to cover the interior walls of the bomb mold with strawberry ice cream (see illustrations on page 203). Store it in the freezer 30 minutes. Spread the ice cream up to the brim with a spoon again and put it back in the freezer for another 30 minutes. Repeat the process if the ice cream sinks to the bottom.
3. Freeze the sorbet, fill the ice cream bomb with it, and hit it against the table to get rid of any air pockets. Place the frozen mazarin bottom on top and press it firmly into place. Store the bomb in the freezer for at least 6 hours.
4. Make the nougatine and cut it into little round plates, about 1.6 inches in diameter, with a smooth cookie cutter. Put them in a jar so they don't soak up moisture.
5. Make the caramel by bringing sugar, water, and glucose to 311° F, use thermometer or do a sugar test (page 232). Brush the inside of the pan occasionally with a brush that has been dipped in cold water to prevent crystallization. Dip the pan bottom in cold water to stop the caramel from boiling.
6. Pour some of the caramel directly onto a baking paper or a baking mat, in the shape of two small plates. Drizzle some color into the remaining caramel in the pan and mix.
7. Pour the majority of the colored caramel into a paper cone with a towel wrapped around it so that you don't burn yourself. Fold the cone carefully at the top so that you don't get hot caramel on your hands. Cut a small hole in the tip.
8. Pipe about 10 slightly tapered drops from one direction and then from the other direction, so that the caramel flows together to form hearts, or pour the caramel into small heart shapes that have been lubricated with oil, if you find it too difficult to pipe them.
9. Heat the remaining caramel without stirring it, just shake the pan over the stove so that it does not crystallize. Dip the tip of the hearts in the caramel and attach two (standing up) onto each plate of nougatine, make a few extra ones just in case you need to practice.
10. Dip the bomb mold in warm water and loosen the ice cream by pressing on one side so that it spins around. Place it on a tray and return to the freezer.
11. Finely chop the chocolate and cocoa butter. Melt it in a plastic bowl in microwave while stirring occasionally, or in a water bath at 122°F. (Never heat white chocolate above 129.2°F, then the casein in the milk powder tends to knot and the chocolate is ruined). Strain it through a chinois or fine sieve. Pour the chocolate into an olive oil syringe with a pumpable pressure, or into a paint sprayer.
12. Remove the ice cream bomb from the freezer, place a sheet of baking paper on the table and put the ice cream bomb on a jar. Spray the white chocolate and swirl the bomb until it is completely covered with the chocolate. Return the ice cream bomb to the freezer.
13. Before serving the bomb, place it in the refrigerator to soften, about 15-30 minutes. Check with a knife to make sure that the ice cream is soft.
14. Place the bomb on a glass plate, wrap around with nougatine plates, and serve the rest of the nougatines on the side. Garnish with some rose petals that you place on the bomb. Gently press the caramel hearts on the nougatine plates onto the ice cream. Make sure that they are attached; otherwise spin them until they stick.
15. Dust with confectioners' sugar and serve with mango coulis on the side.

FROZEN PUDDING AS A WEDDING BOMB

Braun Conditori used to be the finest bakery shop in Malmö when I was a boy, and I remember many of their baked goods from the days when I used to go there with my mom. Their window display was often full of ice cream bombs during the holidays, but they were most famous for their frozen puddings.

Confectioner Master, Calle Widell, says that they would have 200 orders for the frozen pudding on St. Martin's Eve, when many families made it a tradition to serve frozen pudding for dessert. The same dessert was popular on Christmas Eve, and New Year's Eve, or after the crayfish party, when the puddings used to be decorated with crayfish in caramel or marzipan. They were garnished with spun sugar and hippen masse leaves and rolls. Custom garnish according to the holiday was a given, such as geese and willow trees to go with the goose on St. Martin's Day.

In Scania, we baked geese out of petit chouxer dough, filled with raspberry jam and vanilla cream, topped with whipped cream, and dusted with confectioners' sugar. At the time, the bakeries made frozen puddings in many different ways.

I find the classic sugar dome, like in the picture below, to be gorgeous as garnish. It also isn't as difficult to make as it may seem. However, the swans are difficult to pipe, but I could not help myself but flaunting them. You could pipe a few hearts instead.

Serves 12-14 people

1 x 2 liters (68 oz) mold for the ice cream bomb

Day 1
1 batch of macaroons (page 225)

Quick Candied Green Pears:
2 small pears, not too ripe
250 g (1 cup) water
green food coloring
250 g (1 ¼ cups) sugar

Quick Candied Pineapple:
2 slices of canned pineapple
125 g (½ cup) water
125 g (⅗ cup) sugar

1. Make the macaroons. You only need 8 of them, but you cannot cut this recipe down. You can store the left-over biscuits in the freezer.
2. Peel the pears and halve them with a knife.
3. Boil the water with the food coloring, add the pear halves and sprinkle with ¼ of the sugar. Simmer for 15 minutes; add another quarter of the sugar and simmer for an additional 15 minutes. Repeat the procedure two more times, until the pears are the pickled. Pour them into a jar and let them stand in room temperature until the next day.
4. Do the same with pineapple slices, but halve the amount of sugar syrup. Leave them in the syrup until the next day.

Day 2
Nougat Cream

Vanilla Cream:
½ vanilla bean, split and scraped out
125 g (½ cup) milk
30 g (2 tbsp) egg yolks
30 g (2 ½ tbsp) sugar
20 g (2 ½ tbsp) corn starch
10 g (2 tsp) unsalted butter

Nougat:
65 g (approx. ⅓ cup) sugar
5 g (1 tsp) fresh lemon juice
75 g (⅔ cup) roasted hazelnuts

300 g (1 ¼ cups) whipping cream

1. Put the vanilla bean and seeds in a saucepan, add the milk and bring to a boil. Set the pan aside to settle for 10-15 minutes.
2. Whisk egg yolks, sugar, and corn starch fluffy. Add the milk and mix well, and pour everything back into the cleaned pot. Boil while stirring constantly.
3. Beat the butter into the blend until it has dissolved completely, and pass through a chinois or fine sieve. Cool in an ice-cold water bath while stirring occasionally and store in the fridge.
4. Melt sugar and lemon juice in a saucepan to a golden nougat.
5. Add the toasted hazelnuts and stir. Pour onto a sheet of baking paper and let it cool. Crush (coarsely) with a rolling pin into nougat.
6. Whip the cream to a smooth foam in a cold metal bowl. Mix it with the smooth, cold custard to a silky cream and carefully fold the crushed nougat into the cream. Pour it into the bottom of the bomb mold.

Strawberry Cream:
150 g (1⅕ cups) strawberries
150 g (¾ cup) sugar
400 g (1⅗ cups) whipping cream
15 g (1 tbsp) fresh lemon juice

1. Mix strawberries and sugar to a purée and pass through a sieve.
2. Whip the cream to a smooth foam in a chilled metal bowl.
3. Mix the whipped cream with the strawberry puré and lemon juice into a smooth strawberry cream.

5 halved red candied cherries, store-bought
8 macaroons (made on day 1)
6 cl (4 tbsp) kirschwasser (cherry brandy) or cognac
1 tablespoon cooking oil
1 batch caramel (p. 211)
red food coloring

1. Drain and dice the candied fruits. Dip the biscuits in kirschwasser (cherry brandy) or cognac.
2. Spread the candied fruit far out in the mold, and layer fruits, biscuits, and strawberry cream until the mold is full. Cover with plastic wrap and freeze for at least 6 hours.
3. Dip the mold in warm water, and release the ice cream bomb from the dish. Transfer the ice cream to a tray, and return it to the freezer.
4. Wash and dry the bomb mold thoroughly, and use your hand to lubricate it with cooking oil.
5. Cook the caramel and dip the pan in cold water so that the boiling ceases. Leave for 5 minutes to allow the caramel to thicken a little bit.
6. Dip a spoon in the caramel and spin a web inside the mold. Continue until the network looks like in the picture, add a slightly thicker rim around the inside of the dome, it will keep it together better.
7. Check that the dome comes off, lift it out carefully and place it on a baking sheet to solidify. If it doesn't turn out that great the first time, don't worry, with practice you will learn to make beautiful domes.
8. Add a few drops of red food coloring to the remaining caramel and heat it up by spinning it over the stove. Pour the caramel into a paper cone that has been wrapped in a towel so that you don't burn yourself. Cut a small hole at the tip of the cone.
9. Pipe elongated drops of caramel onto a baking paper, make another elongated next to the other drop so that they join, forming a heart. Make a few hearts like this for the garnish.
10. Dip the hearts in the melted caramel and gently attach one or two on top of the dome.
11. I have piped the swans directly onto the baking paper with white caramel. However, it requires a lot of skill and practice.
12. Temper the frozen pudding for 30 minutes in the refrigerator before you serve it. Place it on a glass plate, and gently place the dome over it.
13. Serve with almond tuiles with anise (Page 226), or some other brittle pastries.

Bomb à l'Opéra with Warm Chocolate Sauce

Vanilla ice cream drizzled with warm chocolate sauce is always a hit, although it isn't as common anymore. This delicious vanilla ice cream with crispy almond nougat and warm chocolate sauce serves up a fantastic dessert. It used to be a frequent favorite in the banquet room at the Savoy Hotel in Malmö when I was a young pâtissier.

Serves about 12 people
(To do less, simply halve the recipe).

A 2 liters mold for an ice cream bomb

Day 1
¾ batch of vanilla ice cream (page 32)

Mazarin Bottom:
100 g (⅖ cup) almond paste, with 50 g (⅓ cup) almonds
and 50 g (¼ cup) sugar (see macaroons, page 225)
50 g (3½ tbsp) butter
50 g (⅓ cup) eggs
10 g (1⅓ tbsp) flour

1. Allow the almond paste, butter, and eggs to reach room temperature.
2. Dissolve the almond paste with your hand and work a third of the butter into the paste so that you get a lump-free mass. Work the remaining butter into the paste.
3. Mix the eggs in, in two rounds. Sift the flour over, and mix gently.
4. Draw a circle that is the size of the mold, on a baking paper on a tray.
5. Use a plastic piping bag (cut a hole in the tip) to distribute the mass inside the circle that you drew on the baking sheet.
6. Put the tray in the oven that has been heated to 400°F, bake for about 8 minutes, until the bottom is golden brown. Immediately transfer the baking paper with the bottom to a wire rack to cool. If you leave it on the tray, it will get dry. Freeze the bottom once it has cooled, it will make it easier to handle.

Day 2
500 g praliné mass with roasted almonds (Page 229)

Chocolate:
250 g (1¼ cups) dark chocolate, preferably Valrhona Grand Cru Guanaja 70.5%
300 g (1¼ cups) of milk
75 g (3½ tbsp) glucose

For decoration:
300 g (1¼ cups) whipping cream
15 g (1½ tbsp) sugar
5 g (1 tsp) pure vanilla sugar
optional: chocolate spiral (page 234)

1. Make that praliné mass and allow it to cool. Crush it in a clean towel with a rolling pin so it doesn't fly all over the place. Always store praliné mass (nougat) in a jar with lid, otherwise it will absorb moisture.
2. Freeze ice cream in two batches in an ice cream machine and fold 150 g (1 cup) of crushed praliné into the mass. Store the ice cream in the freezer.
3. Fill the bomb mold with the ice cream, and hit it against the table to get rid of any air pockets. Add the frozen mazarin bottom on top. Make sure that it sits securely, so that it doesn't slide around on the plate when you serve it. Store in the freezer.
4. Chocolate sauce: Finely chop the chocolate. Boil the milk and glucose, and add half of the chocolate and mix with a stick blender to an elastic ganache. Add the remaining chocolate in small portions so that it does not get too warm, which makes the emulsion disappear. Mix vigorously with a stick blender. If you need to keep it warm, do not exceed 95-104°F, to prevent the emulsion from getting ruined.
5. Whip the chilled cream with sugar and vanilla sugar until firm. Fill a plastic piping bag (with a star tube) with the cream.
6. When the ice cream is frozen, dip the mold in lukewarm water until it is easy to release the ice cream. Press down on one side of it so that the ice cream spins around. Use the rest of the crushed nougat to garnish the bomb beautifully.
7. Transfer to a plate, garnish with the whipped cream and optionally a chocolate spiral, but it will be just as good without. Serve with warm chocolate sauce.

FOR THE LITTLE ONES

GLACE AU FOUR AS AN IGLOO

Glace au Four as an Igloo Kids love this delicious and fun dessert, and there is nothing more rewarding than making kids (and adults) happy. If you find the marzipan figurines too difficult to make, you can take this book to a pastry chef, and have him make them for you. However, you'll have more fun if you let the kids make them.

Serves 10-12 people

A round mold, a bomb mold, that holds 2 liters
1 flame burner
1 mazarin cake bottom (page 214)
½ batch strawberry parfait, a mousse glacé (page 68)
½ batch of vanilla parfait with cooked pâte à bomb (page 65)

1. Bake the mazarin bottom and put it in the freezer as soon as it cools.
2. Dress the inside of the mold with strawberry parfait. Then fill a plastic piping bag with the vanilla parfait so that you get an ice cream bomb with a shell of strawberry parfait, filled with vanilla parfait. Apply the frozen mazarin bottom on top and put everything in freezer for at least 6 hours. You could also do this a day in advance.

300 g (1⅕ cups) marzipan
food coloring: yellow, red, green

3. Form a polar bear-like figure with 80 g (about ⅔ of a cup) of white marzipan and shape the eyes and ears with a teaspoon. Use about 1 g (just a pinch) of marzipan to make a nose

that you attach, dust it with cocoa to make it brown. Use about another 30 g (about ⅓ of a cup) of marzipan to make a baby polar bear and put it next to the big polar bear.

4. To make the penguins, make two balls out of 40 g (2½ tbsp) white marzipan. Color 50 g (3⅕ tbsp) of the white marzipan with 5 g (1 tbsp) grams of cocoa and a drop of the food coloring. Weigh up 40 g (2½ tbsp) and make two round balls. Color a piece of white marzipan that weighs 25 g (1½ tbsp) with one drop of yellow food coloring, and a dash of red dye, so that it turns to a pale orange, skin-like color. Put together the white marzipan ball with the brown one and shape them with your hands into a penguin. Cut the wings out with a pair of scissors. Make a beak out of 3 g (⅗ tsp) of orange marzipan and attach it on the penguin. Shape two feet, out of two pieces of marzipan that each weigh 3 g (⅗ tsp). Attach them, and make little dents in the feet with a small spoon. Attach two tiny balls for the eyes and press lightly with a spoon. Put the penguins together so that it looks like they are hugging each other, like in the photo.

5. To make the Eskimo, mix 10 g (2 tsp) of marzipan with a dash of green food coloring. Make a ball. Roll 10 g (2 tsp) of brown marzipan into a little oval and make little dents with a spoon. Shape a ball out of 10 g (2 tsp) of orange marzipan, and attach a little ball as the nose out of 1 g (⅕ tsp) of the orange marzipan. Make a small mouth with a spoon and make to indentations for the

eyes. Push the head into the green ball and add the brown marzipan around it, like in the picture.

½ batch of the Italian meringue, not the baking kind (p. 230)
1 batch of the warm chocolate sauce (page 214)
1 batch of the orange tuiles (p. 226)

Frosting:
150 g (1¼ cups) confectioners' sugar
30 g (2 tbsp) egg whites
5 g (1 tsp) fresh lemon juice

1. Sift the confectioners' sugar and whisk it airy with the egg whites and lemon juice to a firm and fluffy frosting. Use the frosting to decorate a plate like a snowy landscape.
2. Release the ice cream bomb by dipping the mold in warm water and swirl the ice cream around by pressing on one side. Put the ice cream on a serving plate. Use a spatula to spread meringue over it.
3. Fill a small paper cone with meringue and cut a hole at the tip. Decorate the bomb with the meringue and make an entrance to the igloo in the front, like in the picture.
4. Use a gas flame to make the meringue golden brown, like in the photo.
5. Place the Eskimo in front of the igloo entrance. Decorate with the polar bears and the penguins and dust with confectioners' sugar so that it looks like snow.
6. Serve with warm chocolate sauce and crispy orange tuiles. That will make the kids happy, I promise!

Mary Ladybug and the Hedgehog for a Birthday Party

These figures are always very appreciated at the little ones' birthday parties, and they're not very difficult to make. The reward is well worth the work. If you decide to make both of the figures, you'll have enough for about 15-18 people. If you want to serve them with some sort of pastry, I recommend the vanilla macaroons with raspberry jam; see the basic recipe on pages 226 and 227.

2 mazarin bottoms (p. 214)
1 batch of chocolate parfait according to the
crème anglaise method (page 67)
1 batch of strawberry parfait, the mousse
glacé (Page 68)

1. Make the mazarin bottoms and freeze them when they are cool.
2. Make the parfaits and fill each one in a separate 68 oz oblong cake pan.
3. Cut the almond bottoms in the middle, place them on top of the molds and press so that they cover the mold surface. Cover with plastic wrap.
4. Freeze for at least 6 hours, or overnight.

The hedgehog:
100 g (¾ cup) almonds
1 batch of chocolate jelly (page 225)
frosting (see page 216, glace au four-igloo)

1. Preheat the oven to 400°F.
2. Blanch the almonds in boiling water for 1 minute and rinse them cold in a sieve. Remove the shells and cut each almond into 4 strips. Put them on the a baking sheet, roast them golden brown for about 10 minutes and leave them to cool.

3. Release the chocolate parfait from the mold by dipping it in tepid water. Transfer the parfait to a wire rack. Cover your hands with plastic bags, and use them to shape the parfait more oblong and drop-shaped. Insert the almonds so that it looks like a hedgehog. Put it in the freezer for 1 hour.
4. Transfer the parfait to a wire rack and glaze it with the chocolate jelly, allow any excess jelly to drip off. Fill a paper cone with a little bit of cold jelly, and cut a hole in the tip. Give the hedgehog a pair of frosting eyes, and pipe some chocolate jelly on. Be careful so that you don't pipe on too much. Serve on a plate.

Mary Ladybug:
Frosting (see page 216, glace au four-igloo)
80 g (⅔ cup) dark chocolate, like Valrhona
Grand Cru Manjari 54.5%
½ batch of the strawberry jelly (see page 207,
New Year's Eve Bomb)
½ batch of the chocolate jelly (page 225)

1. Pipe a pair of eyes with the frosting on a baking paper and allow it to dry.
2. Finely chop the chocolate and melt it in the microwave, or in a water bath, to 122-131°F. Temper the chocolate (see chocolate techniques, page 234).
3. Use a paper cone to pipe a dot of chocolate jelly onto each frosting eye. Pipe dots with the tempered chocolate on parchment paper, and allow them to solidify.
4. Release the parfait from the mold by dipping it in lukewarm water. Cover it with a plastic bag and shape the parfait with the heat of your hands. Freeze for another hour.
5. Dip half of the ladybug in the melted chocolate jelly and allow it to solidify on a wire rack. Dip the backside in melted strawberry jelly, and place the parfait on a wire rack. Decorate the red parfait with chocolate dots, and make a pair of eyes the same way as for the hedgehog.
6. Serve on a plate.

MERINGUE POODLES AND ICE CREAM CONES
LIKE AT THE TIVOLI IN COPENHAGEN

Day 1
1 batch of chocolate ice cream with milk
  chocolate (page 37)
1 batch of vanilla ice cream (page 32)
1 batch of raspberry jam (p. 227) but replace
  the raspberries with strawberries

Day 2
Freeze the ice cream in an ice cream
machine, and store in the freezer

1 batch of the Italian meringue for baking
(p. 230)

1. Trace the drawing on the last page in
   this book with two baking sheets as
   two mirror image halves. A total of
   4 parts.
2. Preheat the oven to 200°F. Fill a
   plastic piping bag (with plain tube
   number 14) with the meringue. Pipe
   the meringue inside the drawing; try
   to pipe it a little thicker at the
   stomach and the back legs.
3. Decorate the legs, ears and tail with
   a star by using tube number 12. Pipe
   a little bit of meringue directly onto
   the baking tray, just beneath the feet
   so they won't be straight.
4. Dry them in the oven for about
   3 hours or until they are completely
   dry.

Frosting:
300 g (2½ cups) confectioners' sugar
15 g (1 tbsp) lemon juice
60 g (¼ cup) egg yolks
200 g (1 cup) dark chocolate, preferably
  Valrhona Grand Cru Guanaja 70%

1. Sift confectioners' sugar and whisk
   together with lemon juice and egg
   whites to a solid frosting with an
   electric mixer. Keep the frosting
   covered with plastic wrap so that it
   doesn't dry out.
2. Turn the meringue halves with the
   flat side up, and put icing in a plastic
   piping bag with a star tube 12. Pipe
   frosting onto both halves and press
   them together. Scrape the feet with
   fine sandpaper so that the poodles
   stand up straight. Be careful not to
   break them. Fill the seams with
   frosting until the poodles look
   complete. Pipe on a nose and eyes.
3. An hour or so later, when the
   frosting has solidified, finely chop
   and melt the chocolate in the
   microwave or in a water bath at
   122-131°F. Temper the chocolate
   (page 234).
4. Dip the feet on the poodles in the
   chocolate and place them on a
   baking sheet to solidify.
5. Fill a paper cone with the chocolate,
   cut a small hole in the tip. Pipe eyes
   that are as big as a nickel, and a nose
   that is slightly larger directly
   onto the paper, let them solidify.
6. Attach the eyes and nose with a bit
   frosting.

Chocolate Rolls:
200 g (1 cup) dark chocolate, preferably
  Valrhona Grand Cru Pur Caribe 66.5%

1. Melt the chocolate in the microwave
   while stirring occasionally, or in water
   bath.
2. Spread a ladleful over a marble or
   metal disk back and forth until the
   chocolate hardens, use a metal
   scraper to scrape chocolate rolls (see
   chocolate technique on page 234).
   Continue until all chocolate is used
   up. Set the rolls aside.

2 cups whipping cream
20 g (1⅗ tbsp) sugar
10 g (2 tsp) pure vanilla sugar
ice cream cones, purchased or homemade
  (page 224)
foam balls dipped in chocolate and rolled in
  shredded coconut
500 g (4 cups) fresh raspberries

1. Whip the cream with sugar and
   vanilla with an electric mixer to a
   smooth foam in a chilled metal bowl.
2. Add a scoop of smooth vanilla ice
   cream in the cones, add a dessert
   spoon of strawberry jam, pipe some
   whipped cream on top and place a
   foam ball on top. These cones are
   always served at the Tivoli.
3. When the cones are eaten, it is time
   for the chocolate ice cream coupe.
   Put two scoops of chocolate ice
   cream in a coupe glass and pipe
   whipped cream on top, garnish with
   fresh raspberries and stick some
   chocolate rolls into the ice cream.
4. The children usually eat the poodles
   at the end.

SIDES

VANILLA SUGAR

Dry the vanilla beans that you used for the ice cream. Weigh 1 part dried vanilla beans and 9 parts powdered sugar. Mix to a powder in a mixer. Strain through a sieve, and store in a jar. Use when making pastries.

ICE CREAM CONES
To be baked on a waffle iron.

100 g (7 tbsp) salted butter
375 g (3 cups) household flour
2 g (½ tsp) of baking powder
200 g (1⅗ cups) confectioners' sugar
10 g (2 tsp) pure vanilla sugar
1 g (⅕ tsp) salt
350 g (1½ cups) milk
300 g (1¼ cups) water
20 g (4 tsp) egg yolks

1. Melt the butter and set it aside.
2. Sift flour, baking powder, confectioners' sugar, vanilla sugar, and salt through a sieve. Add the milk, water and egg yolks while you whisk everything to a smooth batter. Add the melted butter at the end. Allow the batter to swell for 1 hour.
3. Bake in waffle iron, roll them into cones and place them in glasses and let them stiffen.

BUTTER STRUESEL "CRUMBLE"

This delicious crumble can be flavored with spices such as cardamom, cinnamon, and vanilla. You can even replace the almond flour with hazelnuts, pistachios, etc. If you want to make chocolate crumble, replace 25 grams of flour with fine cocoa, like Valrhona. Crumble also works great as a bottom underneath ice cream or sorbet, to prevent them from sliding around on the plate.

100 g (7 tbsp) butter
100 g (½ cup) sugar
100 g (¾ cup) plain flour
100 g (1 cup) almond meal

1. Mix the cold butter with the other ingredients into a crumbly dough.
2. Spread on a baking sheet and bake golden brown for about 10 minutes at 400°F.
3. Use as a topping on crumb pies, and crumble cake.

WAFER LEAF, "HIPPEN MASSE"

The dough should be mixed a few hours in advance to avoid blisters from forming during baking.

Hippen masse is always baked in two rounds so that it is baked evenly, and without irregular spots.

75 g (½ cup) peeled almonds
75 g (⅗ cup) confectioners' sugar
75 g (⅓ cup) milk
25 g (⅕ cup) flour
30 g (2 tbsp) egg whites

1. Mix the dry shelled almonds with confectioners' sugar to a fine powder.
2. Add milk and flour and mix to a pulp.
3. Add the first half of the egg white. Mix it smooth and add the rest. Cover with plastic wrap and leave to rest for 2 hours.
4. Preheat oven to 400°F. Cut stencils out of 0.04 inch thick rigid paper. Cut different shapes such as leaves, baskets, butterflies etc. Use them as templates when you spread the pulp onto the baking tray.
5. Put the tray in the oven and remove it as soon as the leaves have hardened but haven't gotten any color yet. Allow them to cool and bake them another round until the figures are golden brown. Store in an airtight container, so they don't soften.

TULIPS, CRISPY BASKETS

You can also make these baskets with hippen masse, if you want them to have a nutty taste. This mass is crispy and neutral and is suitable with most flavors. If you want to make chocolate tulips, just replace 0.9 oz of the flour with cocoa powder, preferably Valrhona.

Makes 6 pieces

75 g (⅓ cup) unsalted butter
75 g (⅓ cup) egg whites
60 g (⅕ cup) confectioners' sugar
15 g (1 tbsp) pure vanilla sugar
75 g (⅗ cup) flour
a few drops of bitter almond oil

1. Use a sharp knife to cut a template that is about the size of a saucer. Use rigid paper that is about 0.04 inch thick.
2. Make sure that butter and egg whites are at room temperature. Preheat the oven to 400°F.
3. Sift powdered sugar, vanilla sugar, and flour together. Mix with butter and add the egg white in small portions until you have a smooth batter. Season with bitter almond oil.
4. Place a sheet of baking parchment paper on a baking tray. Put a tablespoon of the batter in the middle of the stencil and spread the batter as evenly as possible with a pallet. Lift away the stencil, and repeat this procedure until you use up all the batter.
5. Bake about 4 bottoms per plate for 5 minutes or until they are beautifully golden brown around the edges.
6. As soon as you have removed the tray from the oven, place the bottoms on upside down turned glasses, and allow them to solidify.
7. Store them in an airtight container with a lid so that they don't soften.

MACAROONS

You can reduce this recipe if you don't need as many biscuits.

Makes 20 biscuits

125 g (⅘ cup) sweet almonds
125 g + 125 g (⅗ cup + ⅗ cup) sugar
60 g (¼ cup) egg whites

1. Blanch the almonds in boiling water. Rinse them cold and remove the shell. Dry them with a clean kitchen towel.
2. Pour the almonds and 125 g (⅗ cup) of the sugar into a food processor and mix for 1 minute so that you get an almond paste.
3. Transfer the almond paste to a bowl. Add the remaining sugar and a third of the egg whites and work into a lump-free mass. Add the remaining egg whites in two rounds until you have a smooth batter. You may need to strain it through a sieve to get rid of lumps.
4. Preheat the oven to 350°F.
5. Pipe quarter-sized macaroons onto a baking tray that has been covered with parchment paper. Use a piping bag with smooth tube number 8, or cut a little hole at the tip of the bag.
6. Bake the macaroons until they are golden brown, about 10 – 12 minutes. Allow to cool and turn the paper on the tray. Brush the paper with cold water and allow to sit for 5 minutes.
7. Loosen the macaroons from the paper and freeze them in an airtight jar.

BISCUIT À LA CUILLER

Makes 32 biscuits

120 g (½ cup) egg yolks
50 g (¼ cup) sugar
10 g (2 tsp) pure vanilla sugar
180 g (¾ cup) egg whites
60 g (⅓ cup) sugar
5 g (1 tsp) fresh lemon juice
120 g (approx. 1 cup) flour
sugar to sprinkle

1. Preheat the oven to 450°F. Beat the egg yolks fluffy with the sugar and vanilla sugar.

2. Beat the egg whites, sugar, and lemon juice into a stiff meringue. Begin whisking at a medium speed, and increase the speed thereafter.
3. Sift the flour through a sieve onto a paper. Fold the yolk foam and the flour into the meringue, so that you get a light and airy mass.
4. Fill a piping bag (with a plain tube) with the fluffy mass, and pipe oblong macaroons onto a baking paper. Sprinkle with a little bit of sugar. Allow them to sit for 5 minutes.
5. Bake the biscuits for 8 – 12 minutes until sugar beads begin to form on the surface. Transfer to a wire rack and allow it to cool.

NOUGATINE

100 g (¾ cup) peeled and sliced almonds
80 g (4 tbsp) glucose
120 g (approx. 1 cup) confectioners' sugar
25 g (1 ¾ tbsp) unsalted butter

1. Preheat the oven to 350°F.
2. Roast the sliced almonds on a tray in the oven until they are golden brown, stir occasionally, and reduce the heat to 300°F.
3. Boil the glucose until it begins to crystallize, add a third of the confectioners' sugar and stir until the caramel turns golden brown. Add another third of the confectioners' sugar, and allow it to dissolve until golden brown, while continuously stirring the caramel. Add the remaining confectioners' sugar and repeat the process.
4. Remove the pan from the heat and add the butter. Stir until the nougat absorbs the butter. Add the almonds and mix thoroughly.
5. Pour onto a baking mat or a silpat mat. Use a rolling pin that has been oiled to quickly roll the nougat as thinly as possible over the baking mat. Immediately cut round shapes with a cookie cutter (press hard). If the mass solidifies before yo have time to cut out all the disks, you can reheat it in the oven until it softens, and continue.
6. Store in an airtight jar, because the nougat absorbs moisture in room temperature.

CHOCOLATE JELLY

Valrhona cocoa adds a beautiful red-brown color to the jelly that regular cocoa doesn't. Chocovic, and Barry Callebaut also carry a red-brown cocoa.

This jelly retains its luster even after it has been frozen. This recipe was created by the head confectioner at NK in Stockholm, and me, when were preparing to represent Sweden in the first World Championship within the confectioner profession in Stuttgart in 1993.

5 gelatin leaves (10 g)
185 g (⁹⁄₁₀ cup) sugar
250 g (1 cup) water
40 g (2 tbsp) glucose
60 g (approx. ¾ cup) cocoa, preferably Valrhona Grand Cru Guanaja 70 %
150 g (⅗ cup) whipping cream

1. Soak the gelatin in plenty of cold water for at least 10 minutes.
2. Bring sugar, water, and glucose to a boil. Sift the cocoa into the mix, and add the chopped chocolate, and the cream. Bring everything to a boil, and reduce the heat until it only boils a little bit. Carefully boil like this for an hour, while stirring occasionally.
3. Do a drop test: Dip a whisk into the solution; if there is a drop hanging form the whisk when you lift it up, it is time to stop boiling the jelly. Then you'll know that it will be able to cover a surface.
4. Lift the gelatin leaves out of the water and add them to the jelly. Stir until they dissolve.
5. Strain the jelly through a chinois or a fine sieve into a bowl. Immediately cover the bowl with plastic wrap to prevent a crust from forming on the surface. Allow to cool to 95°F, which is the ideal temperature when you want to use the jelly for glazing. If you don't want to use up all the jelly right away, you can store it in the fridge for several weeks. You can also freeze it, and thaw it when you need to use it.

Fruit Jelly

5 gelatin leaves (10 g)
200 g (⅘ cup) clear apple juice, or French
    apple cider from Normandy
150 g (⅗ cup) fresh lemon juice
150 g (¾ cup) sugar
100 g (⅓ cup) glucose

1. Soak the gelatin in plenty of cold water for at least 10 minutes.
2. Bring apple juice, or cider to a boil with the lemon juice and sugar, and skim well. Add the glucose and bring to a boil again.
3. Add the gelatin leaves to the jelly, and stir until the gelatin has dissolved. Skim the jelly thoroughly so that the jelly is absolutely clear.
4. Pour into a jar and cover with plastic wrap to prevent a crust from forming on the surface. When the jelly has cooled, it can be stored in the fridge for about 1 week, or in the freezer for 1 month, and you can thaw it when you need to use it.

Orange Tuiles

Makes 20

These deliciously thin biscuits are one of my favorites. You can serve them with pretty much any dessert; they go well with ice creams, parfaits, sorbets, and many other yummy treats.

40 g (⅓ cup) flour
125 g (⅗ cup) sugar
½ orange, the zest
50 g (3½ tbsp) soft butter
65 g (¾ cup) sliced almonds
5 cl (approx. 3¼ tbsp) freshly squeezed and
    filtered orange juice

1. Preheat the oven to 350°F.
2. Mix flour, sugar, orange zest, butter, and almonds in a bowl. Mix well with a ladle. Add the orange juice and work into a pliable mass.
3. Take 4 sheets of baking paper and spread 20 piles of the mass over the 4 sheets. Make sure to leave a lot of room in between each pile, because these biscuits will spread thinly. Dip a fork in water and flatten the batter with it. The thinner you press the

batter, the more brittle and crispy the biscuits will be.
4. Bake the biscuits for 4 – 5 minutes until they look even and have a light brown color. Remove them from the oven, and allow them to sit for 1 minute.
5. Use a spatula to lift the biscuits, and place them onto a rolling pin or a wine bottle, where you let them settle. If they stiffen so that it is difficult to bend them, you can heat them up in the oven for 1 minute. Bake only one tray at a time, otherwise you won't have time to transfer them before they stiffen.
6. Store these biscuits in an airtight container until it is time to serve them.

Almond Tuiles with Anise

The anise and the almonds cut the flavors nicely in these brittle little treats.

Makes 25

20 g (1½ tbsp) butter
30 g (¼ cup) flour
100 g (½ cup) sugar
2 g (½ tsp) pure vanilla sugar
1 g (⅕ tsp) fleur de sel
3 g whole anise
50 g (⅕ cup) eggs
50 g (½ cup) sliced almonds

1. Melt the butter and set aside.
2. Mix flour, sugar, vanilla sugar, salt, and anise. Add the eggs and the melted butter. Stir the almonds into the mixture.
3. Preheat the oven to 325°F. Use a teaspoon to drop 6 little piles of the batter on 4 sheets of baking paper. Dip a fork in water and use it to flatten the biscuits.
4. Bake them golden brown in rounds (one tray at a time). Transfer the biscuits to a rolling pin, or a wine bottle, where you allow them to stiffen.
5. Store the biscuits in an airtight container until you serve them. They are delicious on their own, or just with a simple scoop of vanilla ice cream and warm chocolate sauce.

Raspberry and Vanilla Macaroons

This is one of the most delicious dessert sides that I can think of. You can flavor

the basic mass in many different ways, and it can be filled with various creams, ganache, or anything else that your imagination can dream up.

Makes 30 double macaroons (60 individual pieces)
100 g (1 cup) almond meal
180 g (1½ cups) powdered sugar
20 g (4 tsp) pure vanilla sugar
100 g (⅖ cup) egg whites
5 g (1 tsp) fresh lemon juice
30 g (2½ tbsp) sugar
1 drop of red food coloring

1. Preheat the oven to 350°F.
2. Sift almond meal, powdered sugar, and vanilla sugar together onto a paper.
3. Beat the egg whites with the lemon juice into fluffy foam in an absolutely clean metal bowl. Add sugar and beat to a firm and supple foam.
4. Sift the almond sugar blend and fold into the foam with a spatula until you have a smooth mass. Add a drop of food coloring.
5. Place two sheets of baking paper on a tray each. Fill a piping bag (use the plain tube, nr. 10, or cut a hole in the tip) with the mass.
6. Pipe 30 equal sized bottoms onto each plate, about 0.8 inches in diameter. Make sure that there is a distance of 1 inch between each bottom, so that they don't float together in the oven. Allow them to dry for 30 minutes, until they have a light crust.
7. Bake the bottoms for 5-7 minutes with an extra tray underneath, so that they don't get too much color on the bottom. Vent the oven twice to get rid of any steam that could cause the biscuits to burst. The surface should be shiny and spring back when you press on it and the macaroons should be soft inside.
8. Immediately remove the macaroons from the trays by sliding the paper off of them, so that they don't continue to bake and harden. When they have cooled for about 30 minutes, place a paper on top and turn them upside down. Brush with water so that the macaroons will release from the paper more easily.
9. Put two macaroons together with raspberry jam (p. 227) in between. The macaroons are already sweet, that's why I think a classic raspberry

jam adds too much sweetness. Serve the macaroons the same day, or freeze them in a jar and thaw them. They almost get a little bit more chewy and delicious when you freeze them.

RASPBERRY JAM

500 g (4 cups) raspberries
250 g (1¼ cups) sugar
juice of 1 lemon

1. Mix all ingredients in a saucepan and cook to 225°F. Use a sugar thermometer, or do a jam test on a chilled plate - if you run your finger through the jam, it should not coalesce.
2. Immediately pour into a warm, rinsed jar, screw the lid on right away and turn the jar upside down. Store in the fridge because the sugar content is low.

COULIS

Fruit coulis and berry sauces go well with all kinds of desserts, from ice cream, sorbet and parfait, to pies. Also try adding a few tablespoons of berry coulis to a glass of ice cold champagne, it makes a great aperitif.

Almost all berries are suitable in a coulis. Try adding fresh herbs for exciting flavor combinations. Try adding a little bit of peppermint, basil, cinnamon basil, or lemon verbena. Consider mixing different berries, try black currants with raspberries, raspberries and blueberries, strawberries and red currants, or strawberries and gooseberries. You can also freeze coulis. Mix it with a hand stick blender, after it has thawed, until it has a good texture again. If you want a thinner coulis you can dilute it with sugar syrup. Count on ⅖ cup coulis per person if it is served on the side.

BERRY COULIS WITH RED BERRIES

For every 1 kg (8 cups) of berries, you will need to add between 180 g, approx. 1 ½ cups (strawberries) and 250 g, approx. 2 cups (lingonberries, cranberries) of sugar. Mix and pass through a sieve. Add the lemon juice to balance the acidity. Strawberries often need more acidity than, for example, raspberries.

BERRY COULIS WITH YELLOW BERRIES

Here you will need to add 250 g – 300 g (1 ¼ cups – 1½ cups) of sugar per 1 kg (approx. 8 cups) of cloudberries, ripe apricots, or yellow plums. Mix and pass through a sieve. If you want, you can enhance the flavor by adding liquor. Carefully add the lemon juice.

CLASSIC MELBA SAUCE

French master chef Auguste Escoffier's creation Pêche Glacé Melba is one of the world's most famous ice cream desserts. Vanilla ice cream with vanilla poached cold peach, covered with melba sauce. This sauce doesn't drain off the peach, but it actually keeps it covered.

500 g (4 cups) raspberries
150 g (1¼ cups) powdered sugar
½ lemon, the juice
150 g (approx. ⅗ cup) red currant jelly
6 cl (4 tbsp) kirschwasser (cherry brandy)

1. Mix the raspberries with the powdered sugar and lemon juice until the sugar has dissolved. Pass through a sieve.
2. Also pass the red currant jelly through a sieve and mix everything with the liquor into a covering sauce.

STRAWBERRY JUICE

You can use other soft berries the same way to make juices to serve with your desserts. Strawberry juice is absolutely delicious with strawberry ice cream, pancakes, rhubarb sorbet, and fruit salad.

For 500 g (2½ cups) of juice:

1600 g (13 cups) fresh, ripe strawberries, preferably Sengana, or any other kind with intense flavor. You can also use frozen strawberries of high quality.
100 g (½ cup) sugar

1. Combine the hulled strawberries with the sugar and put them in a large bowl.
2. Place the bowl over a simmering water bath and let it sit and simmer for 60-75 minutes until the strawberries have given off all its juice. Strain

the clear juice through a chinois or fine sieve.
3. Allow to cool, fill in bottles and store in the refrigerator until ready to use.

FRUIT CHIPS

Sugar syrup:
100 g (⅖ cup) water
135 g (approx. ⅗ cup) sugar
25 g (3½ tsp) glucose
1 lemon, the juice
Fruit options:
Apple, pear, pineapple, kiwi, strawberry, mango, banana, etc.

1. Preheat the oven to 150 - 175°F.
2. Boil water and sugar in a small saucepan, wash down the inside of the pan with a brush dipped in water, add the glucose and boil again. Add the lemon juice.
3. Cut the fruit as thinly as possible. Put them in the warm syrup and soak for 30 minutes.
4. Spread the fruit slices over a baking mats, or silpat mats, or greased baking sheets. Dry them in the oven for 2-4 hours, or until they feel dry.
5. Store the chips in a jar with a tight-fitting lid so they don't soften.

CITRUS CHIPS

2 citrus fruits

Sugar syrup:
100 g (⅖ cup) water
135 g (approx. ⅗ cup) sugar
25 g (3½ tsp) glucose
1 lemon, the juice

1. Preheat the oven to 400°F.
2. Cut the fruits into very thin slices, preferably with a cutting machine. Put them in an ovenproof dish. Cover with water.
3. Place the dish in the oven and blanch lemon slices for about 30 minutes. Remove them and let them cool.
4. Boil water and sugar, brush down the inside of the pan with a brush that has been dipped in water. Add the glucose and boil again. Remove the pan from the heat and add the lemon juice. Add the drained orange slices to the syrup and soak for 30 minutes.

5. Spread the fruit slices over baking mats, silpat mats, or greased baking sheets. Dry them in the oven at 175 °F for 2-4 hours, or until they feel dry.
6. Store the chips in a jar with a tight-fitting lid so they don't soften.

QUICK CANDIED PINEAPPLE FOR ICE CREAM AND PARFAIT (DEMI-CONFIT, OR HALF PICKLED)

If you want to use fresh pineapple instead you must blanch the slices for about 5 minutes in boiling water before you pickle them.

You can do the same with pieces of apples, pears, peaches, apricots, cherry, mango, and papaya.

1 can of Del Monte canned pineapple in its own juice
1000 g (4⅕ cup) water
1000 g (5 cups) sugar
1 bourbon vanilla pod, cut and scraped out

1. Boil the water with 250 g (1¼ cups) sugar, vanilla bean, and seeds.
2. Add the pineapple slices and let them simmer just below the boiling point for 15 minutes.
3. Add 250 g (1¼ cups) of sugar and simmer for another 15 minutes. Repeat this procedure twice until the solution contains 1000 g sugar and 1000 g water.
4. Always lift the slices with a fork and they will last longer. Pour into a glass jars and store in the refrigerator. If you want to make large quantities, sterilize the glass jars in a water bath that is 176°F for 30 minutes. This will make the fruit last a lot longer. Store in the refrigerator.

QUICK PICKLED CITRUS PEELS (CALLED DEMI-CONFIT, OR SEMI-PRESERVED)

1 kg (2.2lbs) beautiful oranges with thin peels
lemons or grapefruit
1000 g (4⅕ cups) water
1000 g (5 cups) sugar
1 vanilla pod

1. Brush the fruits thoroughly under running water. Notch the peel in 4 parts and pull it off.
2. Squeeze the juice from the fruit and freeze it for the sorbet.
3. Place the peels in a saucepan. Cover with water. Bring to a boil and simmer for at least 30 minutes or until they are soft when you prick them with a knife.
4. Boil 1000 g (4⅕ cups) of water with 250 g (1¼ cups) sugar and add the drained, blanched zest. Continue as you would with the quick candied pineapple (the recipe next to this one). Store in the refrigerator in a glass jar. They can be stored for several months.

PRESERVING BERRIES FOR ICE CREAM AND SORBET (DEMI-CONFIT OR HALF PICKLED)

Fill jars with berries, such as strawberries, raspberries, blackberries, cloudberries, strawberries, cranberries, blueberries. Cook a simple sugar syrup (see sorbet, page 44). The amount depends on how much berries you are using; 250 g (2 cups) of berries per ¼ of sugar syrup. Pour the boiling sugar syrup over the berries, and immediately screw on the lid tightly. Let stand for at least 24 hours for the sugar to permeate the berries. The berries are half pickled at this point, and will remain soft, even when added to the frozen ice cream. You can marinate candied fruit in various liquors, such as rum, Grand Marnier, Cointreau, etc. The alcohol marinade makes the fruit a bit less sweet and releases their flavor into the ice cream.

CARAMELIZED ALMONDS AND NUTS

There are three ways in which you can caramelize nuts and pits:

1. Melt the sugar and add the nuts, and cover them with melted sugar.
2. Add powdered sugar to the warm nuts and stir until they are covered in golden-brown caramel.
3. Boil the sugar with 40% water to 224.6°F. Add the nuts and stir until they are covered in golden brown caramel.

Tip
Add 1 teaspoon of lemon juice to the sugar, and it will dissolve easier and faster.
Add 5 g (1 tsp) of butter at the end and stir properly so that the nuts are separated.

Pour onto a silpat mat, or a baking mat and separate the pits with your fingers. Store in airtight container when cooled.

Quantities:

Walnuts, pecans:
*   200 g (1½ cups) per 50 g (¼ cup) of sugar*
Pistachios:
*   5.3 oz per 50 g (¼ cup) of sugar*
Hazelnuts, roasted and peeled:
*   250 g (1⅘ cups) per 50 g (¼ cup) of sugar*
Regular almonds, lightly roasted in their skins:
*   250 g (1⅘ cups) per 50 g (¼ cup) of sugar*
Large almonds and macadamia nuts:
*   300 g (2 cups) per 50 g (¼ cup) of sugar*

If you need smaller quantities, reduce the quantities in the recipes.

PRALINÉ

Praliné should only be made with hazelnuts for the hazelnut ice cream. However, you can make it with walnuts, pecans, or macadamia nuts for other ice cream flavors.

If you are looking for classic praliné flavor, mix 2 parts praliné mass with 1 part of melted chocolate.

400 g (2 cups) sugar
200 g (⅘ cup) water
1 bourbon vanilla pod, cut and scraped out
500 g (3½ cups) lightly toasted, shelled almonds, preferably Spanish or Italian

1. Boil sugar and water with the vanilla to 239°F. Add the toasted nuts and cook until they begin to snap. Stir with a spatula until the sugar begins to "die" and whiten.
2. Caramelize the mixture until it is golden brown. Pour onto baking paper and let it cool.
3. If you are going to make nougat that you can use to roll ice cream scoops in, or if you are going to mix it with vanilla ice cream to make nougat ice cream, crush the mass with a rolling pin to a nougat that isn't too coarse.
4. Store in an airtight container because nougat absorbs moisture easily.
5. If you want to make praliné ice cream, blend the mass in a food processor at a temperature of 158°F. It goes pretty fast. Store it in a jar until you are ready to use it.

GIANDUJA

500 g (approx. 4 cups) confectioners' sugar
500 g (3½ cups) of roasted, shelled hazelnuts, preferably Italian, from Piedmont, or Spanish
500 g (2½ cup) milk chocolate

1. Mix the icing sugar and hazelnuts in a blender or mixer to a soggy mass which becomes liquid at a temperature of 158°F. Add the chocolate and mix until it dissolves.
2. Allow to cool, and store in jar until you use it.

NUT CRÈME TO FLAVOR HAZELNUT ICE CREAM, PARFAIT AND MOUSSE

Roasted, peeled, fine hazelnuts, preferably Italian or Spanish, are mixed in a blender to a crème at 158°F. Store in a jar in the fridge.

PISTACHIO PASTE

Try to get a hold of some really nice pistachios, preferably from Sicily. They are beautifully green, unlike the ones from Iran. Make the same way as the hazelnut cream but use pistachios instead.

CITRUS CONCENTRATE

Fantastic when you want to enhance the flavor of the ice cream, sorbet, parfait, mousse, ganache, and various doughs and whipped blends. Thanks to the high sugar content, it is very sustainable.

1. Wash the citrus fruits thoroughly, and cut them into pieces and measure them.
2. Add as much sugar as the amount of the fruits, and mix in a food processor about 10 minutes, until the mixture is thin and completely broken down.
3. Pass the mass through a sieve. Store in glass jars in the refrigerator.

FRUIT PURÉE FOR ICE CREAM, SORBET, PARFAIT, AND MOUSSE

For berry purées, weigh the berries, add 10% sugar, and mix in a blender and pass through a sieve. You can freeze the purée in 1 kg (2.2 lbs) containers and thaw them in the fridge.

Avoid heating purées, because it is detrimental to their freshness.

Fruits like pears, apricots, and peaches must be blanched prior to being mixed with 10% sugar, and passed through a sieve.

You can also make juice with a centrifuge juicer and use it as a base.

MERINGUES

CLASSIC FRENCH MERINGUE

A classic formula is to use twice as much sugar as egg whites.

100 g (⅖ cup) egg whites (refrigerated)
5 g (1 tsp) lemon juice
50 g + 50 g (¼ cup + ¼ cup) granulated sugar
100 g (⅘ cup) powdered sugar
A little bit of sugar to sprinkle over the meringues to make them extra crispy.

1. Preheat the oven to 250°F.
2. Whisk the cold egg whites with lemon juice in an absolutely clean metal bowl, or preferably in a copper bowl that has been washed with vinegar and salt and then rinsed with cold water. Use a dense egg white beater. Whip to a light foam and sprinkle 50 g (¼ cup) of sugar into the foam. Beat with large strokes, or on a low speed if you are using an electric mixer.
3. Sprinkle the remaining sugar into the foam and increase the speed if whipping by hand, or use the fastest setting on the electric mixer, until the foam is rigid.
4. Sift the powdered sugar and fold it gently into the meringue with a spatula.
5. Pipe meringue or meringue bottoms on parchment paper, a baking mat, or a silpat mat. Sprinkle sugar on the surface, it makes the meringue more brittle and crispy.
6. Bake the meringues for 10 minutes with the throttle open, lower the temperature to 200°F and leave meringues in the oven until dry, about 90 minutes.

Tip

As soon as the oven temperature is above 200°F, the meringue mass expands. If you want it to retain its shape completely, lower the temperature.

Tip

Short whipping strokes produce a fine elastic foam. However, it is unstable and liquefies. Longer whipping strokes provide both elasticity and a rigid foam. If you beat the meringue for too long, you'll get a hard foam that isn't elastic, and it could liquefy, depending on how the proteins change.

ITALIAN MERINGUE (NOT FOR BAKING)

A classic to use for parfait and mousse.

200 g (⅘ cup) water
450 g (2¼ cups) sugar
250 g (1 cup) egg white
50 g (¼ cup) sugar
5 g (1 tsp) lemon juice

1. Weigh water and sugar in a saucepan that holds 2 liters (68 oz). Stir with a whisk until the sugar has dissolved. Bring to a boil and remove any foam. Brush the inside walls of the pot with a brush dipped in water occasionally while boiling.
2. When the syrup reaches 230°F (use a thermometer, or take a thread sample page 232), begin whipping egg whites, sugar and lemon juice into a stiff meringue on medium speed.
3. When sugar thermometer shows 251.6°F (Or take a ball sample, page 232), pour the boiling syrup into the meringue in a stream while beating the mixture continuously. Mix on low speed until the meringue is cold.

ITALIAN MERINGUE (FOR BAKING)

Use 700 g (3½ cups) of sugar instead of 450 g (2¼ cups), so that the water content in the meringue decreases and it becomes suitable for baking. Bake in 200°F.
The meringue expands and loses its shape in temperatures that exceed 212°F.
The ancient Egyptians were the first to boil honey into caramel and then shaping them into flowers and other figures to decorate their tables during festivities.

SUGAR CRAFTSMANSHIP

The ancient Greeks embraced the skill and became as famous for their caramel art as their neighbors across the Mediterranean.

Caramel ornaments made with cane sugar comes from Venice, where Ms della Pigna in 1574 for the first time in history in a larger context made colored candy decorations for Katarina of the Medici court. In the 1600s, Luigi Fedela discovered the effect of adding acidity with vinegar, or lemon juice. The sucrose would then be broken down into simple sugars, and the caramel became smooth and pliable to work with. Luigi published the majority of the recipes and templates for caramel work in his days, and they were used until the early 1800s.

The method of measuring the sugar's temperature by hand, by using the thumb and forefinger and cold water, was invented over 400 years ago by the Italian, Sanctorius. Confectioners and candy makers have used this method since the 1600s. The sugar syrup becomes more concentrated and the caramel stronger (see sugar test on page 232). A very famous sugar artist, Canova, from Venice lifted the sugar craftsmanship to unbelievable heights.

In the 1900s, the two Frenchmen, Paul Vigreux and Etienne Tholoniat, became world leaders in sugar craftsmanship, and I had the opportunity to learn from both of them during their guest appearance when they demonstrated their skills at the Coba School in Basel. Willy Pfund, who ran International Sugar School in Zurich, was a very special mentor to me when it came to caramel artistry. He was also the head of the décor department at Confiserie Sprüngli in Zurich, one of the leading pastry shops in the world, and he was an amazing cocoa painter. The principal at the Coba School in Basel, Julius Perlia, was of great help during my journey towards becoming a skilled professional. Algot Svensson, who used to be a teacher at the Pastry Trade School (Konditorfackskolan) in Uppsala, was also a very skilled caramel craftsman and he was always willing to share his knowledge.

Basket covered in caramel with blown caramel grapes.

Cornucopia made out of blown caramel with ice cream fruits.

231

BOILING SUGAR

Sugar is cooked to produce a more or less concentrated sugar solution. Glucose (glucose syrup), is added to prevent the sugar from crystallizing. It makes it pliable and easy to work with.

Equipment to boil the sugar:

+ A copper pan (that hasn't been tin-plated) is ideal because it conducts heat well and prevents the sugar from burning. A typical stainless steel saucepan works as well, but it will take longer to cook the caramel.
+ A brush is needed to keep the walls of the pan free from sugar crystals during boiling.
+ A sugar thermometer that accurately measures the temperature, otherwise you can use cold water to test the solution with your hand.

Sugar Temperatures and Sugar Samples

Dip your thumb and index finger in ice-cold water. Quickly catch a little bit of caramel with your fingers and immediately immerse them in the cold water. Then compare caramel with the pictures on this page.

The most common temperatures for sugar boiling for desserts are:

1. *Weak thread test 215.6 – 233.6°F (boiling fruit, jam, marmalade, jelly, sugar syrup, and sugar syrup for candying) and strong thread test 233.6 – 240.8°F (Tosca mass, liqueur chocolates).*
2. *Weak ball sample 244.4-251.6°F (fondant 244.4° F, fudge, marzipan and Italian meringue 251.6°F).*
3. *Strong ball sample 251,6 - 266°F (caramel sample).*
4. *Weak caramel sample 294.8 -311°F (spun sugar, molded caramel, nougat montelimar).*
5. *Strong caramel sample 155-170°. (Pulled and blown caramel.*

CARAMELS FOR DECORATIONS AND SPUN SUGAR

100 g (⅖ cup) water
200 g (1 cup) sugar
50 g (2½ tbsp) glucose

1. First, measure the water correctly. Then add the sugar while whisking.
2. Put the pan on the stove and heat on low heat so that the sugar dissolves properly. Use a tea strainer to skim off any foam on the surface.
3. Add glucose. Boil at the highest heat. Use a brush that has been dipped in water to continuously brush the sugar crystals away when they form on the walls in the pan. You can also cover the sugar solution with a lid, but keep it ajar. It produces the same effect as the brushing.
4. Once the caramel has reached the desired temperature (311 - 320°F with a thermometer or strong caramel sample, please see the sugar temperatures below), quickly remove the pan from the heat. Dip the bottom of the pan in a bowl with

Spun Sugar

cold water for a few seconds to cease the boiling.

Spun sugar: Take two large forks, hold them back to back and dip them into the caramel. Pick up and swing between two objects, such as broomsticks. (Protect the floor underneath you, by covering it with newspaper). Always let the caramel drip off excess a little bit before you swing it back and forth so that thin wires are formed. If you are going to spin a lot of sugar, buy a cheap balloon whisk and cut it so that only the wires remain, it will be much more affective this way.

Small sugar domes: Dip a spoon into the caramel, lift it up and drizzle the caramel back and forth over the backside of a lightly oiled soup ladle. Pull the caramel to create an edge at the bottom, around the ladle. Loosen the sugar domes from the soup ladle immediately, and continue until you have enough of them.

Storage

Caramel decorations can be stored in airtight jars. Spun sugar can be stored up to several days in air-tight pail with a little bit of desiccant in the bottom (so-called dehumidifiers).

If you need to reheat the caramel, heat it gently without stirring it. Instead, spin the pot so that the caramel doesn't burn. If you stir cooked caramel, it crystallizes and "dies."

As a Professional: If You Make Pulled or Blown Caramel

Adding glucose and cream of tartar prevents the sugar from crystallizing and makes the caramel smooth and elastic. At 330.8°F, the caramel reaches a point where it no longer contains any water. At higher temperatures the sugar begins to caramelize and gets a brown color, which isn't good. When the caramel temperature drops to 122°F, the mass turns doughy. Then when you pull the caramel many small crystals are bound together in long chains surrounded by air pockets, and caramels starts shining like smooth silk. At this stage you have a pulled caramel, which is suitable to make flowers, leaves, bows, and braided baskets for decoration. This caramel is also perfect blowing different figures with it.

1000 g (5 cups) sugar
400 g (1¾ cups) water
300 g (⁹⁄₁₀ cup) glucose
3 g (approx. ⅗ tsp) cream of tartar

1. Boil in the same manner as with the spun sugar, but add cream of tartar with the glucose.
2. Boil to 330.8°F. Dip the bottom of the pan in cold water to stop the boiling. Pour the cooled caramel onto an oiled marble slab, silpat mat, or two baking mats.
3. Allow the mixture to cool slightly, and fold it a little bit, back and forth, until it resembles dough. Pull the dough between your palms, back and forth, until the mass is shiny.
4. Place the caramel underneath a 350-watt heating lamp, pulling it between the thumb and the forefinger and shape leaves, flowers, and bows. Assemble them by using a propane torch.
5. If you want to blow the caramel, form a round ball and press an indentation into ball. Attach it to a sugar blower, blow figures of your choice, perhaps fruits, or flowers. Remove from the nozzle with a heated knife or a pair of scissors.

Pulled caramel for a bow.

Caramel is blown into a torch.

Caramel petals are attached together to form a rose.

CHOCOLATE TECHNIQUES

Tempering

In order to be able to make beautiful fans, rollers, spirals, and many other lovely chocolate decorations, you must usually temper the chocolate first, or rather the cocoa butter in it. Otherwise, the chocolate goes gray and dull and does not shrink the way it should.

It is important to be in charge of the temperature. Therefore, use a digital thermometer. In addition, you will need a small marble slab and a spatula/pallet. The easiest way to melt chocolate is in a plastic bowl in the microwave. Stir and check the temperature frequently. You could also use a water bath too, but make sure to avoid moisture from the vaporized water to get into the chocolate.

Dark chocolate is heated to 118.4 - 122°F, cooled to 80.6 -82.4°F, and then heated to 87.8 -89.6°F.
Milk chocolate is warmed to 113°F, cooled to 78.8-80.6°F, and then heated to 86°F.
White chocolate is first heated to 104°F, cooled to 77-78.8° and then heated to 84.2°F.

Method 1
1. Finely chop the chocolate.
2. Heat half the amount to the correct temperature. Add the remaining chocolate while stirring.
3. Stir until it the chocolate cools to the correct temperature.
4. Bring it back to the correct final temperature.

Method 2 (see the picture below)
(Fastest and safest method, and the most common among professionals).

1. Heat the chocolate to the proper temperature.
2. Pour three quarters of the chocolate onto a marble slab. Spread it back and forth with a pallet until the chocolate begins to thicken and solidify.
3. Scrape up the chocolate and mix with the remaining chocolate.
4. Heat to the correct temperature.

Spirals (see Figure 1 and 2)

Temper the dark chocolate. Apply it on a strip of overhead transparency film. Spread it with a glue scraper, as shown. Insert the film into a glass and place it in the fridge to solidify. Remove the glass from the fridge and remove the plastic.

Fans and Rolls (see figures 3 and 4)

(No tempering)

Heat the chocolate to 113°F. Apply it thinly on a marble slab. Apply until you feel that it begins to harden and you can hear slight "crunching" sound. Place your index finger like in the image. Move a spatula quickly forward once with your finger in front. Make sure the chocolate is bending over the top of your finger. Practice a few times and re-melt the chocolate in between.

Confectioner Method: Heat a tray to 113 °F. Heat the chocolate to 113°F and spread it very thinly over the tray. Place the plate in the fridge and let the chocolate solidify.

Take it out and place it in room temperature. Scratch fans or rollers, like in the photos.

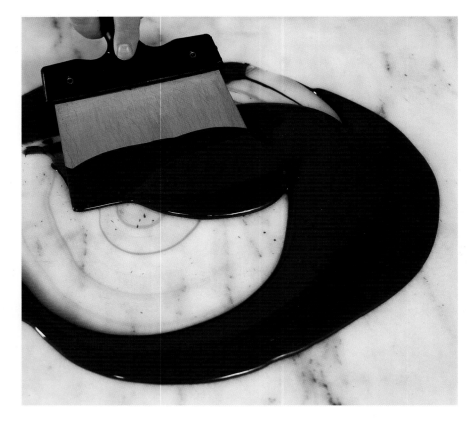

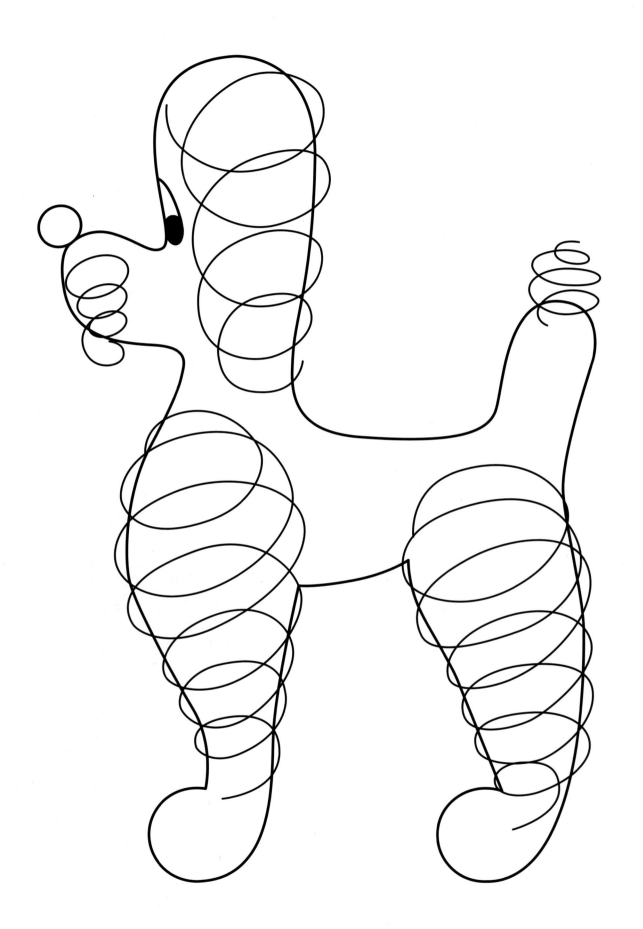